The Best American Movie Writing 1999

★ The ★
Best American
Movie Writing
★ 1999 ★

EDITED BY
Peter Bogdanovich

Jason Shinder, Series Editor

St. Martin's Griffin
New York

ISBN 0-312-24493-2

First Edition: October 1999

10 9 8 7 6 5 4 3 2 1

(continued on page 281)

To Daniel Talbot,

who edited the first important film-writing anthology (*On Film*, 1959, Simon & Schuster), and in whose revolutionary 1960s art house cinema, the New Yorker Theater (now gone), I saw so many wonderful pictures the right way, on the big screen with a sizable audience. Throughout the years, Dan Talbot has been, and continues to be (through New Yorker Films), unquestionably the most discriminating and conscientious of U.S. distributors as well as (with his Lincoln Plaza Cinemas in Manhattan) the exhibitor with the most integrity and the best taste. He also has been to me personally a great friend for nearly four decades, and this small tribute comes with my deepest thanks and love.

—P.B.

CONTENTS

FOREWORD

C an a single annual volume enthusiastically reflect the richness, excellence, and diversity of the best American writing about film? Last year, the debut edition of *The Best American Movie Writing*, guest edited by George Plimpton, answered that question with a spirited yes. And this second edition, guest edited by Peter Bogdanovich, answers the same question with even greater optimism and enthusiasm. Mr. Bogdanovich, the passionate and distinguished director of the Academy Award–winning movie *The Last Picture Show* and such classic films as *Mask* and *St. Jack*, as well as the author of some of the most engaging and insightful books about cinema, had a very clear and passionate vision for this compilation of the year's best writing about film.

There are dozens of obvious topics available in a distinguished piece of writing about film; the approach of the director, the work of the actors, the plot, dialogue, lighting, music. Yet in the very best movie writing even the most familiar subjects can be deeply illuminated, resonating in ways they may have only been suggested to most viewers. The best movie writings quickly establish their authority as pieces that elucidate a movie's content and structure with passion, depth, and poignancy, while at the same time speak to larger issues of the self and society. It is not an easy task: Writers must understand and speak through what Mr. Bogdanovich calls "the craft, technique, and construction, the basic grammar, syntax, and vocabulary of making films." Yet each year the number of authors dedicating their full professional energies toward writing about film, or teaching writing about film, increases—along with the number of magazines dedicating all, or a majority of, their pages to writing about film with full or part-time movie writers on staff.

Tracking the movie writings published in the United States in the last year and a half between November 1, 1997, and October 31, 1998, was therefore a rigorous and instructive experience. Each and every issue of more than 350 general and special-interest magazines was surveyed—almost twice as many as for the previous volume. In addition to our survey, we solicited nominations from the editors of nearly one hundred of the magazines we surveyed. Many authors sent us copies of their published work, or the work of others they admired as well. Writing about film on the Web has certainly become a critical factor, and this year we expanded our survey to include on-line, as well as print, magazines. What we realized soon enough was that it's a difficult task to keep up with what's out there—there is so much of it, and so much of it is good: profiles, memoirs, historical pieces, meditations, academic studies, diaries, essays of all kinds.

With his insistence on excellence as the paramount criterion, and an inclination toward "retrospectively minded material," Mr. Bogdanovich always provided a passioned and magnanimous spirit of response to the genuine article—observation, description, phrase, or word—wherever it was found among the many, many pieces reviewed. His final selections are in the following pages, accompanied by an even larger list of finalists in the "Notable American Movie Writings of 1998" section in the back of this volume. I hope readers will seek out, and read, these notable movie writings for their variety and excellence.

Only two of the authors whose work Mr. Bogdanovich selected for this volume, Martin Scorsese and Geoffrey O'Brien, appeared in the previous, inaugural issue. The inclusion of so many new writers points once again to the abundance of film writers and readers. Mr. Bogdanovich's edition also includes several pioneers in the field of writing about movies—figures without whom there would be no "field," including Andrew Sarris, Robin Wood, Molly Haskell, Jonathan Rosenbaum, Rex Reed, and Roger Ebert. Like Mr. Bogdanovich, their lifelong devotion to the art of films is of the highest quality of intelligence and affection. I'm delighted that this edition recognizes them and, by association, the many others who have for decades tilled the soil of the field of movie writing. Although there is no substitute for the sort of movie writing produced by those committed entirely to the genre, there is always an essential and exciting place for movie writings by authors of other literary genres. E. L. Doctorow and Gore Vidal are among those writers in this edition, for example, who periodically turn their gaze from their usual field of fiction to that of cinema.

As is typical of similar annual anthologies, the rules of selection are simple: A distinguished guest editor makes final selections based on a wide survey of writings published in the previous year. But the selection guidelines are also flexible enough to convey the changing yearly dynamics of the writers and subject being anthologized. This year, to better reveal the conditions and directions of writing about film in America, we've added a new section: a directory of film magazines, which offers a way of assisting readers through the growing maze of movie magazines while recognizing their critical and increasing influence. And, as with the previous volume, this edition of *Best American Movie Writing* permits the guest editor to select one or two pieces from a book or newspaper published within the last year.

Mr. Bogdanovich's movies and writings have a way of setting our external and internal houses in order, of making difficult emotions possible to articulate. It's one of the reasons we have come to depend upon him as a witness during moments of celebration and crisis. How many times do viewers and readers today turn to his award-winning films, highly acclaimed books, or his weekly columns in *The New York Observer,* when it is important to know in one scene, one gesture, one word, what we are going through? I was honored to have the opportunity to turn to him during the process of completing this wonderful edition of *Best American Movie Writing.* Several file cabinets in his New York City apartment are filled with hundreds and hundreds of index cards, each with his hand-written notes about a particular movie: when and where he saw it, what he thought, when and where he saw it again, what he thought, etc. The movies clearly engage and enchant him in the most extraordinary and original way.

In addition to Mr. Bogdanovich, I want to thank his agent, Sheri Arden, for her support of the series and help in securing Mr. Bogdanovich's participation. Thanks also to Katie Adams, senior researcher for the series, whose contributions continue to be invaluable. And thanks once again to George Plimpton and his staff at the *Paris Review* for their continuing critical support, suggestions, and contributions. The series would not be possible without the editorial direction of Cal Morgan and Dana Albarella, editors at St. Martin's. And thanks to Sharon Friedman and Chris Shelling of the Ralph Vicinanza Literary Agency, who continue to work behind the scenes to ensure the success of the series. Finally, and perhaps most important, thanks to the writers and editors who granted permission to reprint pieces in this collection.

—Jason Shinder

P.S. Although unable to reprint Tag Gallager's piece "White Melodrama" (*Film Comment*, November/December 1998) in this collection, it was selected by Mr. Bogdanovich as a Best American Movie Writing.

INTRODUCTION: RETRACING OLDER STEPS
AND NEW

W riting about the movies can change movies. It did in France during the late Fifties and Sixties and it did in America, as a result of the French, in the late Sixties and Seventies. When critics like François Truffaut and Jean-Luc Godard wrote about the U.S. films they liked and the French films they didn't, essentially the entire course of picture history was altered. With their *politique des auteurs*—mistranslated here as "auteur theory"—they fostered a climate that would accept the pictures they eventually directed, superceding the *cinema de papa* with the Nouvelle Vague—that New Wave that swept across the channel and the ocean and affected all of us. Critics and film historians in England and America were inspired to a movement that gave movies back to the director, and so the New Hollywood was born, an eruption that produced a brief renaissance and a slew of young filmmakers who took movies into a new era.

Not everything about this has been entirely salutary. One of the things the French- and English-language critics frequently extolled were the glories of certain genre pictures that revealed a director's often subtly expressed personality. Finding a link between, say, *Baby Face Nelson* (1957) and *Madigan* (1968), and realizing this connection came through the same director's vision, led to an understanding that picturemakers like Don Siegel were able to express themselves in complex subterranean ways that could be as valid and valuable as the more highly budgeted, more highly praised works of social import lauded by the establishment. But Siegel was, nevertheless, often working with material he didn't necessarily like or approve, and indeed, many times it was this particular tension between low-grade material and high-class temperament that resulted in a special noteworthy frisson.

What this eventually deteriorated to, however, was the enthroning of genre for its own sake, forgetting it was usually the director's handling of trash—his subversion of it, transcendence from it—not the trash itself, that was compelling. The unfortunate result today is an endless stream of expensive junk movies with lots of slick special effects and virtually no discernable personality at all. The formally despised, usually suspect genres of science fiction, cliffhanger serials, and crime melodramas are now generally given more attention than the ever-diminishing pictures about people and contemporary society.

Over the last two decades, there also has been, in America at least, a sharp and glaring drop in the level of real film culture. Most of the younger generations seem to think that movies of any interest began sometime either in the early Seventies or perhaps even in the early Eighties. Many new filmmakers, as evidenced in their work, appear to have seen no pictures made more than twenty years ago and so reveal an amazing lack of technical sophistication by their own ignorance, clumsily inventing the wheel each time, unaware of all the wheels already invented. This primitivism is especially disheartening considering the vast treasure trove that (since the videocassette age) lies at their very fingertips. I am speaking of craft here, of construction and technique, of the very grammar, syntax, and vocabulary of making films. The solid silent cinema (circa 1912 through 1928) and the classic sound era (1929 to 1962) did it all, the foundation having been laid ten times over; why are so few learning from it?

The overall purpose of this yearly anthology, as well envisioned by series editor Jason Shinder, implemented and expanded by George Plimpton and his staff at *The Paris Review,* has been to gather together the year's best writing on the movies, and therefore not simply on current pictures. Some of the pieces—like Martin Scorsese's or Steven Spielberg's—are here to show again that a director's personal life does make a difference in what they choose to make. But if anything, in my suggestions, I have pushed to bring in as much retrospectively minded material as possible, because of my concern about the general lack of attention paid to what has preceded us. This accounts for quite a few of the pieces chosen. In a historical context, Robert Graves once wrote, "We must retrace our steps or perish." I feel the same way about this youngest of all art forms, which seems already deeply threatened with decadence. Exposing children to the greatest pictures of the past, as we do to the past of other arts, is a crucially important step. Making that past exciting and tantalizing is part of our job here, as well as encouraging and interpreting quality in the present (which accounts for the rest of the articles).

Perhaps the second biggest danger in films currently is the substitution of money for talent. With the many filmmakers I've spoken to over the years, and among the eighteen masters taped for publication—from John Ford, Howard Hawks, and Alfred Hitchcock to Orson Welles, Fritz Lang, and Otto Preminger—the one attitude common to them all was their pride in doing things economically, of not requiring millions to achieve their goals. Pioneer Allan Dwan said that whoever thought of spending so much money on pictures had taken them into a bad downward spiral. Art is usually born of limitation. Today's emphasis on what pictures cost and what they gross the first weekend is a disastrous atmosphere for true and lasting achievements. Perhaps some of the writing here may act as antidote.

—Peter Bogdanovich

The
Best American
Movie Writing
1999

A Box Filled with Magic

by Martin Scorsese

FROM *NEWSWEEK*

I've always linked my moviegoing experiences to my family. My parents weren't educated. There were no books in our house. I was constantly ill with asthma, and the only activity we could share was going to the movies. We lived in Little Italy in downtown Manhattan, and I remember the neighborhood movie theaters well, with their tantalizing posters promising dreams, and a rich array of second- and third-run movies. Admission was thirteen cents for children. The first film I remember seeing by title was *Duel in the Sun*. I was four years old. My mother said she took me to see it because I liked Westerns, but actually it had been condemned by the church, and I suspect that's the real reason she took me. The movie was overpowering with its hallucinatory color imagery, violent music, hysterical melodrama, and intense sexuality. I wasn't ever the same after that.

When I was a boy, there wasn't much direct communication between my father and me. But at the movie theater, the two of us shared the remarkable images and strong emotions that emanated from the giant screen, emotions we couldn't otherwise articulate to each other. Together we saw such pictures as *The Red Shoes, I Shot Jesse James,*

Rear Window, The Thing, The Day the Earth Stood Still, The Bad and the Beautiful, Jean Renoir's *The River, Sunset Boulevard, The Greatest Show on Earth,* a re-release of *The Public Enemy, War of the Worlds, The Heiress,* and *Shane.* They left such an impression on me that today, much of the desire and need to express myself on film comes from that early loving experience with my father. Movies fulfilled a desire to communicate with those I loved.

The impulse to make movies began in 1951 when my father took me to see a British film, *The Magic Box,* directed by John Boulting. It starred the wonderful actor Robert Donat as William Friese-Greene, one of the unsung pioneers of the invention of cinema. A photographer at the turn of the century, Friese-Greene was obsessed with making pictures move. In a scene that was pivotal to my life, he demonstrates the concept of moving pictures to his girlfriend, played by Maria Schell. He picks up a book she's reading in the garden and flips through its pages. On each page is a drawing of stick figures he'd made in the margins. The images of a little girl and a dog were static when seen separately, but when he flipped the pages, they *moved.* This was miraculous to me as a child. Friese-Greene explained that this phenomenon was called "the persistence of vision." Through this principle an optical illusion is created that makes the pictures appear to move. I went home and tried it myself with telephone books. I was transfixed. I wanted to make movies.

I wanted to create images that reflected the life around me: what I saw in the streets, at home, and, in particular, in my church. There I found the images very powerful, transcendent, and, at times, lurid and erotic. The church in my neighborhood was a historic one: the first Catholic cathedral in New York, St. Patrick's Old Cathedral, built in 1809. Imposing and grand, it provided a refuge from the streets. And it was, in its own way, a very theatrical place. Light coming through the stained-glass windows created color and drenched the atmosphere. Gilded chalices and monstrances and incense added to the effect. I was fascinated by the plaster statues of Saint Teresa of Avila and Saint Rocco, and by the giant crucifix over the altar. Candles were lit in front of two large plaster tableaux. One of them depicted souls in purgatory, naked bodies caressed by bright orange and yellow flames, looking up to heaven where angels were dripping the most precious blood of the crucified Jesus from a golden chalice. The other tableau was a life-size figure of Jesus, his body wounded and broken, lying dead in his sepulcher.

There was also a statue of Saint Lucy, my father's favorite saint— he had eye ailments and she was the patron saint of eyes. My mother told the story of Saint Lucy this way: A young girl with beautiful eyes was pursued by a man who was obsessed with her to the point of violence. But her virtue was so great that she plucked out her eyes and defiled her beauty to put an end to his pursuit. God rewarded her by giving her back her eyes. The statue showed Lucy's beautiful face with her wonderful, innocent eyes gazing up to heaven. In her outstretched hand was a gilded plate, and on it were two human eyes. These images, as well as those from my home and my neighborhood, all found their way into the drawings I had started to make, drawings that—only in my imagination—moved. Later they found their way into my movies.

After going to the movies, I'd listen to my family talk about what we had seen together. Often I'd hear them say, "It was good, but you know what would've really happened in that story . . ." And they'd discuss what they thought would have been a more interesting scenario, usually a much more realistic one. Then my father would add, resignedly, "But they can't do that in movies." I often thought, "What if they *could*?" And as I got older, I wondered, "What if I could?" That impulse was so strong that I secretly drew my own movies after school. They were series of frames—like comic strips or story-boards—with opening credits and stories that were inspired by different Hollywood genres, including epics.

Years later, when I started to make movies for real, I found I couldn't be a part of the cinema that created that strong emotional bond between my father and me—entertainment from the "golden age" of Hollywood. The studio system had started to fall apart in the 1950s and had completely disintegrated by the time I began making movies in the Seventies. So even though I thought along the lines of the movies I'd loved as a child, the movies I made came from a different place. Entertainment became secondary. (Even when I tried to make a film like those of the great era—*New York, New York* in 1977— it turned out quite differently.) When I accepted the fact that I wouldn't make old-style movies, I reconciled the situation by having my father and mother become a part of my films. My mother cooked for the cast and crew, my father helped out in the costume department, and often they both played small parts.

The 1950s, when the old system was changing, had a strong artistic impact on me. Something new was happening in the movies. Censorship broke down with the films of Otto Preminger, Fred Zinnemann, Billy Wilder, Stanley Kramer, and others. They attacked the taboos. I think what struck me most in these movies was a new emotional power and honesty. And of foremost importance, the fourth wall between the audience and the camera was knocked down by the films of Elia Kazan. The acting of Marlon Brando, Montgomery Clift, James Dean was revelatory in its naturalness. I was mesmerized by *On the Waterfront*. For the first time I saw on the screen people I knew in real life, similar to those in my world of the Lower East Side. They reflected emotions and realities I knew intimately. At the end of the Fifties, I thought if I were ever to make movies, I would want to create scenes as emotionally powerful and memorable as those in Kazan's films.

By 1960 my film viewing changed. I had seen foreign films on TV, particularly Italian films by Roberto Rossellini and Vittorio De Sica. A new cinema was being created abroad, by Ingmar Bergman and Andrzej Wajda and, of course, in the New Wave works coming from Italy, France, and England. Add to that the "discovery" of Japanese cinema in the West, and the new American cinema shepherded by critic Jonas Mekas—experimental cinema and the new narrative films of Shirley Clarke and John Cassavetes. When I look back now, I realize that it was seeing Cassavetes's *Shadows* and a re-release of Orson Welles's *Citizen Kane* at the same time that were the defining moments for me. Over coffee afterward with fellow film students at New York University, I knew I really *had* to make movies. And today the impact both films made on me is still powerful. In a way I think some of the approaches in my own films are attempts to reconcile the disparate styles of those two seminal filmmakers. At the same time, I found I had one foot in European cinema and still can't seem to retract it.

Up to now I have not lost the intense desire to say something in film or, at times, the sheer exhilaration of working in the medium; nor have I lost the sense of challenging myself against the work of the great masters. From working on the script and designing shots in pre-production to mixing the score in postproduction, each stage of moviemaking is a collaborative process. On the set itself, there's an excitement that comes from working with great collaborators. It ranges from raucous fun in scenes where actors perform freely, playing off each other like musicians in a band, to moments of almost religious serenity. In a sense, I've been able to re-create my early movie-viewing experience by making movies with a film family.

But the quiet concentration and sense of fulfillment I felt drawing my own movies as a child I can now find only in the editing room. It's where you deal with the very essence of film. When you take two pieces of film, one piece moves and the other piece moves, and when they are cut together, the cut itself creates another kind of movement—an emotional and psychological movement in the mind's eye that creates an emotional and psychological reaction, shared by the filmmaker and the audience. After twenty-five years, I think of each film as a new chance, an opportunity to explore new and different ways of expression. Still, I may never entirely get beyond the simple amazement of watching still pictures move and come to life.

The Moviegoers

Why Don't People Love the Right Movies Anymore?

by David Denby

FROM *THE NEW YORKER*

It's very possible that the terrific crime thriller *L.A. Confidential*—the recipient of two Oscars as well as many critics' awards (I have no hesitation in shilling for it as the best movie of last year)—will someday earn a profit. It hasn't yet; it has struggled in the theaters. But *L.A. Confidential* should do well (so I am told) in the Elysian fields of cable and video, where marketing costs drop almost to nothing and a movie sometimes just earns and earns. Even if that happens, however, the movie's difficulty in finding a large theater audience will remain a matter of some chagrin to me and a number of other movie critics I've spoken to. What remains of vanity has dropped another notch, for here was the latest and most obvious sign of our sorry lack of sway. Clearly, the audience was not listening—not to us, at any rate. And in my case the commercial problems of a good movie stimulated many other disagreeable and rebellious thoughts about the movie scene in general and criticism's place in it.

"Movie criticism has become a cultural malady, a group case of chronic depression," James Wolcott wrote last April in *Vanity Fair*. Critics, of course, are only a minor part of the action, so why should anyone care whether they are demoralized or not? Wolcott himself thought that critics were becoming whiners, and a friend has said to me that "movie critics are like spotted owls," by which he means that the fate of so specialized a creature will never stir a general outcry. True enough, but please notice the flaws in my friend's remark. If a species is threatened, it may be a sign that something is degraded in the environment—something that will affect the rest of us sooner or later. Anyway, critics and moviegoers live together in the same forest, not in separate habitats.

Perhaps we can agree that everyone living in that forest, that magical Arden, is engaged in a lifetime romance, a passion without end—the love of movies. This may seem a lofty way of describing a tired citizen's slinking off to *Con Air* after a long day at the office. Yet the longing to escape from routine is also a form of passion, and passion of any sort is always an absorption in the erotics of shape, texture, and contour. As moviegoers, we care for this movie or that movie, this performance or that one: the ripe *L.A. Confidential* and the austere *Sweet Hereafter*; Julianne Moore's red-lipped, Expressionist anguish in *Boogie Nights*; and Matt Damon's pale, tough-vulnerable mug in *Good Will Hunting*.

But who among us could now love "the movies" as they confront the public in the media—the movies as a system of publicity and commerce? Every week, as new commercial movies open, vast armies of promotion storm the beach—an invasion leading, often, to a sudden withdrawal—and all this happens again the following week, with another set of movies, a new beachhead, and, often, another collapse, the rapid cycle itself producing its share of cynicism and disgust. The audience is buffeted by the anxiety of a system that can never sell hard enough or fast enough; it is trapped in Hollywood's seeming contempt for its own products.

If a new movie doesn't catch on in the opening weekend, studio executives may immediately cut off the expensive TV ads for it and then restrict the film's distribution; and theater-chain owners, who make a good part of their money from the concession stands, and who consequently long to get hungry bodies into the multiplexes, quickly dump a weak performer and move a strong one onto three, or four, or as many as six screens in a single complex. A movie that cannot sell popcorn and Coke at high prices disappears from the 'plexes in a few weeks—often too fast for word of mouth to rally on its behalf. Given more time, the audience might have "saved" the picture, but it's gone.

None of this is new. But in the past decade the selling of movies has grown both deafening and senseless. The promotional system rarely sells the particular qualities of a given movie—the tone, the temper, the body. It just sells, period. Warner Bros., tailoring its campaign for *L.A. Confidential* last fall to look like every other campaign for violent thrillers, could not convey to women that they might enjoy the movie. That campaign (it has recently been revised) was no more than another set of disposable images on television. Miramax alone among distributors understands that if promotion isn't as sharp as a knife, it may never penetrate the barrier of audience fatigue.

A medium that was once the movies' feared rival, television, now functions as a busy ad-pub division of Hollywood. Oprah, Barbara, and Kathie Lee—and, of course, MTV and E!—compete with one another for sell-the-picture "interviews" with the stars; and cable outlets run promotional "documentaries" about the making of a new film. As for print journalism, a good many editors, feature writers, and hack critics—these last handing out rave quotes like free candy on the streets—have simply been pressed into the marketing operation for movies. With what effect? Again and again I have sat before some meaningless Hollywood thriller or comedy convinced that the picture wasn't even made with an American theater audience in mind. Such movies—in the past couple of months, *Hard Rain, Desperate Measures, Sphere*—may fail in the theaters, but the original push in the media establishes the picture's name for the ancillary markets (Blockbuster, HBO, Bangkok), and that may be what matters most to the people who made it. Twenty years ago, critics complained that marketing considerations were determining the content of movies. Now a subbranch of marketing—the clangorous media promotion system, including journalism—is helping to determine the content of movies. The dog is being wagged not by the tail but by the fleas on the tail.

It's the critic's job to straighten things out: He can seize, loverlike, on the particulars, the tone, the succulent difference between one movie and another—at least, when there is a difference. "Evoke, evoke!" a Henry James of movie criticism might cry out; any fool can have opinions. But the flood of media promotion overwhelms the voice of a good critic; and the commercialization of routine reviewing—in TV-preview shows and newspaper-ad blurb writing—turns criticism into mere opinion, another cheerfully meaningless bit of noise, the whooshing of thumbs, up and down. Yes, serious critics continue, with gravity or wit, to announce their opinions. But such people (including me) have been buried by a widespread perception of their naïveté. *They don't get it.* They don't understand that the marketing-and-promotion system is now less a means of bringing products to consumers than a law of existence, a metaphysics of momentum which either turns the critic into a huckster or reduces him to a crank.

L.A. Confidential was cast without stars, but it was precisely the unfamiliarity of two of the actors, Guy Pearce and Russell Crowe, as well as the originality of Kevin Spacey's performance, that made possible one of the movie's strongest effects—the sense that the police-detective heroes were changing and growing under the pressure of experience. So the movie's sluggish box-office performance might be explained by another possibility, one more unpleasant than the failure of an ad campaign: Was the movie too good to take off? Did the complex characterization, the layered plot, and the velvety, soaked-in-noir visual style make the movie too much work for an audience accustomed to simpler demands? If the answer to the above question is yes, or maybe, we are all in trouble. (After all, the picture, however brilliant, was conceived in commercial terms, not as an art film.) And critics are *really* in trouble. In good times a critic can ignore the marketplace, and even the struggles of a good movie, and do his job of expounding and analyzing; he can celebrate art and pleasure and applaud new talent; he can evaluate the traffic and sustain a conversation with moviegoers.

But such high-minded solace will hardly be possible if the culture in which criticism makes sense as an activity is beginning to fade. So, before dismissing the critical malaise as a parochial whine—mere screening-room blahs—consider certain aspects of the movies themselves. Consider whether the last fifteen years or so haven't witnessed dismaying shifts in sensibility and tone—a deadening of vital impulses that make good movies possible and criticism valuable.

As I listen to people talk (well, let's say older people) I get the sense that many moviegoers who loved the French, Italian, Japanese, British, and Eastern European films of the Sixties and the American films of the Seventies (the early work of Coppola, Altman, Scorsese, Spielberg, De Palma, and many others) have simply stopped going to the movies, or go with limited hopes, with a sickened sense that the house is sliding down the hill and can never be pulled back to the top again. It's not just "art" (always rare) that older moviegoers miss. It's emotion. After all, some very sophisticated people have cared about movies in a primitive way. They have cared about characters and stories and gestures, and the strength of their involvement has produced a remarkable intensity and variety of moods—pangs of regret and despair; voluptuous enjoyment of lowlife pessimism and inadmissible snobberies; a winged exuberance; a flowing sense of well-being. The more knowing may have told themselves that the emotion-flooded products of Hollywood—Bette Davis as a blind woman on the stairs in *Dark Victory*—were kitsch; they may have felt themselves seduced, even gulled, by movies. But that realization hardly ended the power of enjoyment. In *L.A. Confidential*, set in the early Fifties, the swank Beverly Hills pimp played by David Strathairn provides his wealthy clients with whores made up as Lana Turner or Veronica Lake, and in a way, that's what we've always wanted from movies: the erotic power of illusion. Movie love puts people in touch with their own instincts and pleasures. Movies can lead to self-reconciliation, and that is one reason they have inspired an almost unlimited affection.

Even to speak of movie emotion in such terms is now extremely awkward. In so many Hollywood movies nothing much is at stake—no particular meaning, no powerfully articulated temper, no arrogantly singular sense of style, no fully achieved narrative. Indeed, many big-studio movies are consciously fashioned so as to take involvement *out*—the entire range of emotions jettisoned in favor of one emotion, physical excitement. Why? It has apparently become a commonplace among Hollywood filmmakers that a given emotion, if done straight, will simply seem a dim and sentimental retread of some cherished moment from an old movie, so it's safer not to try for it. But isn't that fear a covert way of admitting that one has little conviction about whatever one is doing? Emotion grows out of belief in a subject, a character, a dramatic situation. In art, emotion always entails risk—the risk of imprecision—whereas spectacle is a matter of technique and production values.

The cinema, having replaced the public executions and bare-knuckle fights of earlier ages, is the modern arena of peril, sadism, and death. But most of the spectacular, violent new movies are amazingly impersonal—a rush of frenetic images that have little in common with, say, the heart-stopping dangers and last-minute rescues in Griffith, the tumultuous waves of frenzy in Gance, the stately displays of massed power in Lean, or even the physically eccentric, hiccuping movements in Spielberg's *Raiders of the Lost Ark*. A car or a boat, ramped into the air, glides in slow motion before crashing. A couple holding hands runs away from an explosion, or runs down a corridor as flames (or floods) chase after them. How many times have we seen those action tropes? Repeated again and again, they have assumed a purely formal meaning, like the cherubs and folded drapery in bad religious painting.

The old light, sure, happy self-confidence of Hollywood moviemaking is gone, perhaps forever. Instead, a jangled, derisive atmosphere of cynicism and self-mockery now surrounds much of the stuff coming out of the big studios. Suddenly, everyone has become an ironist: The postmodernist smirk of diddled reference and weightless play is the form of a new universal knowingness. Traditionally, irony divided the audience into those who understood and those who were left out, but the irony of, say, *Independence Day*—a reworking of old invasion-from-outer-space movies—comes without any point or object. Your not believing for an instant in any part of the fantasy—your reveling in the intentionally crappy movieness of it—is meant to be central to the fun, and for many people it is. *Independence Day* is a festival of spangled, kidding clichés—and a perfect example of the new corporate irony. The picture's status as a media event depends on its being dumb enough not to leave anyone out but knowing enough not to make the audience ashamed of the dumbness.

The hits and flops of corporate irony—the third and fourth *Batman* movies, *The Last Hero, Wayne's World, Dumb and Dumber, True Lies, Independence Day, Mission Impossible, Men in Black, Starship Troopers*—are cases not of parody but of pastiche: the merging of ransacked older styles in a play of surfaces. *Ghostbusters,* I suppose, stands behind *Men in Black,* and behind *Ghostbusters* stand *Dragnet* and other old cop movies and TV shows, but only vaguely—the referents trail off into media nowheresville. Big movies are now spoofs without a target; they draw in a generalized facetiousness. Corporate irony, which ridicules the very thing that it is selling—and ridicules the act of selling, too—is the deadliest weapon ever leveled against artistic seriousness (including comic seriousness). A clever picture like *Men in Black,* which is really about nothing at all, inverts the commonplace, but the success of such witty movies about nothing has the effect of making it much harder to say anything even halfway consequential. Cynicism, like bad currency, drives more authentic products from the scene.

A pox on irony! At the end of the twentieth century, despite such brilliant examples as *Pulp Fiction,* irony has become the refuge of the gutless and the accommodating. It functions not as a way of provoking and cleansing but as an attitude of solidarity among consumers who would like to feel hip while they are doing what everyone else is doing.

And corporate irony effectively disarms criticism. Anyone who gets too angry at self-mocking triviality risks looking stiff-necked or merely out of it. A critic may corkscrew himself into the proper joshing attitude, but doing so makes him less a judge than someone hoping to maintain balance with his limbs all askew. He's in danger of ironizing *himself* out of existence.

A new generation gap has opened up between older moviegoers, who are holding on to the remnants of modernist seriousness, and younger ones, who are often satisfied by spectacle alone. I know a variety of young intellectuals and advanced media whizzes who go blank whenever their older friends, through some lapse of decorum, speak of the moral valence of a given piece of behavior in a movie—say, the obvious exploitation of sadism and disgust (those putrefying corpses) in David Fincher's hypocritically "moral" police melodrama, *Seven*. Lighten *up*, they say. After all, these are just images. And so they are. But photographic images that move in real time still carry a freight of actuality that other images do not. At least that's the way many older moviegoers feel. Sorely literal, we cannot shake the naïve habit of reacting to images as if they actually referred to something; we still quail when a woman gets punched in the mouth.

Growing up in the violent wards of industrial pop, younger moviegoers have had the dismay pummeled out of them. This is not an intellectual failing; the same moviegoers may express the most refined distinctions about movies. A thirtyish intellectual I know was enraged by Jack Nicholson's saying, at the climax of *As Good as It Gets*, that Helen Hunt's criticism of his character has made him "want to be a better man." A novelist suffering from compulsive disorders, Nicholson declares that he will now do what he has failed to do in the past—he will take his pills. And my friend was indignant because he thought that a movie should stick to one thing or another and not mix together a moral conception of character and a clinical-pharmacological conception of character. That this same moviegoer can sit through the cartoon violence of *Replacement Killers* without annoyance suggests not dissociation but a set of responses learned from the media, at a safe remove, before they are learned from life.

The young audience for industrial pop talks about character and plot as if these things were just retractable formulas, a series of strategies to be manipulated toward a given end. To them, identity is a put-on, like a celebrity's riff on the Letterman show. A good part of the young audience wants the euphoria of weightlessness, of not feeling a thing ("I hate *drama*," a friend of my fourteen-year-old son told me with some heat). For older moviegoers, though, the weightlessness may produce not euphoria but nausea. Certainly a critic who comments on the quality of imagery when there is neither emotion nor conceptual daring behind the images—as there wasn't in a high-tech glossy shell like *Mission: Impossible*—is becoming a connoisseur of gleaming rot. He's falling into the chic irony of emptiness.

The trouble isn't that a number of meaningless movies have become hits; such things have happened throughout movie history. The trouble is that critics can no longer appeal to a commonly held set of values. Arguing with pleasure is a mug's game. If people say that they are having good sex, you can hardly tell them that they should give up lovemaking for sunsets. You can only tell audiences satisfied by *Mission: Impossible* or *Men in Black* that there are pleasures they are not experiencing, and then try to say what those pleasures are. But it becomes hard to do so when there's little new art around to offer as an alternative. Unwilling to play the killjoy, a critic may suffer a kind of internal collapse and simply go with the flow of commerce—or, flowing in the opposite direction, he may become a haughty contrarian, retiring from the mainstream movies in favor of Kazakhstani cinema (or whatever) that he encounters at film festivals.

It is perhaps too late to lament the disappearance of the foreign film from a major place in our culture. After many depressing conversations, I have found that younger moviegoers, reared on little but American movies, imagine that mourners for the foreign cinema are talking about some fool's paradise of zinc counters and cappuccino, a pretentious refuge for bearded losers and solemn girls in black. "Ciné-astes"—isn't that what they used to call them? It is worse than useless to tell such moviegoers that Bergman and Kurosawa, Antonioni and Fellini, Godard and Truffaut—to name just the most obvious figures—defined our moods in late adolescence, enlarged our sense of romance and freedom and passionate melancholy as well as the expressive pos-sibilities of movies, and that their influence was so pervasive that *Bon-nie and Clyde* as well as the careers of Woody Allen, Paul Mazursky, Robert Altman, and a host of other American directors and writers would not have been possible without them. The promotion onslaught creates so dominating a sense of *now* that the past loses all reality; it seems merely a discarded consumer style, faintly ridiculous.

One must quickly add that the current French, Italian, German, and Japanese cinemas are but a remnant of their former selves, and that the new movies from China, Russia, Finland, and Iran, however fascinating, cannot replace the old masterworks in excitement or glam-our. "Where are the great foreign films?" a friend asks, by which he means that he refuses to feel guilty about not going when there are no masterpieces to see. He has a point, but even when a good French movie opens here (like Claude Chabrol's *La Cérémonie*, in 1996) it's hard to scare up much of an audience for it.

Some would argue that the films of the American independents—strong, small-scaled movies like *Safe* and *Big Night* and *Swingers*—have replaced foreign films, fulfilling the same needs. But it hardly seems fair to mention the independents in the same breath as Kuro-sawa or Bergman. The American independent filmmakers, reacting to the impersonality and waste of Hollywood, don't work on that scale or seek that kind of vision. The indie movement exists as a perpetual promise—a slippery Sundance of dreams—and not as an achieved body of great work.

An intellectual life devoted to film has become harder and harder to support. As a student at Columbia in the early Sixties, I used to walk down Broadway with a friend to the Thalia, on Ninety-fifth Street, and see two Marx Brothers movies, or two René Clair films. But the old revival houses have been chased out of business by the video stores, and so have the 16-mm rental companies servicing university film-history classes, so that students now end up looking at a masterpiece by Jean Renoir or Jean Vigo on a mossy videotape that turns the movie's unique redolence into something as faded as pressed flowers discovered in an old book. A certain pathos attaches itself to earlier movies trapped in inadequate means of presentation: They seem merely decrepit, as if they had been made for people with a hunger for sensuous excitement smaller than our own. As consumerist irony replaces history, nostalgia is forbidden us.

Thirty years ago, a variety of film cultists turned their obsessions into a way of life; they broke up the massness of mass culture, casting a delirious, purplish light of humor and gossip on specialized passions and outlandish tastes. The cultists are mostly gone, and there are now fewer venues for "underground," or avant-garde, movies, many of whose techniques have simply been pulled above ground, into TV advertising and music videos. The recent outbreak in New York of cafés, nightclubs, and former factories exhibiting movies one or two nights a week is a lovely development, and Film Forum is an oasis. The museums and art institutes are always there, too, but one can't simply drop into such places on a whim the way moviegoers dropped into revival houses thirty years ago.

Young people create fashions in moviegoing. But do the young now have any special tastes or moviegoing habits of their own? Do they have anything comparable to the old appreciation of, say, Forties Hollywood for its passion-fruit camp qualities or of B movies for their lack of hypocrisy? In the late Sixties and early Seventies, young moviegoers gathered around rock documentaries or such counterculture movies as *Easy Rider* and *Alice's Restaurant.* What is the equivalent now? At the recent Sundance Festival distributors and exhibitors were publicly complaining that, apart from *Pulp Fiction* and *Chasing Amy,* few independent movies mean anything special to college students.

A new counterculture has grown up on the Internet, not at movies, and passionate connoisseurship now finds its home among TV watchers. Film has not died, but that ornery exasperating thing film culture has been seriously weakened. With some exceptions, smart kids simply join the mass-movie culture the same way that everyone else does. They go to movies not at individual theaters but at malls and twelveplexes, among the video games and roller rinks, where they absorb the quick-turnover attitude toward merchandise that mall life imposes on everyone. Taste as a specialized inside affair ("we" versus the eternal, undifferentiated "them") has largely disappeared, and as a result, moviegoing has lost its wickedness, its humor, a good part of its savor.

The critics, at their best, can still provide a little salt and pepper. Yet the ones with temperament, the ones with a feeling for the flesh and bone of a movie, have been largely drowned out by the salesmen and shouters.

If you look at the Sunday *Times* or at any major newspaper, you will see ads for movies that haven't yet opened. These ads are frequently garlanded with raves—not words from reviews that have already been published or broadcast but quotes given over the telephone to publicists after an early screening. Critics whose identity depends on blurbs have no incentive to dislike a movie, or even to moderate their praise, because unless they rave, their names will not appear in the ads. Some critics have even been asked to select among blurbs offered by publicity people ("How about 'You'll howl with laughter'? Is that good for you?"), and still others may hire ghosts to write their blurbs or set up reviewing "services" that generate raves in bulk.

Considered as a racket, this sort of thing lacks flair, the grandeur of audacity; it's so familiar that it has become a kind of national joke. *Mad* magazine, hanging in there after all these years, recently sent subscribers an issue wrapped in a mailer covered with blurbs for *Mad* itself. The best blurb: " 'Every once in a while a magazine comes along. This is such a magazine!'—Hecky Peckersmith, Peckersmith Press." You may wonder how someone like Hecky can possibly survive as a movie critic. But who's going to tell him he's a fake? The movie companies? The newspaper or the TV station that employs him and obviously finds him useful?

Hail Hecky! Junketing twenty weekends a year at good hotels in Los Angeles or New York, Hecky Peckersmith hardly seems like an absurd man. On the contrary, he seems to know exactly what he's doing. And if Peckersmith is happy, and if his editor or his producer doesn't much care how silly he is, then why make a fuss? One makes a fuss because honest praise is devalued when the studios fill the ads with manufactured raves; the language of criticism has become so debased that the public may not notice any difference between the ads for *L.A. Confidential* and those for trash like *Kiss the Girls*.

In the last fifteen years or so, the studios have largely taken control of the coverage of movies. Outside of the trade journals, one can hardly find an analysis of how the command structure of Hollywood makes decisions—routine decisions that often squeeze the art out of movies. The badness of most of our movies is simply accepted with a shrug as a given—as an element in the atmosphere that only a fool would deplore. The waves of promotion, the climate of selling overwhelm some newspaper publishers and their editors, and this may cause them to pressure their critics to shorten or punch up their reviews, to drop reasoning and evocation, to stop reviewing independent films and documentaries. Such editors have allowed themselves to become convinced that serious criticism is an annoying encumbrance—an élitist fraud—which most people can do without.

Movie critics dip in and out of shadows, seeking enchantment amid long spells of sardonic disaffection. Much of the time, they slouch and vegetate, cultivating endless memory and strange loyalties. But critics also cultivate hope. Obsessed with a performing art, they need to feel that something is breaking out, that something good is *opening*. They may be outsiders, but the surge of excitement surrounding a new movie sweetens their mood as much as it does that of people working in show business. And, like players everywhere, they hope to get lucky: They would love to feel, exultantly, that they were riding the crest of a movement, or helping some new taste or sensibility make its way in the world, or at least marking the stages in a great director's or actress's career. Handing out grades is never enough.

Critics seldom make things happen, but they can spark the dialogue, the good talk that is one of the prime pleasures of moviegoing. Aroused, they may long to find a way of preaching to their readers, and so they examine small bits of evidence—the spoor and flower of an entertainment system—and offer their modestly immodest comment on the moral life of the country. If they forget that all this matters, and that it matters, too, when bad movies triumph and good ones falter, they will amount to little more than horseflies on the great rump of movie commerce. And if that happens irony will no more save them than it has saved the movies.

Movie love is the critics' resource, their gaiety, their only possible victory. As lovers, they are surely equipped to rescue from its current embarrassment the belief that movies are an art form. And only as lovers can they re-create the fervent connection with bodies, faces, and stories that drew so many people to movies in the first place.

A Touch of the 1940s Woman in the '90s

by Molly Haskell

FROM *THE NEW YORK TIMES*

In the legendary women's films of the Thirties and Forties, much-loved throb specialists like Bette Davis, Margaret Sullavan, Joan Crawford, and Barbara Stanwyck played gallantly miserable women in stories where love was a vocation with its own rules and heroics. Vexed relationships and outsize emotions claimed center stage, and the tears they generated provided catharsis for female moviegoers who felt trapped by fate and domesticity.

The genre, revolving as it does around a sense of limited options, would seem to have outlived its raison d'étre in the rush of women's newfound freedoms. We supposedly live in a liberated era of multiple choices, high-powered careers, chic out-of-wedlock pregnancies, and serial marriage. Yet here, in modified form, is the woman's film staging a comeback, suggesting at the very least that our horizons are narrower and our options fewer than we think.

In *Stepmom*, which opens on December 25, the homey ex-wife and the hip wife-to-be butt heads over the kids until Mom gets cancer and career woman learns to be motherly. In the new British film *Little Voice*, opening on December 4, a daughter is driven to near catatonia by her loud-mouthed, man-chasing mother. The recent *One True Thing* features a stay-at-home mom and a career-oriented daughter who clash over values until the mother's dying initiates a rapprochement. It is characteristic of the genre that the male for whom the women compete is more significant as a trophy than as a flesh-and-blood character: William Hurt and Ed Harris, two of our more incandescent actors, play spear carriers to the drama of the dames, played respectively by Meryl Streep and Renée Zellweger in *One True Thing* and Julia Roberts and Susan Sarandon in *Stepmom*.

The actresses lend charisma to roles that might otherwise feel programmed, for the earnestness with which these two movies confront "life-choice" issues—the "stepchildren" problem, the "career woman" conflict—tap very different feelings from their more modest, yet oddly luminous, predecessors.

As another example of *plus ça change, plus c'est la même chose*, what new movie is a disguised update of that classic 1945 noir woman's film *Mildred Pierce*, with Joan Crawford as the pie-baking hausfrau turned restaurateur? Two free tickets if you guessed *Beloved*! Consider the plot resemblances: A mother prefers one daughter—the wrong one—to another; the bad daughter enjoys an incestuous relationship with the mother's lover. As punishment for the mother's behavior, the "good" daughter leaves.

In *Mildred Pierce*, the leave-taking is actually a death: Dear little Kay sickens and dies while Mom is gallivanting at the beach house of Zachary Scott. And the spoiled and poisonous Veda (Ann Blyth) takes up with Scott where Mom left off. In *Beloved*, Sethe's daughter Denver finally walks out of the house usurped by her monstrous sister, who has returned to insinuate herself into the arms of her murderer-mother and seduce her mother's newly acquired lover.

Of course there are differences. *Beloved* is nothing if not serious, a three-hour-plus adaptation of Nobel Prize–winning Toni Morrison's savagely ornate novel about the consequences of slavery, directed by the Academy Award winner Jonathan Demme and brought to fruition by Oprah ("This is my *Schindler's List*") Winfrey. By contrast, the source of *Mildred Pierce* was a darkly entertaining story by that specialist in the upward strivings and perversities of the Southern California middle class, James M. Cain, and directed by that quintessential Warner Brothers journeyman, Michael Curtiz. Yet the makers of *Beloved* might have learned a thing or two from *Mildred Pierce* about streamlining a plot, clarifying character, and building toward a climax. Ms. Winfrey, who is used to playing it low key on television, where the show is built around her, might have taken a leaf from Joan Crawford's book about the grandstanding of a star, how she moves front and center to claim our attention with an emotional transparency.

We can't go back to the studio film, nor would we necessarily want to, but the artificiality of back-lot shooting and the personalities of the stars created a distance that allowed us (and our heroines) to endure tragic events without succumbing to depression or being forced into analogies with our own lives.

The greater realism of today's movies, and the more visceral impact of images on the screen over those on the page, impose a burden on viewers that can finally sabotage a movie before it opens. For a number of reasons, among them the high profile of AIDS and breast cancer, dying is very much in the public consciousness, and in the movies, death is not what it used to be.

In *No Sad Songs for Me*, the Margaret Sullavan movie on which *Stepmom* is loosely based, the actress develops a fatal cancer but manages to look decorous and enchanting until the end. A *Time* magazine reviewer's snide dig that she looked as if she were suffering nothing worse than a migraine was obviously written by someone who'd never had one. But the complaint about divas who refused to spurn their glamorous makeup and hairdos for the verisimilitude of illness was a common one.

Now we get shaved heads, pale faces, shadows under the eyes, weight loss and gain—the whole nine yards of deterioration and disfigurement, enough to plunge us helplessly into memories of everyone we've known who has endured the indignities of dying. In *The Theory of Flight* (set to open on December 25) Helena Bonham Carter, as a woman fatally ill with Lou Gehrig's disease, gives such a convincing rendering of the muscular disorder's contorted speech that she's almost impossible to understand. Movie producers and marketers know that death is a commercial downer—hence the apparent popularity of homo resurrectus in ghost and afterlife movies and the disappointment of *One True Thing* at the box office despite good reviews.

One True Thing, Stepmom, and *The Theory of Flight* work as hard as they can to play against sentimentality and avoid the manipulation inherent in the material, but most of the old women's films didn't need disease to create pathos. In the 1937 Depression-and-class-conscious *Stella Dallas,* Barbara Stanwyck's struggle to promote her daughter socially pits Stella's own robust vulgarity against the refined world of the girl's father. Under the full-throttle direction of King Vidor, Stanwyck enacts some of the most emotionally charged scenes in the history of women's film, showing us Stella at her most outlandishly tacky, and Stella transfigured by a mother's love. The mutual wounds inflicted by mother and daughter touch on universal sins of insensitivity, and Stella's final surrender of her daughter breaks the most hardened heart; yet the movie doesn't weigh us down with guilt. Instead, it leaves us with a lift, much like Stanwyck's own curious expression of elation at the end, the mother having completely entered into the daughter's joy.

The new women's films want to help us with our lives but have no such faith in the outcome. Pregnancy is no longer a "fatal misstep," nor is extramarital sex a matter of sin and retribution (except, of course, where wives and mothers are concerned). We don't much believe in the majesty of sacrifice, nor the permanence of endings, happy or otherwise. There are just intermediate truces, provisional loves, a muddling on.

The difference between *Mildred Pierce* and *Stella Dallas* is between the heroically altruistic mother and the misguidedly altruistic mother; the same "problem," the spoiling of the daughter, has an opposite result. But there is never any question of the essential maturity or nobility of the mother. Compare Stella, who, for the sake of the sensitive Laurel, gives up carousing and her bibulous beau, with Mari Hoff (Brenda Blethyn), the unquenchably vulgar, me-first mother in *Little Voice*. Mari makes Mommie Dearest look like Mother Theresa. Sympathy in this British film is entirely with the repressed daughter (Jane Horrocks), who magically metamorphoses through the songs of Judy Garland and Ethel Merman, while the man-eating widow is loud, brassy, and whorish—a Stella unredeemed by mother-love, or by star casting.

The point in the old weepies was that in a world with the cards stacked against them, the heroines were seen as survivors because they were infused with the indomitability of the stars themselves, women who had succeeded in a tough profession and would make another film, and another, and another.

There's a continuing paradox in Hollywood films, a tension between actress and role: Mary Scott (the Sullavan character) dies; Margaret Sullavan lives. Now the underlying sense of the future has changed along with the nature of filmmaking. Women's lives today, despite political and economic gains, are more uncertain: Mothers do die; and, in Hollywood, women have fewer and fewer strong roles, thus "dying" professionally as they grow older.

If some things never change, others do. What hasn't changed is the taboo against full-bodied sexuality in the mature woman. In the choice between career and personal life, you can't "have it all." Even Elizabeth Tudor in *Elizabeth*, the new movie starring Cate Blanchett as the great Protestant queen, has to choose, as Papa Henry never did, between a sex life and the crown. Shedding her femininity, jettisoning her lovers, she puts on the virgin's genderless mask to establish her authority as queen. Yet, finally, there's a feminist triumph in her self-enforced solitude, something that Bette Davis's virgin queen was never permitted to feel as she sent Errol Flynn's Essex, the love of her life, to the executioner's block.

I Fired Capra

Hollywood, D.C.: For a Dreadful Moment, It Looked as if
The Best Man *Was Going to Be Turned into* Mr. Smith
Goes Back to Washington

by Gore Vidal

FROM *NEWSWEEK*

Several years ago, as I entered the theater on Venice's Lido, the
flower of the Italian press burst into hearty boos. I was president
of the Venice Film Festival jury that had just awarded the first prize:
The—what's the adjective?—*coveted* Golden Lion to Tom Stoppard
for *Rosencrantz and Guildenstern Are Dead*. The press knew that I was
responsible for this terrible homage to the unloved English language.
Graciously, I accepted the boos and catcalls, then murmured a few
words to the effect that, once a decade, simply as a novelty, the best
film in competition should win first prize. The decibel count grew.

Afterward, my fellow juror Gilles Jacob, head of the Cannes Film
Festival, reminded me that in 1964 my film *The Best Man* had won
the Critics' Prize at Cannes. "What was your happiest experience," he
asked, "in regard to this film?"

That was an easy one. "Firing Frank Capra." Had my colleague not clutched a passing console, he might have fallen to the floor. *"You . . . fired . . . Capra!"* He choked out the words. I might have finished him off had I said that I had also tried, but failed, to fire Jerry Lewis from *Visit to a Small Planet. La France, toujours.*

Capra. Political movies. Washington, D.C. Hollywood. At century's end, the symbiosis between the two is now a given. *Primary Colors* on the screen, with Bill and Hillary, while John and Emma are en route to Camp David. Or is it the other way round? From the beginning, politicians have used the movies. Woodrow Wilson appeared in two silent films just before the 1916 election: He would, he assured the audience, keep us out of the European war. Once re-elected and at war, he sent a master publicist, George Creel, to Hollywood to make sure that films were made demonizing the wicked Hun. But for a long time, Hollywood was far too shy or too ignorant to use Washington for its own ends: Of course, its ends were entirely commercial and an attack on those who had brought about the Depression would have been thought communist, and the Eastern banks that financed the studios would have been irritable. Then along came the exception, Frank Capra.

Born in Palermo, Capra arrived in America at the age of six. The Capra family were not huddled masses; they were fairly well off and settled in Los Angeles, where Capra graduated from high school in 1915, year of *The Birth of a Nation,* the first film to impress him. At a Pasadena college, Capra did well scholastically, but he was developing, if not a sense of inferiority, a fair-size chip on his shoulder: short, dark Sicilian in a world of WASPs. But he proved a natural for the movies, the local cottage industry. He worked as an editor, then directed dozens of silents and talkies, with ever-greater success.

Graham Greene, a film critic in his early days, regarded Capra as a technician of genius. Greene was a proto-auteurist who seldom took into account the writer's contribution to a film. But, as it turned out, it was two writers who invented the legendary Frank Capra and made of his curiously divided nature something much more interesting than it was to begin with. The first writer was Robert Riskin. He was a droll figure with a sharp wit who had come to the movies from the New

York theater. The Depression had driven him politically to the left, while Capra himself had not gone anywhere except to Columbia Pictures, the studio that brought Riskin and Capra together. They made movie history with *It Happened One Night* (1934) and *Mr. Deeds Goes to Town* in 1936, the year that Riskin voted for Roosevelt and Capra, by now in his heart if not in his vaguely populist films a man of the right, voted for Alf Landon.

It was also in 1936 that the other inventor of Capra, Myles Connolly, appeared on the scene. A Boston newspaperman, Connolly was a crusading Roman Catholic with a messianic mission. In a novel, *Mr. Blue* (1928), Connolly wrote, "If you want to reach the masses you can reach them through pictures. These new children can be bent and molded as they sit in the dark enrapt before the magic of the mobile [*sic*] screen.... Here is a destiny for art second to none in history. For it is given the motion picture to save the soul of a civilization." Thus, Capra-corn was first popped, as it were. Through Capra's technical skill, Connolly would save the world. Paradoxically, the first picture that Connolly worked on was *Mr. Smith Goes to Washington,* whose screenwriter was a genuine communist, Sidney Buchman. Capra was now between heaven and hell. As hell has the best dialogue, the film was a great success.

The gala 1939 opening in my hometown of Washington, D.C., was full of ironies, perhaps wasted on Capra. As the Wise Hack at the MGM writers' table used to say, politics is show business for the ugly. Washington has always been acutely aware of Hollywood, whose stars it regards with such awe that it even tried one out as president; hardly anyone noticed.

Mr. Smith is the story of a virtuous young man who arrives in the Senate, where a wicked senator is trying to build a river to go with a dam or some such self-serving skulduggery. The senators at the premiere managed to keep straight faces until the villain, bested by the passionate Mr. Smith, cries out to the Conscript Fathers, "I'm not fit to be a senator. I am not fit to *live*.... Expel *me!*" Senators hardly knew which way to look. Capra, ever the self-dramatist, reported in his biography that a third of the audience walked out. They did not.

But the *Chicago Tribune* denounced the film, and Ambassador Joe Kennedy warned Columbia that this was not the right sort of message to send abroad as war clouds gathered over Europe. Even so, the movie was a hit, thanks to Jimmy Stewart and Jean Arthur at their best.

A decade later, Capra again used American politics as background to a film. *State of the Union* was a solid middlebrow Broadway play about a presidential candidate with a wife and a mistress, the situation that the Republican candidate, Wendell Willkie, had found himself in during the 1940 election. The dread Connolly coauthored the screenplay and is duly credited. Where the play's core was standard Broadway liberalism, the film's protagonist, as played by Spencer Tracy, is a sort of holy fool—he's new to politics, he keeps telling everyone. Capra's biographer, Joseph McBride, notes: "Capra puts into [Tracy's] mouth a nonsensical jumble of contradictory political opinions, particularly on business and labor issues, on which he flip-flops from Republican to Democrat within a single sentence." Actually, this could be the basis for a truly ironic study of an "independent" candidate today, artfully dodging his way to the White House. But Tracy's character is incoherent. The Riskin formula demanded a moment of self-revelation; unfortunately, Connolly's religiosity ruins it. The senator in *Mr. Smith* roared like a lion about his sins; poor Tracy whispers, as if in confessional, "I have as much right to run for president as a gutter rat . . . I lost faith in you [he means The People], I lost faith in myself . . . I forgot how quickly the Americans smell out the double-dealers and the crooks." Though this film is no more dimwitted about politics than the successful one, Capra without Riskin has lost his mastery of image and, most unsung of his skills, his ability to get the best from actors.

In 1960 my play *The Best Man* opened on Broadway. Sometimes billed as a comedy, sometimes as a melodrama by those who could not accept a realistic play about the maneuvering that used to go on at presidential conventions before multiple primaries ruined the fun. Ever since *You Can't Take It with You*, Capra had liked to adapt successful plays for the screen. Now he was intrigued by politics again, and by *The Best Man.* He asked United Artists to buy it for him to produce and direct, with Myles Connolly in the priest's role. Capra wanted one last hit in the old *Mr. Smith* vein. United Artists made me an offer. I was still the snotty hometown Washington boy who knew just how corny and untrue Capra's political movies were. On the other hand, political films usually have a bad time of it commercially. So I sold the play to UA and went on to other things. Then Capra and his chaplain presented UA's Max Youngstein with a screenplay. Youngstein noted that their protagonist "spouts clichés at the rate of one a minute, and while many of these clichés have great truths behind them, no one can take that many, back to back, without vomiting." Plainly, Riskin and his wit were now history.

UA called me in for "consultation." I met Capra. A bright-eyed, amiable little man. Eyes like black olives. "Quite a guy your Kennedy . . . exciting stuff at the convention . . . of course I'm for Nixon . . . he's better on communism. . . ." I asked to see the script, but Capra wanted a fresh start. "Now I've got this idea. The good guy should go down on the convention floor . . . you know, just before the vote. He's dressed up as Abraham Lincoln, and he makes this speech and wows the delegates. . . ." It was now I who clutched at a passing radiator to keep from falling. "What, uh, does he say?" Capra was airy: "Oh, you know, some 'fourscore' stuff." I reported back to Youngstein that Capra was not capable of making the film, and I advised UA to drop the project. They had another idea; if Capra walked the plank, would I write it, with a director of choice? So I did, with Franklin Schaffner, and we ended up with a film that went from rave reviews and prizes to classic without an intervening success. Perhaps if our star, Henry Fonda, *had* worn a Lincoln suit . . .

Anyway, that was the end of Capra but hardly the beginning of a cycle of political films. Even so, in the thirty years since, we have had several splendid movies like *The Candidate, Bob Roberts,* and now *Bulworth* and *Primary Colors,* whose scenarist, the philosopher Elaine May, put our politics in a nutshell years ago when she told critic Edmund Wilson, who took notes, as we all do when she speaks, "I like a moral problem so much better than a real problem." So do I, and that is why I made no fuss when Mr. Anonymous lifted the plot of *The Best Man* (to use or not use a sexual smear in order to become president) for his novel *Primary Colors*. Travolta did; Henry Fonda did not. Other times.

I Would Toss Myself Aside

Confessions of a Catholic Film Critic

by *Richard Alleva*

FROM *IMAGE: A JOURNAL OF THE ARTS AND RELIGION*

I am a film critic for a Catholic magazine, *Commonweal,* written and published by the laity. This has allowed my love of movies both to flourish and to become articulate. Thinking about my job has induced a curious fantasy. Suppose a time machine could whisk the sixteen-year-old Richard Alleva out of 1964 and off to a well-stocked library of 1998. That rabid movie buff, eager to learn the state of his beloved art, would begin riffling through current issues of *The New Republic* in search of Stanley Kauffmann reviews (and would find that gray eminence still there and as eloquent as ever), would seek in vain the now defunct left-wing journal the *New Leader* in pursuit of John Simon, only to find him still applying the acid test in the pages of the right-wing *National Review,* and would be dumbfounded by the absence of Pauline Kael, now retired and babysitting her grandchildren in Massachusetts.

What would the teenager-I-was do if he came across a pile of *Commonweal* magazines? I know all too well. He would toss them aside.

Not out of disrespect for Catholicism, for he was (and, more anemically, still is) a Catholic. Not out of disrespect for Catholic writing in general or *Commonweal*, in particular. After all, that sixteen-year-old did read Chesterton and other Catholic writers, and yes, he did read, with sporadic interest, *Commonweal*, among other Catholic magazines. But to read the *movie columns* in a Catholic magazine? No! He had read a few once, but—nevermore! He wouldn't even bother to look at whose name was on the by-line. If any movie critic was writing in any Catholic magazine, *ipso facto* he must be a bore.

Yes, I would toss myself aside. To make you understand exactly why, I have to talk about the birth of my love for movies.

Infatuations are born in the most banal places. My infatuation with movies began in a barber shop in my home town, Waterbury, Connecticut. This was no unisex hair boutique but just a neighborhood place that didn't schedule its clientele; you went in, took a seat, and when your turn came round, you got in the chair. As a thirteen-year-old schoolboy, I had to go for my monthly shearing on Saturdays when the shop was always full. And, due to various circumstances, I always showed up between eleven and one, when the place was most busy, and I would have to wait for a couple of hours. I was already a great reader, yet—and I haven't got any explanation for this except that kids are weird—I never brought a book, not even a comic book, to while away the waiting, so I had to read the magazines that the barbers had stacked on a long table. And, amidst the issues of the *Police Gazette* and *Sports Illustrated* (the clientele was mainly male) I found *Esquire*.

This was the *Esquire* of Harold Hayes's editorship. Never really a pin-up magazine like *Playboy*, *Esquire* had its reputation as a guide to the male sophisticate further upgraded by Hayes's hiring of classy talents such as Capote, Talese, Mailer, Baldwin, Plimpton. The regular critical columnists were Dorothy Parker, Malcolm Muggeridge, and, fatefully for me, Dwight Macdonald on movies.

Macdonald, a Trotskyite turned anarchist, one of the founders of the *Partisan Review*, editor of *Politics*, friend of Dorothy Day and big-brother-in-spirit to James Agee, had pretty much abandoned his political commentary for the creation of the best cultural criticism ever written by an American. His articles (collected in *Against the American Grain*), defining and excoriating our ersatz approaches to life and art, are as pertinent today as they were in the Fifties. Yet Macdonald never let sociological generalization come between him and the unique life of each movie or book he focused on.

I don't remember what made me pick up that issue of *Esquire*, but it certainly wasn't Dwight Macdonald. Maybe Yvette Mimeux in a bikini was on the cover. In any case, when I saw the column titled *Film*, I began reading and stayed with it and carried it into the barber's chair.

For I had the same interest in movies that virtually all Americans in the twentieth century have had and which only now is being usurped by video games and the Internet. I went to them in the same spirit of pop consumption with which I read comic strips and watched TV. Movies were available. They were fun. They constituted the official American idleness. And unlike TV or radio, they were a night out. What struck me as weird as I read Macdonald's piece was that here was an obviously intelligent man taking an obviously intelligent pleasure in what was supposed to be sheer distraction.

I knew what aesthetic discrimination was (though I wouldn't have called it that) because I had seen book reviews in the *Saturday Review of Literature* to which my mother subscribed. But the idea of distinguishing good movies from bad ones and offering specific reasons why—well, this was something new.

In the piece I chanced upon, Macdonald was considering some classics which had just been re-released: *Gone With the Wind*, which I'd seen, and two I hadn't, *The Public Enemy* and *The Birth of a Nation*. He explained why *Gone With the Wind*, for all its romanticism about the dear, dead antebellum South, was an adult movie. The tension between Ashley's conventional Southern chivalry, which Scarlett revered and told herself to love, and Rhett Butler's pragmatism, which both disgusted and attracted her because it was just like her own pragmatism and animal vitality, was what made the film something more than a soap opera like one of those Joan Crawford movies I despised. The contradiction between what people wanted and what they told themselves they wanted, psychological complexity in short, was what made a movie adult, and I sensed this was so even at the age of thirteen. But I hadn't been able to formulate my feelings until Dwight Macdonald did it for me. (This might be the chief delight of reading criticism: not being told something you didn't know, but being told something you sensed but couldn't say.)

Then he moved on to *The Public Enemy* and explained the difference between gangster movies that wallowed in violence and a subtle gangster movie like this Jimmy Cagney masterpiece. The very idea of a subtle gangster movie startled, almost disturbed me. My snobbery about the genre (too much like the covers of the *Police Gazette*) was checkmated by the concrete example the critic gave: the killing of a stool pigeon not shown but indicated by an off-screen report and—this was the master stroke—since the victim had been desperately playing the piano to distract and placate his executioners, we heard the tune he'd been playing suddenly go wildly discordant, then the crash of keys as the dead man's face slammed down. We didn't see the violence but instead a distillation of it, and the distillation was more pungent than the literal sight. It's a familiar enough device now but, at the age of thirteen, the idea that Less Is More was a revelation.

Finally, Macdonald took a look at what is pretty much the first major movie ever made, *The Birth of a Nation*. Actually all he did was analyze one shot which the movie's title calls "The Mulatto's Mad Proposal." D. W. Griffith's racist horror at the idea of a black man proposing marriage to a white girl saturates the shot but, as dreadful as it is, the racism also fills the screen with a sort of malevolently mythic horror. Macdonald's point was not to expose the racism—for a progressive like Macdonald it was laughably self-evident—but to show how the racism resulted in a luridly exciting shot that could be studied as if it were a nineteenth-century Victorian print (so many intense emotions, vibrant and repugnant, in a single composition!). That's basically what movies were, this critic was saying: images, single or edited in a sequence, that had to be *read*.

That was the decisive revelation for me. All my life I had been told by teachers that reading was greater than moviegoing because you had to work at reading, had to decipher the words, turn them into images in your mind, had to work at understanding what the author had to say, and it was the *work* of reading that consecrated that activity and made literature a greater art form than film, which was scarcely art at all, since movies just flowed in front of your eyes and did all your imagining for you.

But here was Macdonald telling me that the viewer who merely let images flow before his eyes simply wasn't watching the movie at all but submitting himself to a zombie-like condition. To truly watch a movie was to *read* it, i.e., to see all that was put before you and to question yourself about what was shown.

There were, it seemed, many questions to be asked. How was the action framed and where were the characters placed? Why in the fore-ground? Why in the background? Why did the camera look over the shoulder of one character rather than over the shoulder of the character being looked at? Why was another character kept off-screen while speaking? Why was the camera moving in a given shot but kept still in another? Why was music used at one moment and not another? Why was one scene told with rapid cutting while another consisted of one shot held for five minutes?

I learned that film could be seen as a sort of conglomerate art. It had musical rhythms, novelistic storytelling, theatrical acting (modi-fied for the camera), the composition and color of painting, political and metaphysical ideas made concrete and dramatic. And the very thing that made film not just a junction of all the other arts but a distinct art form in itself—editing—also made each truly good movie impossible to absorb at one viewing. Editing made the movie flow before you and enchant you, but it also made the film flow away from you and escape you. At any rate, movies ceased to be for me an easy activity that you indulged in instead of doing something worthwhile, like reading. In fact, movies for me became the most difficult reading of them all. Without ceasing to be fun.

Thus was born an irredeemable movie buff and thus began many trips to the Lincoln Theater in New Haven to see the films of Truffaut, Fellini, Antonioni, Godard, Varda, Kurosawa, Malle, John Schlesinger,

Lindsay Anderson, and Tony Richardson. And to be a movie buff, at least in those days, was to be a reader of certain film critics because, though American films weren't yet sparked by the exciting innovations of the Europeans, the excitement was already there in American movie criticism. To read Pauline Kael on Godard, Stanley Kauffmann on Antonioni, and John Simon on Bergman, was to be made to feel that you were present at the creation of art that would sooner or later (surely sooner) take on classic status. As different as they were from one another and as much as they quarreled with each another, the best critics all had one thing in common: They got at the meanings of their favorite works by thoughtfully examining their surfaces. When Kael wanted to convey the amusing perversity of Joseph Losey's *Accident*, she told us that the sunlight in that film "is terrible, it's *rotten*, because it makes the characters feel sexy. Joseph Losey uses sexual desperation and the beauty of Oxford in summertime to make our flesh crawl." Kauffmann made the reader see the originality of Antonioni's *Red Desert* by carefully describing how the colors of that movie portrayed the heroine's state of mind in a way that no other color photography had ever done. "Caress the details," Vladimir Nabokov urged his Cornell students when he unveiled the wonders of literature to them. The best American film criticism of the Sixties did precisely that, and it fed the flames lit for me by Dwight Macdonald.

This, at long last, brings me to the reason why the adolescent I was scarcely ever bothered with the film criticism in Catholic magazines. I did read some reviews at first in the *Sign*, the *Catholic Transcript*, *Catholic World*, and others, but soon stopped. Why? I was sympathetic to the effort to get at the spiritual core of a film, but I think I also sensed that the essence of art can't be reached by skipping over its materiality, its sensuous surface. In any good or great movie, a camera pan, a dolly forward, a splash of color, the expression on an actor's face or the intonation in his or her voice, an apt line of dialogue, are never decorative, but reveal something about the inner lives of characters and, of course, the inner life of the filmmaker. I never received a taste of this excitement from Catholic critics.

Instead, the reader would get a plot summary and superficial comments along the lines of "well paced," "beautifully acted," concluding with a thumbs up or thumbs down. (It's the sort of thing Elizabeth Hardwick complained of in *The New York Times Book Review*—"the flat praise and the faint dissension.") I sometimes wondered why such reviewers had to see the films before writing such stuff. Why couldn't they simply obtain plot summaries from the film companies and proceed from there? For often it appeared as if their judgments were strictly verdicts on the moral decency or indecency of the plot. Hitchcock's 1957 remake of *The Man Who Knew Too Much* was well received in the Catholic press (a father searches for his kidnapped son—good family values!) while *Psycho* was abominated (Janet Leigh in her bra and short slip plus slashings in the shower—horrors!). You would never have guessed that *The Man* was a pretty stodgy piece of moviemaking while *Psycho* was Hitchcock at his innovative best, a movie that forever changed the way directors of chillers handled plot and characterization.

As the Sixties proceeded, Catholic critics and academics often latched on to certain films to explore or exemplify theological matters, but always the same films: *La Strada, La Dolce Vita,* and—always, always—*The Seventh Seal*. I respect these movies but, as written about in the Catholic press, they weren't so much works of art as just so much symbolic ore to be mined for the sake of theological nuggets. But the real being of any good movie resides in the way it moves in time. You can talk all you want about the monster fish on the beach at the close of *La Dolce Vita*, but you get closer to the temperament, yes, even the essence, of that movie when you notice how the camera hovers, seemingly hypnotized, near the face of Anita Ekbert as, with rock music blasting away, she dances herself into a sort of kinetic stupor. You feel that if a camera could pant, then Fellini's camera would pant as it tries to position itself on the neck of the amazonian film star, and this enthrallment of the camera by so much flesh and heat has more to do with the much noted ambivalence of *La Dolce Vita* than any symbolic fish.

By concentrating only on those elements that lend themselves most obviously to religion-related discussion and by neglecting the expressive surface of a film, a critic can actually blind himself to the filmmaker's vision and whatever spiritual qualities that vision might possess.

But let us say that a critic writing for a Catholic periodical does respond to the sensuous surface of a film. What then? Is he doing anything for his audience that the reader couldn't get from an agnostic critic writing for, say, *The New Yorker* or *The New Republic*? I'm afraid the answer is no, or at least not insofar as purely aesthetic analysis goes. However, his religious upbringing (or instruction, if he's a convert) should strengthen his criticism in at least two ways.

First, Catholicism has an inherently dramatic vision of life. Unlike certain Protestant sects, Catholicism does not smile upon the notion of doom, to put it mildly. Though circumstances may do their best to damn you, you can resist, and resistance is dramatic. I was taught that grace could be an aid in the struggle, but even grace had to be won by prayer, and prayer itself is a sort of struggle.

I think that the popular, secularist view of Catholicism as a religion that devalues, even demeans, life probably derives from Christianity's vision of life as a struggle, because the struggle itself is perceived as a refusal to enjoy the goodness of life. What's missed by secularists is that the struggle can be heroic, energizing, life-enhancing. (The Protestant *Pilgrim's Progress* got this right by picturing the search for salvation as a sort of chivalric adventure story, but no one reads Bunyan anymore.) You are the protagonist of your own drama. This view of life makes the Catholic critic of film or drama or fiction look for certain things that the non-Catholic might not so instinctively seek. Who is the protagonist of the film? (Who struggles?) What is his or her objective? (What is he or she struggling for?) What is he or she doing to reach the goal? And this leads the critic on the classic Aristotelian hunt for the incitement of the main action—development, climax, and denouement. This classic view of drama must be kept flexible to accommodate the work of innovating artists whose instincts may lead them away from this framework, but it remains a sound bulwark against trendy nonsense. (Let it also be said that the best practitioner of this approach is the *New Republic*'s Stanley Kauffmann, Jewish and agnostic; not incidentally, Kauffmann was the staunchest American champion of Antonioni, whose time-stretching and time-eliding movies stretch the Aristotelian concepts to their limits without shattering them.)

Second, there is the democracy of Catholicism, or rather of Christianity. I'm not talking of political but spiritual and eschatological democracy. Any Christian must acknowledge not only the inherent dignity of other human beings but also their unshunability. This isn't the same thing as tolerance. It's rather a kind of humility before the glory and misery and wonder of life that might make the Catholic critic pause a second before condemning a dramatist or director for constructing a story around a seemingly worthless character. (A serious Catholic doesn't keep the word "worthless" on the tip of his tongue.) You have to take the trip through the drama before you can say whether or not a character is a truthful distillation of some aspect of humanity. A drama is not a cocktail party with guests you may choose to greet or ignore. It's a reflection of the passage through life. And all the elements of moviemaking—camera, cutting, design, dialogue, acting—contribute, or don't contribute, to that journey. To refuse to revel in those aesthetic elements is like taking a train ride with the windows boarded up while wearing a blindfold and earplugs. You may get off at your destination but you don't know how you got there, and therefore, you really haven't had a trip at all.

The Catholic critic always writes *out of* his or her own Catholicism, *not toward* what he perceives as the reader's Catholic concerns. He does not bring to film his intellectual passion *as a Catholic,* or his sense of moral obligation *as a Catholic.* He does not have to rouse his Catholic conscience every time he sees a movie. He does not stoke up his Catholic sensibility when he enters the theater. He does not say to himself, as the lights go down and the screen lights up: "And now, it's time for the Catholic perspective." Rather, he goes to a movie or to a play or reads a novel or listens to a concert with his entire being, with all the passion that is in him. He watches from the perspective of his entire life. He does not, in fact, experience a work of art as a Catholic but as the human being whose Catholicism is now part of his being

. . . or isn't. The religious sense will not spring to attention on cue as he watches the film but always subtly informs the way he takes it in. If it does not, he is simply the wrong person for the job. The Catholic critics I read as a boy did seem to consciously rouse their Catholic sensibilities; they did put their Catholic outlook on the alert. And that may have been why their criticism seemed to me so uninspiring, so boring. They were writers who had filtered their souls. In effect, they weren't being truly Catholic, or catholic, critics.

The best American film critic was James Agee, who was Episcopalian and who wrote for a completely secular magazine, *The Nation*. His religious sense was at one with his passionate response to life, and that passion made his criticism still the best film criticism ever written in English. His childhood friend Dwight Macdonald wrote that Agee "was deeply religious, but he had his own kind of religion, one that included irreverence, blasphemy, obscenity, and even Communism (of his own kind)."

Macdonald's description of his friend informs my vision of a serious man and a serious critic.

Afterwards

The Sweet Smell of Success

by James Mangold

For all the cynicism it portrays, *Sweet Smell of Success* is a film directed by an idealist, a perfectionist, and an innovator. In 1981, when I was seventeen and in my first week of art school, I met Sandy Mackendrick. He was a giant presence at Cal Arts. Students, professors, deans, cafeteria workers, everyone was in awe of him. Though seventy years old, Sandy was a strapping, broad-chested genius with little patience for ignorance and even less for talent unmarried to discipline. Fresh out of suburban high school, my only reference for a man like this was the John Houseman I had seen on Seventies TV as Professor Kingsfield in *The Paper Chase*.

I had a pile of Super 8 films under my arm and was desperate for Sandy to become my mentor. I watched all his movies (*The Man in the White Suit*, *The Maggie*, *The Ladykillers*, *Whisky Galore*, and *Sweet Smell of Success*, to name a few), but he wanted nothing to do with such a youngster. I was persistent. I forced him to watch my collection of shorts. I will never be as proud of anything as changing his mind that day.

As I sit here, over fifteen years later, I profoundly miss Alexander Mackendrick. He taught me more craft than I could articulate, but beyond that, he showed me how hard one had to work to make even a decent film. He demonstrated—on a daily basis—the sharp elbows, passionate heart, and evangelical tongue required to defend and nurture innovative projects.

The innovation of *Sweet Smell* is often credited to Ernest Lehman's courageous portrayal—in his original novelette and screenplay—of the underbelly of the post-war American media machine. But the dazzling achievement of the film springs not merely from its politics—many mediocre films of the Fifties took on important political concerns—but from its swirlingly brilliant screen-narrative and language, verbal and visual. Sandy supervised all the rewrites on the film. When Ernest Lehman fell ill, Sandy chose Clifford Odets to do the rewrites. The collaboration of these three continued through production.

"What I really enjoyed about working with Clifford," said Sandy about Odets, "was his craft in the *structuring* of scenes. One of Odets' passions was chamber music. Particularly string quartets. He took great delight in the craft of the composers who knew how to interweave the five 'voices' of the instruments so that each has its own 'line' throughout the work, each distinct from the others but all of them combining to make sure the whole was greater than just the sum of the parts."

Mackendrick's office at Cal Arts was adorned with nearly thirty framed aphorisms that ran the circumference of the room. They were rendered in a faux needlepoint style (Sandy was a wonderful illustrator), and they said things such as:

1. A character who is intelligent and dramatically interesting THINKS AHEAD.

2. EXPOSITION can only be dramatic when it emerges in the context of DRAMATIC CONFLICT.

3. A FOIL CHARACTER is a figure invented to ask the questions to which your audience needs answers. (*It may be more important to have the questions clearly asked than to provide an immediate answer.*)

4. In movies what is SAID is less effective than what is SEEN HAPPENING.

5. The "action" of the ANTAGONIST(S) is often more important to the structure of the PLOT than the intentions of the PROTAGONIST.

6. Don't expect audiences to register the names of characters mentioned in the dialogue but not shown on the screen.

There were no aphorisms about eyelines or blocking or camera placement. Sandy was a director who built his films from the script up. He believed a film's value and style, its jazz and its meaning, all stemmed from the screenplay. And he knew, as most decent filmmakers (but few outside the process) do, that a script is more than a libretto of zippy dialogue. It is *what is seen happening* in *what order to whom, where.*

To that end, I want to examine the front end of *Sweet Smell* through the introduction of J. J. Hunsecker (Burt Lancaster) at the "21" Club. Of the selected aphorisms above, the first five are all clearly implemented in these sequences. Ernest Lehman's exposition in *Sweet Smell* is artfully dispensed (given the bewildering world of the press agent); we are told only what we must know to survive the current scene.

From the moment Sidney Falco (Tony Curtis) is introduced, we see a man in crisis. The exact nature of this crisis is indistinct, but it clearly emanates from a columnist named J. J. Hunsecker. Even without understanding the exact nature of Sidney's profession, we see in his artful maneuvers that he is clearly a man who thinks ahead (Rule #1). We (the audience) are continually catching up with him. We learn about this world as (a) Sidney spars with frustrated clients, (b) responds to the romantic whinings of his assistant, (c) slinks his way toward Susan and Steve, maneuvering past Steve's manager and a cigarette girl desperate for a favor—both characters to be used effectively later—and (d) escorts Susan home, discovering her engagement. Each dollop of exposition religiously follows Rule #2. Every scene has a present purpose and conflict, as well as serving to dispense more and more backstory.

Sidney's assistant is the first "foil character" introduced (Rule #3) and asks him *"Why is Mr. Hunsecker trying to squeeze your livelihood away? What do you stand this kind of treatment for?"*—this charged with the lingering feeling that Sidney has taken comfort in her "meaty arms" in the past. He responds with a passion-charged monologue about getting *"up there where everything's balmy"* and no one snaps their fingers and says, *"Hey—kid—rack up the balls."*

However, the essential load of exposition (Just what *is* a press agent? What does Sidney Falco do for a living, and why is he necessary?) is denied us. Without it, we (the audience) are living fully through Rule #4. We watch both the Machiavellian and the ass-kissing *behaviors* of a press agent without much explanation or comment upon the rationale behind them. It makes the movie smart. Lehman and Odets make us work a little. Something we experience rarely these days. In fact, in this age of intensive audience previews where everything needs to be fully comprehensible at every moment (unless you are making a mystery), this kind of slow-spooned exposition is nearly impossible to get through the system.

And this is where a whole second tier of structural brilliance comes into play. Sandy chose to defy his own rule (#6). But to our benefit. For the first twenty minutes of the film, everyone is talking relentlessly about J. J. Hunsecker with nearly religious fear and respect. But he goes unseen.

Sweet Smell's build-up to the introduction of J. J. Hunsecker at "21" yields one of the great character introductions in the history of film. Lehman, Odets, and Mackendrick boldly chose to force us to deal with J. J. in every possible perceptual way before introducing him as a live human presence on-screen. Equipped (as he was) with an awareness that he was breaking one of his own cardinal rules, Sandy compensated for the gamble with a breathless pace. He knew Hunsecker was being played by one of the biggest stars of the day and the longer his arrival was delayed, the more it would build suspense and appreciation of J. J.'s supreme status in the world of the story.

1. In the very *first image* of the film we see J. J.'s name and face slathered on the side of the newspaper trucks leaving the warehouse.
2. In the first scene, we see J. J. Hunsecker's likeness on the banner atop his column as Sidney reads it with disgust at a hot dog stand.
3. We then follow Sidney through a night's work—all the time hearing J. J.'s name invoked with fear and/or reverence.
4. Sidney goes to "21" and asks, "Is he here?" A maître d' nods and we see a table in the dining room with a man's back to us (J. J.). Ever thinking ahead (Rule #1), Sidney measures his moves. He chooses *not* to plunge into the club and confront J. J. Instead, the brilliant indulgence of this tease is tested one more time as . . .
5. Sidney calls J. J. on a house phone. It is now, for the first time, that we hear the sinister voice of Hunsecker. "You're dead, son. Get yourself buried." Sidney now, with some hesitation, marches into the dining room where . . .
6. Lancaster (J. J.) is finally unveiled. Sandy worked this first image of Hunsecker out very carefully with James Wong Howe (the cinematographer), who top-lit Hunsecker in his horn-rims so that his head resembled a skull. J. J. tells a waiter to have Sidney escorted out—until, that is, Sidney (thinking ahead once again) lets Hunsecker know that his sister is about to become engaged.

This is brilliant filmmaking. The movie up to this point has been dancing through a dark parade of major and minor characters. There is no one left to introduce. We have met *everybody*. Only J. J. remained veiled. And no one previously introduced failed to discuss J. J., the great unseen monster. Lehman claims this choice came from his subconscious, without planning. Many bold ideas come to a writer quietly and without fanfare—a feather falling in the night—but when they fly in the face of accepted practice, it requires real courage for the writer and the team that follows to maintain the bold choice and avoid back-sliding.

This unique first act structure is not merely a stylistic device. The holding back of J. J. until all other story forces have been set in place (all of these plot lines reactive to his power) is what *makes* J. J. Hunsecker so impressive upon his introduction. It is not just Lancaster's searing portrayal. It is not merely Howe's cadaverous lighting. It is not simply the sparkling dialogue of Lehman/Odets, nor Sandy's swinging dark camera and furious blocking. J. J.'s power comes from the film's core architecture. The sum that is greater than the parts. Hunsecker's introduction is the arrival of the missing link. Once we confront him, we retroactively understand everything that preceded this moment. And the movie structurally unites with its own setting and theme. We have not been merely told that the world of the press agent is a dark labyrinth, we have been *shown it* (Rule #4); we have felt, first-hand, the humiliating scramble for the access to power.

And who is at J. J.'s table? Not only a talent manager, Manny Davis (expected), and a pretty actress (expected) but a United States senator who is apparently trying to get his "Jersey" mistress (the "actress") a gig through J. J.'s influence. With such a table setting any confusion over the level of J. J.'s power (or "the system") is quite literally demonstrated. What might be another movie's authority figure (senator) is witnessed groveling before J. J.'s power to anoint. Says J. J., at the scene's climax, "God willing, Senator, you might want to be President one day. Yet here you are, out in the open, where any hep cat can see that this one (Manny) is toting around that one (actress) *for you.* Are we friends or what?"

Dialogue—no matter how clever or poetic—plays like this only when the architecture of the film supports it. The elements (narrative, performance, visual, verbal, musical) have to *dance.* The crafters of this film—Lehman, Odets, and Mackendrick—were not just smart, they were very smart and they gave the senator an additional purpose here. The senator asks Sidney to explain what it is he does for a living—what is a press agent? And so it is that we finally (Rule #3) get a foil to ask the question that we've been dying to understand. What exactly is Sidney doing? And instead of a merely verbal response we also get to *see* the relationship on the other side of the table, between a press agent (Sidney would now be called a publicist) and an influential columnist. Sidney sits to J. J.'s side, just a bit behind him. It is immediately understood. They may snipe at each other, but Sidney is an ally, a junior officer in "the war."

There is a Shakespearean aura to this film. It is rare in modern movies to follow characters who are so irredeemable and ambitious. But as we see in Sandy's Rule #5, antagonists drive a story. And this story's particularly intense drive comes from the fact that our central characters are conniving, cunning, methodical, lying—in short, innately evil. Throughout the film, there is a tenuous dance between elaborate scene constructions and economical story-telling—we move from location to location, club to TV studio (an amazing scene of five-step manipulation) to club to office without confusion, just momentum. Notice the beautiful symmetry of the two cigarette girl and Herbie Temple scenes.

The spiral toward the climactic triple-cross is a beautiful narrative sculpture of bluffs, lies, and counter lies with the seemingly innocent Susan proving to be every bit up to the twisted methods of her adversaries. According to Sandy, this final conflict in the penthouse was the source of several battles between the producers (including the star, Burt Lancaster) and the writer/director team. Odets rewrote it several times. Sandy shot it twice and recalled staging it in such a complex series of movements and linking shots that—should the producers seize the movie—would make it impossible for them to cut the footage any other way.

Like many innovative masterpieces, *Sweet Smell of Success* was unappreciated when it premiered. Sandy believed there were several reasons for this: "One, I suspect, was that many of the reviewers, particularly those from the Hearst papers, were outraged by what they felt—rightly—was a pretty savage attack on one branch of their profession, the press agents and gossip columnists, believing that the central figure was a libelous (portrayal) of a very famous journalist who was extremely powerful during the era of the blacklist. Another may have been because it offended the fans of Tony Curtis, who had, up till that point, appeared only in quite sympathetic roles, the juvenile lead in light romantic comedies. Tony himself had accepted the role enthusiastically, but the moviegoing public was clearly unprepared for the shock of seeing one of their favorite young leading men presented as a reptilian figure who, in the end, emerges as even more corrupt than his villainous associate played by Burt Lancaster. There were some commentators, indeed, who saw the whole subject as an attack of the 'American Way of Life' and the 'success ethos.' "

I find Sandy's point about Curtis particularly interesting as I had a similar experience on *Cop Land*. Instead of his archetypal super hero role, Sylvester Stallone portrayed a more hesitant, damaged character. In previews, we experienced a "disconnect" between Stallone and his core audience. We made some attempts to correct for it, but it didn't change the reality that the fan base of an iconic star can get frustrated if their hero takes a severe departure from type. When one Rambo fan in a focus group was asked how he would describe *Cop Land* to his friends, he replied concisely, "I'd tell 'em that Stallone's a fat wimp."

Beyond the "glamorous-stars-playing-flawed-characters" problem, there is yet another issue that certainly hurt *Sweet Smell*'s box-office prospects. This is not a story about a dark hero changing his ways (redemption), this is a film about his *undoing* (tragedy). This is mitigated only by the triumph of a second-tier love story. Some find the film depressing. However, when you mention *Sweet Smell* to many filmmakers, it brings a profound grin. Despite Sidney's tragic end, there is such structural genius and moment-to-moment wit and humor, not to mention the pleasure derived from watching Susan (the depressive waif) outmaneuver Sidney and J. J., that *Sweet Smell*'s proud swagger overwhelms the story's dark outcome for Sidney. One could even mount a decent argument that Susan is, in fact, the movie's true (but rarely seen) protagonist.

Barry Levinson made fond references to *Sweet Smell* in both *Rain Man*, where a clip from the film plays on a television in a hotel room

Cruise and Hoffman are staying in, and in *Diner*, where a supporting character continually spouts J. J. Hunsecker dialogue. Levinson told me he thought *Sweet Smell* might have been overlooked, both at its initial release and over time, partly because its setting and characters were so hard to sell to an audience. "I mean, I just happened to see it. I just walked in the theater. But I was absolutely knocked out by the movie. What got me was the dialogue. There was such a stylistic naturalism. It was amazing."

Martin Scorsese told me he also remembered seeing *Sweet Smell* upon its initial release at the Astor in New York City in 1959. "The thing we loved about it was the toughness. It was such a tough film. The way it was written. It was vibrant, alive. The images of New York, the location work were all brilliant. And of course, the amazing performances. We loved Tony Curtis. It was a world of operators I knew very well—except of course I never knew anyone like J. J. Hunsecker."

I mentioned *Sweet Smell* to Paul Thomas Anderson because I thought I had heard one of Chico Hamilton's jazz pieces from *Sweet Smell* in *Boogie Nights*. He confirmed the "quote" and also said that when he was in England a reporter asked him what he thought might be the greatest screenplay of all time. He thought a second and said, "You know, I think I'd pick *Sweet Smell of Success*." The reporter was stunned. "That's amazing. James Mangold was here last week and he said the same thing."

Of course I did. While, in truth, one could point to a bias on my part (as my teacher made the film)—and it can get plain ridiculous, even nauseating, making "best of" lists in any category—I can't diminish the inspiration I have gotten from this film. Lehman crafted a truly original story, a great morality tale. Odets danced with some of the scene structures and dialogue till it sang. Elmer Bernstein's score was swank, brassy, bold, and moving. "No one would let you get away with a score like that today," Bernstein told me. "To get that out in front—people would cringe." James Wong Howe's brooding, smoky, low-angle black-and-white photography was revolutionary, as was his low-light location shooting of Manhattan. Burt Lancaster was maniacal and controlled. Tony Curtis leapt headlong against the currents of his "boy with the ice-cream face" career and made arguably the greatest performance of his life.

This synergy, these bold choices and collaborations, all these musical strands coming together in one remarkable film must have something to do with the brilliance and leadership of the conductor. And because I knew Sandy, I know it did. And because I have worked in this business, I also know the answer to the next question. *Why didn't he make ten more films like this?*

In truth, Sandy made a dazzling run of films in the U.K. at Ealing, which culminated with his arrival in America to make *Sweet Smell of Success.* However, his emigration (not really an emigration as he was Boston-born) also marked the beginning of a difficult period.

I asked Elmer Bernstein about the environment on the set of *Sweet Smell.* "I wasn't privy to everything, but the combination of people on that movie—Harold Hecht, Burt Lancaster, Cliff Odets, who was crazy—good crazy, but crazy—it was a snake pit. There was a cultural distance between Burt and Sandy. It was like Sandy's heart beat at a different rate. Burt was really scary. He was a dangerous guy. He had a short fuse. He was very physical. You thought you might get punched out.* I mean, I was in the projection room once and I saw Burt chasing someone around. Sandy was a lovely man. It was a miracle that he finished that film. In fact, I think that film is what finished Sandy— as a filmmaker."

The same perfectionism and vision that can yield a brilliant film can also assist in the cooling of a career. One can become a "problem" director. Particularly in the absence of Oscars or dollars. Sandy did not give up making movies after *Sweet Smell,* in fact he signed on to direct another Hill/Hecht/Lancaster project (*The Devil's Disciple*). However, Bernstein was right, this was a turning point for Mackendrick. And the projects to follow were often troubled.

Burt Lancaster fired Sandy from *The Devil's Disciple.* He was taking too long. "Sandy told us not to worry, but after shooting a week we

---

*Ernest Lehman adds: "At one point Lancaster muttered to me, 'I oughta punch you in the jaw right here and now.' To which I replied, 'Go ahead, Burt, I need the money.' "

had only two days of film," said Lancaster, "so we called him in and let him go. It's ironic that his two days of the film are the best in the picture."

Then, Edward G. Robinson had a stroke on *The Boy Who Was Ten Feet Tall*, forcing Sandy to shoot half the film with a dubbed photo double. Sandy prepared to shoot *The Guns of Navarone* (he performed uncredited rewrites and designed the film—his beautiful sketches of the great gun in the mountain were all over his office) but left the project a few weeks before production. *A High Wind in Jamaica* (with Anthony Quinn) was not a hit. And a stunt man tragically died on his final feature film, a comedy, *Don't Make Waves*.

Upon these misfortunes, was an atmosphere of contraction and confusion in the film business (it was the mid-Sixties and TV was making everyone scared and drying up production). Sandy directed some television—*The Defenders*. In declining health, he contracted emphysema. When offered the chance to run a film school, he jumped. I caught him twenty years later.

Sweet Smell of Success is one of the great American films. Ask Martin Scorsese. Ask Paul Thomas Anderson. Ask Barry Levinson. Ask me. I have watched it a dozen times. I will surely see it again soon. It is a miracle of craft and passion and it was directed by my great teacher. I am supremely proud to have touched his genius and his heart.

Moving Pictures

The Author Encounters the Ghost of the Silent-Screen Legend
Billie Dove and Delves into the Mystery of
Her Relationship with Howard Hughes

by Bruce Wagner

FROM *THE NEW YORKER*

Most people in the business of making movies have never heard of the Motion Picture & Television Fund's health-care and retirement village, in Woodland Hills. For a town that makes hagiography of its heritage via tearjerk Academy Award–night montages, one would think that awareness of the place's existence might be more prominent. Instead, its low-slung buildings and cottages reside in the collective consciousness of Angelenos as "the old actors' home," a kind of ephemeral, oddball hideout where bygone nearly-made-its live out their anachronistic days. There is something almost quaint about *The Los Angeles Times'* routine inclusion of the institution's better-known denizens in its obituary pages (after all, this is a company town); the attendant studio photographs of luminous vamps and benevolent cowboys conspire to lend the setting a hazy, anomalous, Garden of Allah vibe. Add the fact that no one seems to know where it is—

mention Woodland Hills and watch the time-warpy stares, as if getting to that onion field of a place might entail a dusty day trip by roadster—and you've got a fairly serious public-relations problem. Well, not a problem, really, but a challenge, because the people responsible would like to see perceptions change. The bearish Screen Actors Guild's president, Richard Masur, thinks he knows the trouble. "It's the name," he says. "Did you know some people still call it the Home? And we're talking active fundraisers!" Masur raises a rascally eyebrow. "*The Motion Picture and Television Fund*—I mean, they should just call it Omega! Or something."

I was researching a book on Hollywood's early days and felt compelled to make the trip. The retirement community itself is fifteen minutes northwest of the Getty Center, by freeway. I'd heard that there was a chapel, and that Thursday-morning services were open to the public. It was there that I met the veteran character actor Hal Riddle, who told me his story about the silent-screen star Billie Dove.

"There's a statistic," the remarkably nimble Mr. Riddle says, from his memorabilia-filled cottage. "See, an insurance company did a survey. It said people usually die around twenty-two months after they retire, because they're cut off from what they did. Well, we don't do that here. We're still surrounded by the business. Yes, we don't work any-more—the idea is not to take away jobs from the older people still out there—but we are surrounded by the industry." The rain had stopped—it was one of those California days when the sun keeps shining through the downpour—and we'd walked back from the morning service at the John Ford Chapel. Dressed in jeans and cotton shirt, sporting a white brush mustache, Riddle looks sixty but is closer to eighty, and talks a blue streak. His alacrity is such that he feels politely compelled to repeat himself, just in case the listener's lost the thread.

Kentucky, 1931: An eleven-year-old boy went to the movies and fell in love with the silent-film queen Billie Dove. Although the reels of *Adoration* are long lost, for Hal Riddle they burn still—in particular, a scene in which a white cape is thrown on the floor and two lovers, one of them Miss Dove, go to bed while the camera lingers on the garment. Had it panned a bit farther, a breathless boy in a fold-down seat would have been found, the crumpled cape trapped within the virgin lens of his eye—an emblem of cosmology. When he told his mother that he wanted to write Miss Dove a letter, they thumbed through *Photoplay* and found an address. In time, a signed picture arrived. (It might as well have come from the Pleiades.) That ethereal, barely faded five-by-seven travelled with Hal Riddle everywhere, like a fetish. It hung on the wall of his college dorm, and in the hotel room he shared with Jack Lemmon, when he was young, doing summer stock in Pennsylvania; it flew with him to L.A., when he took a crack at the movies. By then, Hal says, all the greats were gone—the Warner Bros. commissary was "like a ghost town." The portrait of Billie Dove is with him now, for the last leg of the journey. It is almost seventy years old.

We go into the garden, where Hal shows me his irises, a flower that is popular with cottage residents because the rabbits avoid it. The rain has come and gone again, leaving a washed and scrubbed, absurdly Technicolor world. We settle into a couple of chaises. "You know, I wasn't the first to chase after Billie," he says sardonically. "She was the love of Howard Hughes's life—the great love, people say. There are *lots* of stories about Billie and Mr. Hughes. Mr. Hughes showed her a yacht once, with a crew of sixteen. Sixteen! And he asked, Did she like it? She said, 'Oh, yes, it's beautiful'—and Mr. Hughes said, 'It's yours.' I really do think she loved him as much as he did her. He asked her to marry him, but I think Billie just saw he wasn't the one. She eventually got involved with someone else and moved to the desert—Rancho Mirage. Married a wealthy rancher. You know, she was at her peak when she left the business. They said she quit because she wanted to start a family, but there's another story. See, her last film was *Blondie of the Follies,* with Marion Davies, in 1932. Irving Thalberg asked her to do it. A great part—she knew it was great, and she couldn't turn it down. When Mr. Hearst—Marion's lover—saw the finished film, he said, 'Well, it's a good Billie Dove picture.' Billie knew what that meant. They wound up recutting and reshooting, making her the villain—you can still see it on cable. I think that broke her heart. She'd had enough."

Back home, I download from the ether (http://www.uno.edu/ ~drcom/Silent/PDove.html) images of Billie Dove that confirm the Kentucky boy's acuity: a phantom mosaic of pixels reveals a delicate, strangely modern girl next door. They called her the American Beauty, after one of her films; the world was sending this woman nearly ten thousand pieces of mail a week. I compare a digital portrait with several photographs in *Heart of Hollywood*, Bob Thomas's slim red history of the town. The star of more than forty silents and talkies (*The Black Pirate, The Painted Angel, Madness of Youth*) stands beside Zasu Pitts in a 1926 group shot of the Our Girls Club. Billie smiles sunnily. The second photo is more telling—a coed ensemble, only this time she's on a tier, above and behind Howard Hughes. She looks straight at the lens, incandescently melancholy, a flapper with heartbreak in her eyes. The impossibly handsome Mr. Hughes pivots away from the camera's attention like a boyish saboteur.

From the Web-site bio, one learns that she was born Lillian Bohny in New York City in 1903, that Billie was her nickname, and that she changed "Bohny" to "Dove" when she began working as an extra at studios in Fort Lee, New Jersey. Billie was sixteen when she appeared in the Ziegfeld Follies, and in 1922 she was brought to Hollywood on a one-year Metro contract. A film director named Irvin Willat cast her in a small part, expanding and highlighting the role through flashbacks. They soon married and moved into a white stucco house filled with stained-glass windows, on North Harper Avenue, in West Hollywood.

A few days later, I meet Irvin Willat's son, Boyd, who is living not too far from that house—the one he grew up in. Handsome and open-faced, Boyd Willat, who is fifty-three, is an entrepreneur who founded Day Runner, the American version of Filofax. He tells me that, in the twenties, Howard Hughes, flush from his inheritance and recently arrived in town, "targeted" Billie, after taking movie-directing lessons from Irvin Willat in the living room of the house on Harper. "Hughes didn't have a lot of boundaries," Boyd says. "He was probably just about twenty-five years old. And Billie was ambitious. She was an adolescent! I think she stayed that way most of her life. And her mother was—well, her mother was high-maintenance. By the time Billie met Hughes, my father had become her personal manager. I think the roles got blurred—husband and manager. For example, Dad didn't want her to smoke. He forbade it. He was conscious of the image. So there was friction there, and Hughes took advantage."

Boyd drives me to the site of the former Willat studio, in Culver City, a few blocks from his corporate office. The street signs are still in place—Willat Avenue and Ince Boulevard—but little else indicates the bustling intersection of movie history: what Boyd calls the "geomancy" of the place. We sit in the car and soak it up.

"Thomas Ince"—one of the early movie moguls—"had a little studio here," Boyd says. "He knew my Uncle Doc, from New York. Doc Willat had built one of the first all-glass film stages in New Jersey, in Fort Lee. Ince was out here making a picture called *Civilization,* and he was having some trouble. Doc told him my father could probably help. So Ince brought Dad out, probably around 1916. The problem Ince was having was with the effect of a materializing Jesus. They couldn't fade Jesus in. His entrance was jerky. Dad solved it—he was kind of a mechanical genius. After that, Ince let him direct second unit. Dad was mostly an adventure director—biplane dogfights, submarines, Houdini."

Boyd remembers sitting with his father in the Harper house in 1976, as the old director lay dying. When the death of Howard Hughes was announced on television, Irvin Willat immediately began writing a kind of confession; he was now free to divulge the circumstances of his separation from Billie Dove.

"People said," Boyd begins, with a cool eye and a calm voice, "that Dad sold his wife—that Dad sold Billie to Howard Hughes for money." Boyd is protective of his father's memory. After all, Willat had helped create Billie Dove; had smoothed her entrance to Babylon as surely as he had that of Jesus before her.

"Dad and Billie were already in trouble," Boyd says. "I knew my father—he was very much the director. Things had to be his way. Dad could be a real son of a bitch. But he had a warm spot. Howard Hughes had lured her; the evidence shows as much. And there was a law against luring another man's wife—it's not on the books anymore. They called it 'alienation of affection.' Dad's brothers approached Noah Dietrich, Hughes's confidant. I don't think my father knew anything about it. They told Dietrich they were going to sue. You have to understand— Billie and my father were going to make movies together forever. That was Dad's plan. She was, in that sense, his livelihood." He pauses before getting to the heart of the matter: "The Hughes people were known for making payoffs. And a deal was struck—a valise *was* dropped off at the Harper Avenue house. The fact is, Billie had signed a contract with Hughes to make four pictures. They gave her a hundred thousand dollars, and she always said my father got three times that. Dad didn't work much in films after Billie left; his heart wasn't in it. He eventually got into real estate. Owned a lumber mill. He was one of the original developers of Coldwater Canyon. Dad never married again—he *couldn't*, after Billie. In fact, a lot of people don't know it, but he never actually married my mother. And when he died my cousins contested his paternity—they said I wasn't his son. That hurt. I finally told them, 'All I want is the house on Harper.' And I got it. Lots of things have been born in that house—great geomancy. My kids were born there, right in the dressing room Dad built for Billie, with the *Romeo and Juliet* stained-glass window. I'm an old hippie; we did like the Russians and delivered them underwater. Built a tank and put it in there. We were only the seventh recorded couple in America to have an underwater birth."

There were also fifty acres of land that Irvin Willat had owned in Palm Springs; Boyd wound up with ten. He was out there in 1986, and a Realtor must have made the link with the Willat name, because she told Boyd that Billie was living nearby and gave him the number. Soon afterward, he called. "I'm Boyd Willat," he offered when the intensely theatrical voice on the other end uttered an eccentric hello. "I've heard about you all my life, but we've never met. I'd like to come and visit."

I needed to take a breath. My intention had been to write about the hospital itself, not about a silent star; it's a long way from Sunset Boulevard to Woodland Hills. Yet the mood of my monograph was shifting: the campus—whose buildings include a full-service medical center with outpatient services and I.C.U., a theater and library, a state-of-the-art Alzheimer's-care unit, and sixty or so cottages for the ambulatory retired—was exerting a powerful tug. As a living trust of this century's singular, spectacular dream and the industry that grew out of it, the very grounds and structures constitute a kind of organism. For the first-time visitor, the place has a floaty, timeless, epiphanic aura, a feeling enhanced by a vaguely Rockwellian town-square motif, with an architectural nod to gazebos and bandstands. The chorus of memory that resides there has genuinely altered the locus of the spirit of place, and the voices sang to me. It's an authentic memory palace: as you pass through the entrance you shiver. I checked myself from making another appointment with Hal Riddle, even though I knew he had a story to tell—I couldn't drop another nickel in the nickelodeon just yet. So I borrowed some books from the Woodland Hills library and boned up.

The organization that paid for all this—the Motion Picture Relief Fund of America—was born in the early nineteen-twenties, along with its official motto, "We Take Care of Our Own." The Fund helped out-of-work players find jobs and fronted them rent money. It even paid for funerals. Throughout the Thirties, the Fund helped actors, writers, and directors who were marooned by the demise of the silents, and raised money by hosting costume and skating parties, Brown Derby Bamboo Room benefits, and Turf Club Balls at the Ambassador Hotel. In 1932, when these efforts fell short, a payroll-deduction plan went into effect. Studio workers were asked—well, forcefully encouraged, sometimes by Jack Warner himself—to tithe half of one percent of their earnings. (Ken Scherer, the current Motion Picture & Television Fund C.E.O., showed me a payroll pledge card signed by Marilyn Monroe when she lived at 1301 North Harper, just down the street from the Willat place.) In 1938, the Danish character actor Jean Hersholt was made president of the Fund. Hersholt had always had a hospital and retirement home in mind; when a broker told him that forty-eight acres were available in Woodland Hills, he brought his wife out to take a look and they made a down payment with a personal check. Some of the board members thought it too far from Hollywood, so Hersholt threatened to buy the land himself. The board relented. At 850 dollars an acre, it was a bargain.

A friend of mine mentioned that someone she knew had a strange connection to Billie Dove. She gave me an address, and one azure morning, I drive to a house in the Hollywood Hills, nickel in hand.

The screenwriter and actress Arleen Sorkin (*Picture Perfect, America's Funniest People*) is now married to one of the producers of the TV sitcom *Frasier*. Arleen tells me that when she was starting out in Hollywood her father suggested that she change Sorkin to Dove; he didn't explain why. Like Hal Riddle, he had written a fan letter to Billie in the thirties, and in his case the letter had begun a lifelong correspondence. After he encouraged the star to watch his daughter on a television soap opera, Billie summoned the girl to her beloved desert hideaway. There Billie held court, regal and extravagantly vain—a coquette who, well into her eighties, had had surgery on both knees so she'd be able to do a new dance step. "I knew a doctor who'd moved to the desert," Arleen tells me, "and I asked Billie if he could give her a call. 'Is he attractive?' That's what she wanted to know—at eighty-five!" Billie had the fattest poodle in the world, and a cabinet lined with urns—the ashes of all the dogs she'd lost. "Once I made the mistake of asking if she'd been intimate with Howard Hughes," Arleen says. "She just looked at me and said, 'Don't be naïve.' She said that one day she was going to write down what really happened between her and Hughes. That's a famous mystery—why they didn't marry. I even sent her little tape recorders, to dictate the story. She never did. But she was fabulous. When I told her I'd fallen in love, all Billie said was 'Give, girl. Give.' Sometimes when I'd call, she'd answer the phone like this." Arleen's voice goes into High Mame: "You know, they say you can only love *once*, but I loved three times—completely."

One of those men was Hughes; another a husband; the third a lover. Arleen tells me that when Billie heard that the lover had died she literally blacked out.

At a restaurant called Crustacean, in Beverly Hills, Jeffrey Katzenberg, chairman of the Motion Picture & Television Fund Foundation, is being handed a check for fifty thousand dollars. A glass-topped stream runs under the floor, and it's a little disconcerting to see swollen, giddily expensive koi swimming underfoot. Look down and your mind stutters.

The Next Generation Council was founded for the purpose of raising awareness of the Fund among young Hollywood. The actors Robert Townsend and Illeana Douglas are at the soirée, along with a smattering of executives, one of whom thinks that the hospital has something to do with a charity associated with Will Rogers. Warren Beatty and Annette Bening, both great supporters of the Fund, stand on a bridge that arches gently from bar to dining room. I eavesdrop on Bening as she tells someone about growing up in San Diego. "This friend of mine," she's saying, surreally earnest, "actually lived on Serenity Path. My family lived on Defiance Way."

I corner her husband and, although Beatty is civil, that's how he looks—cornered. (Like Bulworth, he has an endearing dodginess.) After years of this sort of thing, he's well braced for the Three Categories of Strangers: the ebullient ones he's just spoken to; the slightly startled ones currently engaged; and the fidgety ones-in-waiting, taxiing toward him like planes before takeoff. Yet when I bring up the place in Woodland Hills he gets that Freemason look in his eyes, and mentions feeling a weakness in the knees when he and Annette first drove up there. It wasn't just the ineffable that moved him but the fact that the hospital was one of "the few successful examples of socialization. I mean, you're not hearing the 'Internationale,' " he says, his glance skimming the crowd like a stone. "But people are taking care of their own."

Years ago, I'd read of Beatty's interest in making a film of the life of Howard Hughes, but something stops me from asking him about Billie. Besides, he and Bening have been here an hour and he's chafing to leave.

"Darling," Beatty says to his wife as she finds us—he puts a hand on her arm and suddenly I feel like I'm in a Thirties film—"Max will be very angry if we're late."

El Nino is browbeating us: rain falls hard on the John Ford Chapel, in Woodland Hills—a replica of Mount Vernon, which the great director donated to the campus. On Thursdays, the pugnacious chaplain, David Grant, presides. Grant has the charisma of one of those two-fisted movie priests of the Forties. A while back, someone called him a "compassionate hard-ass," and he took that as a great compliment. The irony of his being at Woodland Hills is that, when he was a boy, his father, a minister in the strict Assembly of God in Kansas City, discouraged him from going to the movies. "The first film I ever saw was *Old Yeller,*" Grant says. We stroll through the soggy grounds, past the Louis B. Mayer Theatre. From my guess, that meant that he was pure until the age of thirty. He adds, with a wink, "Or maybe it was *The Ten Commandments.*"

Later, I mention the *Old Yeller* business to Hal Riddle, and he says, "I was the guy who took him to that! I had come to California to act, and I went on one of those retreats Dave was giving when he worked for the Campus Crusade. See, Dave was always attracted to people in the business—and there were lots around, too. Yvonne Lime—remember her, from *The Rainmaker?* Not Mr. Coppola's film but the one with Burt Lancaster and Kate Hepburn. She was Snookie, the cute little blonde. He dated Yvonne Lime. Dave liked show people. And I've seen photographs of him onstage when he was in college, at Bob Jones University—he did some Shakespeare there. Oh, I think Dave always wanted to be an actor. He was even a deejay on the school radio station." ("That was at WMUU," Grant says, looking mischievous. "The World's Most Unusual University.")

Riddle brings me a soft drink and begins to talk, with an actor's eerie, studied casualness, a born storyteller's finesse. One day last year, he says, he was in the lobby of the Louis B. Mayer Theatre, about to watch a movie. He was telling someone the tried-and-true story of the Silent Siren and the Kentucky Kid when a woman near him said, "Billie Dove? Well, she's here, you know. Would you like to meet her?"

A few years ago, Billie Dove could no longer afford to live in a desert sanatorium. The prolonged illness and death of a son had drained her resources. Friends helped her sell off jewelry and lobbied to get her to Woodland Hills. Billie moved into the hospital's long-term-care facility in 1997; she was too frail to have a cottage of her own. It was years too late for that.

"I try to be with her a few hours each day," Riddle tells me. "I usually spend Christmas morning with Lee Meriwether if she's in California—her kids are like my godchildren—and then I visit awhile with Billie. She's got pneumonia now, and it's tough. I'm afraid I'll lose her. Normally, I answer letters that come in. You'd be amazed at all the flowers and letters. One week, there were a few from Germany and I said, 'You're big in Germany, Billie!' Ever since, she says, 'Am I still big in Germany, Hal?' You know, she used to put on lipstick and have the nurses help her get together when she knew I was coming, but now she's too weak. 'I look awful, don't I?'—that's what she says when I see her. And I say, 'No, you don't, Billie. You look beautiful.' The other day, she looked at me and said, 'You won't leave me, will you?' "

What, I ask, could it have been like to see her that first time, after waiting almost seventy years? Hal gives me a Rotarian smile—redolent of barbershop quartets and Kentucky hollers. "Well—my legs just turned to jelly! I was eleven years old again." Emotion overtakes him. "At first, I think she was a little guarded. People want things from her.

They want to see her, get to her—for interviews. They come right onto campus. I think Billie might have thought, Well, who is he—what does he want? And, of course, it was impossible for her to remember sending me that picture. After a while, when she saw I didn't want anything from her—well, she accepted me. She saw that all I needed was to be able to love her."

Billie Dove died on the thirty-first of December last year. A decade ago, the star had spoken to a friend about one of the quotidian horrors of her life: she had "simply lived too long." It was fitting that her body held out until the very last day of one of the final years of a century that had been her shadow or her lover; this time, she blacked out before its expiration.

The drizzly Saturday memorial is held at the Forest Lawn Cemetery in Glendale, a hilly park with a stone castle to hold the dead; it looks like just another Hollywood-heyday Xanadu. I pass the tomb of Jean Hersholt and park outside the Last Supper Window. I spot Pastor Grant, off by himself, quietly mulling. He's spoken at too many services of late and he isn't happy; in the last several weeks, a virulent flu has claimed a number of hospital residents. The funeral director, a ringer for Harry Dean Stanton, ushers us up the hill to the Freedom Mausoleum.

It's cold in the long columbarium. The coffin lies on delicate scaffolding in front of the empty space beside Billie's father, Charles Bohny (1872–1934). A plaque hasn't yet been made for her crypt, so we stare at a small, macabre plate that was affixed some years ago: PURCHASED BEFORE NEED. Billie's adopted daughter, Gail, is there, along with her grandson and nephew. Hal Riddle stands tall and dignified; Boyd Willat enters, hands folded respectfully in front of him. Arleen Sorkin is with a friend, Dana Delany, who wears one of Billie's bracelets. Various fans and caretakers through the years have gathered, and I introduce myself to Lenore Foote, the president of the Billie Dove Fan Club. Lenore wrote Billie a mash note in the late twenties, and attained her post in 1932, the year of Billie's unexpected retirement.

El Greco skies rain down through impromptu eulogies, but the sun also shines, and Dave Grant remarks that the day can't make up its mind. A blown-up photograph of Billie stands on an easel; it will later join the memorabilia in Hal Riddle's cottage. Riddle delivers the last eulogy. Earlier, he had told me that he was afraid he'd break down, but he draws on his actor's muscles and does just fine.

After the service, I catch up with Boyd Willat. We talk about his mother, an actress, who was a murky presence in his life. She left Irvin and Boyd when he was three years old and went to Hawaii, where she was swindled out of money and fell on hard times. Boyd was eighteen when he last saw her.

Billie Dove was the original, the woman Irvin Willat married, then lost to a god—just as in a Greek myth. In a sense, Boyd lost her, too. Unlike the heroes in myths (or the movies), the spurned director wasn't able to gather celestial forces to exact his revenge. For Boyd, the great star had remained the mother of all ghosts, a spectral presence somewhere in the world yet not of it, an epic bit of unfinished business. And still there remained the nagging detail that could have been borrowed, if not from Mt. Olympus, then from Arthur Miller: A valise had been dropped at the Harper house, bringing a bagman's end to a contract that was supposed to be eternal. Boyd had years to ruminate over what a man, any man, might have done—himself included. The stacked bills were said to have added up to 325 thousand dollars, a staggering amount seventy years ago. The powerful brothers had asked for restitution; Boyd's father must have been too angry or numb to consider the alchemical consequences for the soul of such a buyout.

When Boyd finally met Billie, in 1986, she was inordinately gracious. He had come to the desert with no axe to grind and never mentioned what he knew—that his father had loved her, obsessing, to the end. Suddenly, the era of the silent star, the director, and the rich rake must have seemed distant enough to be science fiction. "Still," he tells me, "there's a kind of insanity when something is so real, yet intangible. I was *uncomfortable* until I met her. Meeting Billie grounded me—I was definitely physically affected. I became *personally sane* about the whole subject the moment I looked into her eyes."

A month or so later, I come across a scrap of paper tucked away in a sports coat. Boyd gave it to me at the funeral—the phone number of the caretaker of the house on Harper Avenue.

An actress lives there now, same as it ever was. She doesn't mind letting him give me a tour while she showers upstairs. My affable guide tells me that most of the architectural details have remained intact since that faraway time. As we pass through the living room, he points out the original sconces and ceiling frescoes. On the second story, off Billie's old bedroom, is the dressing area, which once housed a water tank, for birthing. The stained-glass window Boyd spoke of is breathtaking, with its painterly gradations of color. The caretaker remarks that they don't do glass like that anymore. Romeo, in a brilliant harlequin vest, is on bended knee; a phosphorescent moon hangs in the sky. An ethereal Juliet looks down from a balcony of stone.

At the base, a legend: "A thousand times good night."

Mighty Aphrodites

*Used to Be That Feminine Wiles Won a Screen Siren Just
What She Wanted. Why Are Today's Actresses So Scared
of Turning Up the Heat?*

by Terrence Rafferty

FROM *GQ*

This is boys'-movie season, when going to the multiplex to beat
the heat necessarily entails watching tough guys save the world
from computer-generated disasters. There's no use complaining about
the summer action glut: It is, as the saying goes, what it is (that's how
we nineties people convey the idea once expressed by "You can't fight
city hall"), and even if all the critics in the country decided to scream
and stomp their feet at exactly the same time, it's unlikely that Hollywood's studio executives would feel a measurable tremor of doubt.
And when something is so immutably what it is, the most effective—or
at least the pleasantest—defense is to dream about what it isn't. Call
it denial, but while the male stars (and their stunt doubles) are sweating and shouting and exercising deadly force up there on the screen,
I often find myself thinking about Julia Roberts and Michelle Pfeiffer,
wondering what they'll be doing once the summer smoke clears and

the movies make room for them again. The hell with Harrison Ford. Let's talk about women.

But which women? As a representative of the entertainment-news media, I'm required to have an opinion about who really matters and who doesn't and sometimes—although I try to avoid forecasting— even to predict who possesses the right stuff for lasting stardom. And the more you try to handicap these popularity contests, the more you come to appreciate the inscrutability of the moviegoing public's taste. Picking Roberts out of the *Mystic Pizza* ensemble in 1988 may have been child's play, but they're not all such easy calls. In the mid- Eighties, I would have placed my bets on Rebecca De Mornay and Diane Lane as future stars and felt dead certain that Demi Moore would finish out of the money. Prognostication and critical judgment don't mix well. Combined, they become an intellectualized form of wishful thinking: Because I found De Mornay and Lane talented and sexy, I wanted to see them in more and better roles; and because Moore seemed pretty ordinary, I didn't care if I never saw her again. So when I wonder now about the prospects of Gwyneth Paltrow or Cameron Diaz or Claire Danes or Jennifer Lopez or Jada Pinkett Smith or Neve Campbell, what I'm asking myself, really, is, How much am I looking forward to watching her, in large and demanding parts, for the next ten to thirty years?

All the young actresses I've named are, of course, easy on the eyes: a necessary but not sufficient condition for stardom. An extraordinary camera subject, like Paltrow, can, in fact, appear to be a star without actually being one. Beauty isn't everything, but it's a tremendous asset to a performer of either sex: It eliminates some of the hard work of grabbing the audience's attention. Paltrow doesn't have to figure out how to get you to look at her any more than Pfeiffer or Grace Kelly or the young Elizabeth Taylor did. In her first movie role, as a sullen, sexy teenage con artist in Steve Kloves's *Flesh and Bone* (1993), Paltrow made a big impression simply by looking cool and hard and myste- rious: She was—much as Pfeiffer was in her first significant role, in De Palma's 1983 *Scarface*—an icily commanding presence, inviting viewers to project whatever they would onto her gorgeous blankness.

She hasn't come across with anything like that force since. Not in the movies, anyway: In still photographs, in glossy magazines, she looks smashing—every inch the star. Unlike the astonishingly versatile Pfeiffer, who moved easily, and quickly, into warmer, less goddessy roles, Paltrow hasn't found the star part that will enable her to give shape and dimension to the elegant sketch (like a fashion drawing) she dashed off in *Flesh and Bone*. She's still more interesting in repose than in action. Even in the most complex and full-bodied roles she's taken on in the past five years—in the 1996 Jane Austen travesty *Emma* and the recent *Sliding Doors*—Paltrow's personality remains wispy, stubbornly elusive; the enigmatic quality that gave her such allure in her first, small role just isn't enough to carry a movie. As I watched Paltrow working hard, and even fairly skillfully, in *Sliding Doors* and yet failing somehow to come into focus, I realized that part of her problem is that she embodies a type the movies have largely dispensed with in the past couple of decades—the remote, don't-touch beauty of studio-era icons such as Greta Garbo, Gene Tierney, Veronica Lake, Kelly, and, at the type's sadomasochistic extreme, Marlene Dietrich. The sole surviving example of this rarefied species is Catherine Deneuve, who, in her peak goddess years (the Sixties), smartly allowed such unworshipful directors as Polanski and Buñuel to use her uncanny physical perfection ironically. Chiseled features and freezing hauteur, male or female, don't stir much enthusiasm in Nineties viewers. Okay, Ralph Fiennes, but who else? (And I can't help thinking that if Fiennes were an American—or a woman of any nationality—his mock-soulful poses would be jeered off the screen.)

If the studios were to start remaking Garbo's pictures (or Tierney's signature film, *Laura*), Paltrow could thrive; this summer she's starring in *A Perfect Murder,* playing a woman whose husband is plotting to kill her—that is, the Grace Kelly role in *Dial M for Murder*. But no matter how much audiences and filmmakers claim to yearn for old-style romance and glamour, the fact is, no one seems able to imagine these qualities convincingly in contemporary settings. The nostalgia of such turkeys as Sydney Pollack's *Sabrina*—a remake of a 1954 Audrey Hepburn vehicle that was itself an attempt to recreate Thirties romantic-comedy values—is too desperate and willful to be very appealing; audiences smell a con. The reactionary interpretation of the decline of grand-manner romance is that sex, in these "permissive" times, has lost its mystery. That argument, often advanced by people who spend way too much time listening to Cole Porter, is untenable. Sex never changes; it's as mysterious, and as unmysterious, as ever. (It is what it is and was and will be.) All that has changed, really, is the representation of sex, which is obviously franker than it was in the days of Hollywood's stringent Production Code, and there's no fundamental reason why showing sex, or talking about it freely, should be an impediment to romance. *Pretty Woman* proved that beyond the faintest doubt: A Cinderella fantasy can work just as well with a happy hooker as it does with the demure young heroine of *Sabrina* (either one).

The concept of "glamour," however, is genuinely problematic. Glamour, unlike sex, has no objective reality to call its own, but depends entirely on perception, on attitude; and although this decade is rich in attitudes, it's a little light on consensus—one person's glamour is another person's grunge. That's good for real women in the real world; they have lots of options and no single standard of attractiveness to conform to. It's hell on performers, though. Those who strive to stay ahead of—or even keep up with—the fashion curve can wind up looking silly. Madonna, now into motherhood and (of all things) the Cabala, has reinvented herself so many times in her tenacious career that it's no longer possible to take anything but a clinical interest in her transformations. She's the poster girl for multiple-personality disorder. Although pop-culture fashion is ruthless, in the studio era the pace of change was much more stately, more forgiving, so the shelf life of the star's established "look" was a lot longer: Veronica Lake's peekaboo hairdo carried her through the Forties; the hair queen of the mid-Nineties, Jennifer Aniston, recoiffed even while her original style was still popular, as if in terror of swift sudden obsolescence.

The audience, of course, doesn't care very deeply about the fate of individual stars—nor, in most cases, should it. If the people on the screen are just seductive images, incarnations of currently fashionable attitudes, then we're perfectly content to see them replaced by performers who move vividly embody the next cultural style. There's always another pretty woman, another handsome guy, and although it sounds cruel to say it, only a handful of actors at any given time are so distinctive that they deserve to be considered indispensable. As much as I may now enjoy gazing at, say, Halle Berry, I can imagine my life without that pleasure; and although I wish her a long and fulfilling career, I'm not losing sleep worrying about her prospects. One after the other, the models slouch up and down the runway, pausing to allow us (and the photographers) a moment of contemplation, then they quietly disappear. Most of us are satisfied; only a stalker would ask for more.

Except at its highest level, movie entertainment is a luxury, not an absolute necessity, and there's no point denying the ephemeral nature of the beauties it provides. The fact that aesthetic styles come and go more quickly now is a difference in degree, rather than in kind, between today's volatile movie culture and the studio system of Hollywood's bygone "classic" era. The most important distinction between then and now, I think, is that in the old days—during the Depression and the Second World War—movie audiences were entirely comfortable with the idea that this pleasure was luxurious, even frivolous; that's what they wanted from "the silver screen." My parents, dedicated moviegoers in the Thirties and Forties, spoke of films as an "escape," and although most viewers today would probably say the same thing, the getaways that contemporary pictures provide are, for the most part, less elaborate and less exotic; even deep space seems just a day trip away, because the studios, in their market-driven wisdom, now populate the screen with characters designed to flatter us, not dazzle us with their difference. (It's no wonder Frank Capra's shameless populist fables, glorifying the values of "regular" guys and gals, are so highly regarded by today's filmmakers.)

And this shift in the audience's relationship to the people it sees in the movies is, I think, a bigger problem for actresses than for actors. Men can still get away with the strong, silent act, but women, who have always had to project more to register as anything other than mere decoration, no longer have that regal, Garboesque shtick to fall back on. It survives only in the most attitude-drenched postmodern productions, like *Pulp Fiction*, which have been, for the past few years, the movies' last bastion of pure exoticism. Uma Thurman's too-cool allure in *Pulp Fiction*—less a throwback to studio-era glamour than to Godard's intellectualized, Gallicized reinterpretation of that glamour—plays as irony, so it fits right into the picture's tricky semi-parodic tone. The danger of being glamorous in the old-Hollywood style is that it now seems, in a dressed-down, postfeminist culture, perhaps too forceful a statement: either an obvious "signifier" of wealth or an embarrassingly eager announcement of sexual availability. Unusual beauty has often made it more difficult for actresses to be taken seriously, and when they dress up to *enhance* that unfair advantage, contemporary audiences may actually turn on them—resent them for the ego-deflating reminder that, somewhere, someone has more than we do.

Look at Sharon Stone. Playful self-consciousness enabled her to put across her showy vamp number in *Basic Instinct* (1992), but she hasn't managed to repeat that high-wire act since; she keeps tumbling off to one side or the other. When she tries to go drab and ordinary, as in *Last Dance* (1996), all her personality seems to disappear. And when she pulls out the stops and unleashes her full sireny Sharon Stone–ness, as in *Diabolique* (1996), the glam persona tends to read as either inadvertent self-parody or unattractive sexual arrogance: She seems to be saying to women, "I'm Sharon Stone, and you're not," and to men, "Eat your heart out." The funny thing is, neither of those messages would have disturbed a Thirties audience: The women may have dreamed of being Garbo, and the men may have dreamed of going to bed with her, but I doubt many of them felt, as Nineties viewers seem to feel, *entitled* to be or to have any of the glorious creatures strutting across the screen. Those vanished audiences, in other words, recognized movie fantasy *as* fantasy and acknowledged without bitterness the existence of people richer, wittier, and/or more beautiful than they were. The suave playboys and giddy heiresses of Thirties comedies simply inhabited a different world, which was (and to a certain extent still is) pleasant to fantasize about. Sure, that's a pretty passive

attitude—and the class assumptions it's built on don't bear much scrutiny—but it does at least have the virtue of reflecting a realistic
distinction between the products of imagination and the actual possibilities of most people's lives. These days we dream less and envy
more.

That is, on the whole, not a good thing—especially for women on
the screen, who must now manage to be attractive enough to make us
want to look at them but not so "glamorous" as to seem off-puttingly
different. In a sense, they're stranded in a kind of no-person's-land
between the larger-than-life qualities traditionally associated with
movie stardom and the homelier, more accessible traits that audiences
prize in TV performers. *Pretty Woman* aside, the few successful romantic comedies of the past decade have featured girl-next-door types
as heroines: Meg Ryan in *When Harry Met Sally . . .* and *Sleepless in
Seattle,* Sandra Bullock in *While You Were Sleeping.* Pfeiffer's most
recent foray into the genre, *One Fine Day,* mysteriously bombed, although she and her TV-bred costar, George Clooney, worked charm-
ingly together; Roberts's long-overdue return to screwball territory,
My Best Friend's Wedding, was a hit, but, perversely, it required her to
lose her man to a duller, "nicer" woman. (That never happened to
Carole Lombard; the audience wouldn't have stood for it.) And what
are we to make of Helen Hunt in *As Good As It Gets?* Hunt, a likable
and skillful comedienne of the regular-gal type, is compelled to mute
even the friendly, unthreatening sex appeal she displays on TV's *Mad
About You*—in the movie she dresses dowdily, seems to be wearing
no makeup at all, and generally appears very, very tired—in order to
be a plausible mate for the increasingly peculiar-looking Jack Nicholson, playing a dysfunctional jackass twenty-five years her senior.
That's about as modest as a romantic fantasy can be: Look like hell
and land a jerk.

If today's movie actresses are ambivalent about using the qualities
that make them unique—their beauty and their sexuality—that's
partly because they're afraid to alienate viewers who are themselves
ambivalent about the nature of movie-stimulated desire, who apparently no longer know whether they want their female stars to represent
achievable goals or impossible ideals (and may, in fact, no longer care

to admit that there's a difference). When I watch old studio movies, I'm invariably struck by how uninhibitedly the stars of the Thirties, Forties, and Fifties flaunted their assets, how unembarrassed they were about their out-of-the-ordinary physical endowments. Even actresses who weren't considered great beauties or outright sex symbols didn't shrink from turning on some sex appeal if they needed to. When Barbara Stanwyck had to make a fool out of Henry Fonda in *The Lady Eve* or a chump out of Fred MacMurray in *Double Indemnity*, she knew what to do; Bette Davis (whose looks were persistently underrated) is ravishing in Thirties pictures like *Ex-Lady, Of Human Bondage, Marked Woman*, and *Jezebel*. (Even in the 1950 *All About Eve*, Davis, as the fortysomething Broadway queen Margo Channing, gives off considerably more erotic heat than the youthful usurper played by Anne Baxter.) The studio system, for all its many inanities, did at least create and nurture an audience with fairly stable expectations, and that, in a way, enabled the more talented performers to use every resource at their disposal, including sex, without undue fear; it's easier to be sexy when you know the public doesn't quite see you as real.

Elizabeth Taylor, who was one of the last pure products of the studio system, moved from child stardom (in pictures like *National Velvet*) to full adult sex-symboldom without, apparently, ever pausing to consider that her ripe, grown-up beauty might cause her more problems than her youthful beauty had—that there might be danger in exposing herself to a less innocent kind of admiration. When Taylor, all of nineteen, played Montgomery Clift's upper-crust dream girl in *A Place in the Sun* (1951), she inflamed his blue-collar desire as if she just knew that that was what she had been put on this earth to do, and she was so sincere that you couldn't begrudge her that serene self-assurance; it wasn't *her* fault Monty wound up in the electric chair. Through the Fifties and early Sixties, Taylor learned to use her unignorable sexuality with increasing boldness, and gave startlingly good performances in pictures of varying quality—*Giant, Butterfield 8*, and a pair of floridly unconvincing Tennessee Williams adaptations, *Cat on a Hot Tin Roof* and *Suddenly Last Summer*. (Her bracingly direct, out-there style was superbly suited to Williams's material; and to act well—uncampily—in *inferior* Williams is a real feat. In *Cat* she steals the show from more highly regarded actors, like Paul Newman and Judith Anderson, and in *Summer* she quietly acts rings around both Clift and Katharine Hepburn.) After the *Cleopatra* debacle, in 1963, and all it entailed (including the notoriously stormy relationship with Richard Burton), her acting became more strident, but in a handful of films—*Who's Afraid of Virginia Woolf?*, *Reflections in a Golden Eye*, and the little-seen *X, Y, and Zee*—she used her newly hyperbolic style to extraordinary effect, giving off crude erotic energy with an almost frightening lack of reserve.

I've gone on about Taylor because I think her body of work is much more impressive than it has been given credit for, and also because I regret that more screen actresses haven't looked to her career as an example. In a way, she's been overshadowed by her contemporary Marilyn Monroe, who, like Taylor, was a sex symbol who wanted to be a "real" actress. But Monroe, whose greatest gift was for comedy, never got there; and, of course, she died young and unhappy and turned into a martyr figure, the mythic heroine of a feminist cautionary tale about the sad fate of women who arouse too much passion in their audience. The message of Monroe, as it's been handed down to us over the years, is that being a sex symbol can be hazardous to a woman's mental and physical health, and an awful lot of today's actresses appear to have taken that chilling moral to heart—even (perhaps especially) those who, like Roberts and Stone, became stars by playing hookers and vamps. There may well be some truth in this message, particularly now that the audience wants its stars to be more accessible; and performers of both sexes are always, and understandably, reluctant to believe their popularity depends solely on their physical attributes. But there's no sense in being an actor if you're afraid to use everything you've got. Liz did.

Although survivors' stories never pack the narrative punch of martyrs', Taylor's career might serve as a useful countermyth to the tragedy of Monroe's. Taylor, an actress with virtually no training in the technique of her craft, was, it's worth remembering, perhaps the only female star of her era who consistently held her own opposite the brooding male heroes of the Method: Clift, Newman, James Dean (in *Giant*), and Marlon Brando (in *Reflections in a Golden Eye*). Although she never studied at the Actor's Studio, as Monroe did, Taylor actually looked comfortable sharing the screen with those actors: Neither their lofty reputations nor their intense acting styles appeared to daunt her. (Perhaps it was her relative innocence of technique that enabled her to match the hard-won simplicity of their effects.) Elizabeth Taylor as Method icon? As myths go, it's at least as viable, I think, as Monroe's martyrdom—and a hell of a lot more inspiring.

In the past couple of decades, moviegoers have seen a few performances that have evoked the sexy bravado of Taylor at her best: Anjelica Huston in *Prizzi's Honor* and *The Grifters;* Judy Davis in *High Tide;* Jessica Lange in *Crimes of the Heart* and *Blue Sky.* But younger actresses have, it seems to me, become too cautious—too timid, maybe, to take the risk of being either ravished or ridiculed by the audience. Pfeiffer, the most resourceful actress of our time, has managed to forge an expressive style from that wariness. Even in her most overtly "glamorous" parts, in *The Fabulous Baker Boys* and *Tequila Sunrise,* she often appears reluctant to be wooed—embarrassed or defensive about the romantic attention she's receiving. She has a great sizing-up look: less imperious than Bette Davis's, but not so brazenly needy as Taylor's. It's a very attractive persona: She's not *averse* to romance exactly, just prudent. (You can't quite imagine her actively pursuing a man, even in the screwball-comedy style of Lombard in *My Man Godfrey* or Hepburn in *Bringing Up Baby.*)

But Pfeiffer hasn't run away from her physical assets, either. She understands, as well as any movie actress has since Lillian Gish in the silent era, that her beauty enables her to portray the subtlest, most complex emotions by the simplest of means. When an actress has such a strong grip on our attention (fairly or unfairly, who cares?), she can have her way with us, surprising us with a flickering change of expression or an offhand gesture; she's limited only by her imagination.

Not many performers have an imagination as rangy as Pfeiffer's, but it's hard not to feel that an actress like Gwyneth Paltrow should be making more of what she has. The reckless power of Bette Davis and Elizabeth Taylor is probably beyond her, but Pfeiffer's emotional delicacy might not be; we won't know for sure until Paltrow finds a role that allows her to exploit her looks unselfconsciously. In the movie culture of the Nineties, though, that kind of part is hard to come by. So I'm not making any predictions about her here. I'll just wish her luck, because she'll need it; and so will Lopez and Danes and Diaz and all the other young actresses looking for a place in the sun but trying not to get burned by the audience's desire. I'm reasonably certain that Bridget Fonda will continue to delight and amaze in movies too few people will see; that Huston, Lange, Judy Davis, and Sigourney Weaver, along with Pfeiffer, will survive the cooling of viewers' hotter passions; that the versatile young Renée Zellweger (*Jerry Maguire, The Whole Wide World*) will be around—as a star or not—for a long time.

But even these actresses should keep in mind the famous words spoken by Bette Davis in *All About Eve*: "Fasten your seat belts; it's going to be a bumpy night." Better to have that combative catchphrase ringing in your head than, say, Shakespeare's paean to Cleopatra— "Age cannot wither her, nor custom stale her infinite variety"—because *that's* something no actress will ever hear from the studios or from the audience. Of course, that's unfair: one more unfortunate fact that is what it is. But it has a cruel logic. What today's audience wants from a female star is precisely that sort of vague, undefined inevitability, the quality of being no more and no less than what she is. The question is, Will we know it when we see it? Glamour may have had its drawbacks, but it sure was easier to recognize.

The Glory of Cary Grant and Other Girlish Delights

by Elizabeth Abele

FROM *IMAGES*

Recently *Entertainment Weekly* published a special issue—"The 100 Greatest Movie Stars of All Time." Star number 6 was described as follows:

> If Hollywood had its own Mount Rushmore, Cary Grant's profile would be the most prominent: the hair that Katharine Hepburn mussed in *Bringing Up Baby* (1938), the eyes that Eva Marie Saint couldn't quite meet in *North by Northwest* (1959), the lips that locked so breathtakingly with Ingrid Bergman's in *Notorious* (1946), and, of course, the cleft chin that fascinated Audrey Hepburn in *Charade* (1963).

On reading this entry, I was struck at how it contradicted Laura Mulvey's seminal work, "Visual Pleasure in Narrative Cinema," which characterizes the gaze of the camera, and the spectator, as always male and the object of the gaze as always female. Though these looks at

Grant described above are all attributed to an on-screen female, it is obvious from the description that the gaze of the shots described forces male *and* female spectators to look at Grant as an object of desire. Because no other entry in this *Entertainment Weekly* issue presents such a detailed objectified description of an actor's (or even actress's) appearance (the entries on Brando, Redford, Cruise, and Gibson acknowledge their looks but quickly move on to discuss their other qualities), it reinforced my own personal feeling that there might be something special about looking at Mr. Grant.

E. Ann Kaplan (the author of *Women and Film: Both Sides of the Camera*) contends that traditional male stars, like John Wayne, derived their glamour not from their looks but from the "power they were able to wield within the filmic world in which they functioned." Though Kaplan's association with glamour and power may hold for John Wayne, James Cagney, and Humphrey Bogart (or Katharine Hepburn, whose appeal *EW* describes as based on her portrayal of feminine rebellion, "the original liberated woman, on and off the screen, tilting at the windmills of convention and male dominance"), Grant's glamour is directly tied to his objectified beauty, whether it is situationally supported by power or not. *EW*'s entry on Grant goes on to remind us that it was Cary Grant whom Mae West first asked, "Why don't you come up and see me sometime?" in *She Done Him Wrong* (Lowell Sherman, 1933). Grant began his career as the object of an active, female desire.

UNMASKING THE FEMALE GAZE

I remember feeling frustrated and more than a little annoyed the first time that I read Laura Mulvey's "Visual Pleasure in Narrative Cinema." I followed her Freudian and Lacanian reading of the cinematic experience and recognized her description of the frequent scenes in film of female as spectacle, with the action of the film controlled by male figures. But the exclusion of the female spectator both from identification with active images of women and from the erotic contemplation of images of men did not feel complete to me. As a gourmand of old and new Hollywood movies, I could recognize and accept Mulvey's description of films that I watched from a male spectator position, but I felt that I had also experienced distinctly female pleasures—which for me didn't include identifying with passive victims. So I began looking for gaps not ruled by the male gaze in Hollywood movies, remembering movies that had given me pleasure as a female spectator and trying to find a language to describe what I experienced.

Since 1974, much work in feminist film theory has been done to expand and enrich Mulvey's viewpoint. Significantly, work must also be done to update it. Mulvey intended her work as a challenge to Hollywood's monolithic gaze ("psychoanalytical theory is thus appropriated here as a political weapon"), a pluralist and dialectical stance which allows for the reexamination of her theory. Since both the publication of her article and the production of the films Mulvey examines, attitudes toward men and women have gone through many (though sometimes cyclical) changes, presenting another justification for the constant re-visioning of "Visual Pleasure."

But though it may be simpler to describe exceptions to Mulvey's work in recent films, it is worthwhile to examine alternative looks and pleasures that may also have existed in the classic Hollywood era that Mulvey describes. Though 1930–1960 was a period where patriarchy may not have been under open attack, to see gender relations as totally stable seems simplistic. American feminism did not spring fully formed from the head of Zeus in 1968, but evolved from questioning of constructed gender roles dating back to Elizabeth Cady Stanton, if not before. The radical movements of the 1930s allowed space for independently minded women to actively work for societal change; Eleanor Roosevelt modeled the obligation of women to get involved during the Depression. And with World War II, women entered the workforce in large numbers, often in jobs previously closed to women. The Thirties/Forties was a period when women proved their ability to work in partnership with men outside of the home. That Hollywood could consistently create images of women as passive objects during a period when real women were becoming more difficult to contain seems unlikely—especially if Hollywood wanted to sell tickets to these women with the freedom and income to go to the pictures.

Second, filmmaking is a multiple medium, created jointly by writers, cameramen, actors (which includes actresses), editors, etc., as well as the director. The film itself is made of multiple looks, with multiple scenes and shots. To assume that all of these elements would create one, unassailable, controlling look also seems problematic. Even if these multiple looks are generally subsumed by one look, the success of the masculine gaze in subsuming these looks would vary from film to film, depending on the collaborators and other elements inscribed within the film.

Additionally, many films of this era have now been "canonized" as texts of literary value, with their directors dubbed as "auteurs." A common requirement of literary value is a text's ability to bear multiple readings, to contain a polysemy which a single, controlling look would deny. Though standard "movie factory" productions might be expected to conform most closely to Mulvey's description, more complex work in the era would be expected to reflect existing tensions within patriarchy and phallocentric pleasure, and to be more full of contradictions. In "Visual Pleasure," Mulvey focuses on the work of auteurs Josef von Sternberg and Alfred Hitchcock, without noting the contradictions contained within their oeuvre.

In *The Women Who Knew Too Much*, Tania Modleski explores barely contained incoherences caused by female characters in films by Alfred Hitchcock: "His films are always in danger of being subverted by females whose power is both fascinating and seemingly limitless." Modleski examined Hitchcock to understand why female spectators received so much pleasure from the films of a "misogynist": She contends that Hitchcock's unresolved fascination and fear of women led him to create gender roles so complex that his female characters "remain resistant to patriarchal assimilation." Through Hitchcock's use of a "feminine" perspective in some films and frequent portrayals of ambiguous sexuality, Modleski argues that Hitchcock forces male and female spectators alike to experience (the discomfort of) their "bisexual" positions.

SUSPICIOUS LOOKS

In several Hitchcock films during his Selznick period ("Visual Plea-sure" discusses Hitchcock's later work), the action of the film is con-trolled by a woman's active (masculine) gaze, with the male figure objectified—and not coincidentally, Cary Grant was this objectified male in *Suspicion* (1941) and *Notorious* (1946). In *Notorious,* the gaze of the camera actually shifts back and forth, first objectifying Ingrid Bergman's Alicia and then Grant's Devlin, forcing the spectator to identify with active desires for a female *and* a male body. But in *Sus-picion,* the camera only has eyes for Cary.

In *Suspicion,* Hitchcock presents a controlling woman who is un-willing to see her own power or the man under her control. Hitch-cock's alignment of the active gaze with a female character establishes Lina McLaidlaw (Joan Fontaine) as a voyeuristic but unseeing woman, who controls an objectified man, Johnnie Aisgarth (Cary Grant). John-nie first emerges out of darkness into Lina's train compartment. As he talks nonstop, the camera focuses on this handsome, charming man. Johnnie attempts a traditional male gaze at Lina—the camera starts at her sensible shoes, follows her leg up her thick stockings and is stopped short at the book *Child Psychology* held at her chest; Lina's face is obscured by her hat and reflective glasses. Lina's image resists a desir-ing gaze. But as Johnnie goes to sleep, he presents himself as a passive object for her and the camera's gaze, which is reinforced by her si-multaneously finding his likeness in a social magazine.

In the next scene, Johnnie is being photographed with two women, but the male photographer is only interested in Johnnie's image: "Give us one of your smiles, Mr. Aisgarth." At that moment, Johnnie sees Lina, without glasses and in riding habit, controlling a rearing horse. The camera—and Johnnie—sees Lina's hidden beauty at this mo-ment, transformed by the exhilaration of her own power: "It can't be the same girl." Johnnie continues to view Lina as who she is in this moment, a perception of her that he realizes is unrecognized by all, including Lina and her father, General McLaidlaw. As Johnnie says, "I bet they call you monkey-face."

Throughout the rest of the film, Lina's perceptions control the spectator, as she attempts to control Johnnie. When Johnnie appears at her house, he finds in her book his own image, a picture Lina tore out from the magazine. After they have left for a walk, Lina is seen desperately struggling with Johnnie. The spectators' first impression is that he is attacking her, which turns out to be false: "What did you think I was going to do—kill you? Nothing less than murder would explain such a violent reaction." Johnnie was merely going to rearrange her hair, because of the unseen possibilities that he perceives in Lina. When Johnnie asks her to compare him to her horse, Lina replies, "I think if I got the bit between your teeth, I would have no trouble handling you." Her belief that handling a man like Johnnie would be easy becomes significant.

Lina at this point sees no possibilities in herself or with Johnnie. But as she returns home, after refusing a date with Johnnie, she overhears her father predicting she will never marry. To gain control over her life, to escape the house the General does not believe that she can leave, she impulsively and passionately kisses Johnnie. Though she only knows Johnnie as an attractive object, Lina realizes that by possessing this man/object she can gain a degree of control over her life and her future.

After Johnnie leaves town, Lina continues to be motivated by his photographic images, with another magazine photo giving Lina the impetus to track Johnnie down to invite him to the Hunt Ball. Johnnie makes a late and disruptive entrance, his handsome image drawing a crowd of women to him—but he only has eyes for Lina. Throughout the following courtship sequence, the inexperienced Lina is remarkably in control. As they take *her* car to *her* house, Lina professes that she loves Johnnie. Though he admits to sharing her feelings, he knows enough about himself and about her to be afraid. He remarks on her coolness, while saying that he is shaking like a leaf. She replies: "For the first time, I know what I want."

Her self-determination can be seen in her elopement. Instead of being carried away by Johnnie, Lina leaves her house on her own, arriving separately at the registrar's office. But she then allows Johnnie to take her on an extravagant, romantic honeymoon and rent a home for them. Now that she has put the bit between his teeth, she expects him to act like a husband, to live up to the ideal of his photographic image.

However on their return to England, she is surprised to learn that he has no way to pay for the honeymoon or the house: "I don't have a shilling—never have." Her surprise is indicative of Lina's short-sightedness: the first time Lina met Johnnie, he did not have enough money for his train fare and borrowed change from her. He repeatedly warned her that he was no good, sincere warnings that she brushed aside. Everyone else sees and loves Johnnie for who he is—an open-hearted but irresponsible man. But he has chosen to love a woman who does not understand him and expects him to conform to her image of a man, an image that causes him to suffer. She is a McLaidlaw, expecting Johnnie to conform to patriarchal expectations. Lina calls Johnnie a child, but Johnnie is the realistic one.

Johnnie continues to suffer under Lina's refusal to see and accept him. Johnnie's discomfort with the expectations laid out by Lina, and reinforced by General McLaidlaw, is represented by Johnnie's relationship to gifts from the General. Instead of providing the newlyweds with support, the General's wedding gift is two ornate chairs. Lina is delighted by the chairs, signifying her family tradition and structure. Johnnie finds the chairs ugly and uncomfortable, appearing dwarfed and childlike (diminished as a man) when he sits in them. Johnnie sells the chairs at his first opportunity, which upsets Lina so much that he embezzles to get them back for her. The General's "gift" to the couple serves only to illustrate the inadequacies of the groom.

Johnnie's failure as a man in the McLaidlaw's eyes is further evidenced by the General's bequeathing of his portrait to Lina and Johnnie—and nothing else. Again, Johnnie is asked to live with a symbol of his failure as Lina's husband, under the constantly disapproving eyes of his father-in-law. Throughout the rest of the film, Johnnie is watched suspiciously by Lina and her father's portrait. These suspicious eyes push Johnnie farther away from Lina, which only makes her suspect him more. Lina's inability to see the suffering of her husband, to see him as anything but a glittering, romantic object, almost costs both of their lives. Not only does *Suspicion* shift the alignment of the camera's active, desiring gaze from a male to female perspective, it also places the female character in the traditionally male position of the sadistic voyeur, with the male character, our dear Cary, in the role of the masochistic victim of the gaze.

SCREWBALL CARY

Besides the films of Alfred Hitchcock, the genre of screwball comedy, which was particularly popular from 1934–1944, also offered possibilities for female pleasure and power during Hollywood's Golden Era. Despite their surface flightiness, women in this genre were pretty effective in getting what they wanted, including the man that they desired. And the most popular leading man of these screwball comedies was Cary Grant.

The figure of Cary Grant was even more open to active, female desire in the genre of screwball comedies than he was in Hitchcock's films. In *Screwball Comedy: A Genre of Madcap Romance*, Wes D. Gehring describes the balance in these comedies occurring between an anti-heroic male and a dominant female. Gehring defines the anti-hero as an American humorous figure, who is urban, apolitical, child-like, with an abundance of leisure who is frustrated by society in general and women in particular. In screwball comedies, the female character controls the action (often occupying a superior social/financial position to the anti-hero) but preserves her femininity through her "screwball" affect—and a major part of controlling the action is the screwball's controlling of her desired anti-hero. Through the course of the film, the anti-hero often regains (through the capers initiated by the screwball heroine) his agency and/or manliness that he was lacking at the beginning of the story.

Comedy often allows for a subversion of the status quo that is not tolerated in more serious genres. Despite their surface flightiness, women in this genre were pretty effective in getting what they wanted, including the man that they desired. Screwball and other forms of romantic comedy do not just reverse the masculine/active, feminine/passive paradigm (which as Kaplan notes accomplishes little in terms of change), but instead strengthen the female and weaken the male *to put them on more equal footing.* As besieged as the anti-hero is by the screwball heroine, he always manages to hold his own, overcoming some obstacles on his own, revealing himself to be her worthy partner. But unlike the end of Shakespeare's comedies, these strong women are not "tamed" by marriage, but maintain their control of the narrative past the final frame.

Though the narrative and the gaze may attempt to follow traditional male patterns, the screwball heroine continually subverts them. Though she presents herself as a prospective object of the male gaze, she rarely remains motionless or stops talking long enough to conform to the fully objectified position—in Mulvey's terms, the flow of the action cannot freeze to contemplate her erotically because she won't sit still for it. The only time the heroine slows down is to direct her gaze, and the camera's, to contemplation of the anti-hero. Though her desire for the anti-hero generally becomes evident early on, the anti-heroe's awareness of the screwball heroine as the object of his desire is often blocked until almost the end of the film. Similarly, the narrative may anticipate following the direction put forth by the anti-hero only to have the action hijacked by the heroine in another direction entirely.

Earlier I discussed that film was a collaborative medium and as such was subject to subversion from within its monolithic stance. This seems especially true in the realm of screwball comedy. In his discussion of the directors of these comedies, Gehring describes their collaborative approach, citing Rosalind Russell's autobiography as an example:

[Hawks] encouraged us [in *His Girl Friday*] and let us go . . . once Cary [Grant] looked straight out of a scene and said to Hawks (about something I was trying), "Is she going to do that?" and Hawks left the moment in the picture—Cary's right there on film asking an unseen director about my plans.

The fact that Hawks left in Grant's appeal for aid demonstrates that the anti-hero's inability to control the screwball heroine is a part of the genre. The anecdote also demonstrates the freedom that screwball actresses had to shape their characters and the film's action. Perhaps not coincidentally, Gehring individually identifies Katharine Hepburn and Carole Lombard, two of the defining actresses of this genre, as daughters of suffragettes. Other actresses within this genre were also known for their independent personas, on- and off-screen: Claudette Colbert, Barbara Stanwyck, Irene Dunne, and Jean Arthur.

BRINGING UP DESIRE

Bringing Up Baby (Howard Hawks, 1938) is considered a classic screwball text. Grant plays David Huxley, a paleontologist who is trying to finish reconstructing a brontosaurus skeleton, marry his fiancée, and secure a million-dollar gift for his museum in one weekend. As his fiancée presents him with the final and long-awaited bone for his brontosaurus, she runs down his upcoming schedule for him. The camera's gaze pays little attention to Miss Swann, focusing instead on David, who is disappointed to learn that Miss Swann's agenda does not allow for a honeymoon or a marriage with children, to allow them to put all of their energy into his work. He whines like a little boy, but submits to her judgment.

Of course it is implied that Miss Swann's edict against "distractions" includes not only a honeymoon and children, but sex as well. Though Miss Swann refuses to look at David as an object of desire, his full-front, boyishly whiny appeal encourages the audience to see his potential as an object of desire.

The camera has a harder time gazing at Katharine Hepburn in this film. To secure the endowment for the museum, David meets Alexander Peabody for golf. The game is interrupted when Susan (Katharine Hepburn) takes his golf ball and his car. She refuses to acknowledge David or his ownership claims, driving away in his car with David on the running board. The first real close-up of Susan is not presented until the next scene, when she is elegantly dressed—but seated at a bar, trying to catch olives in her mouth (a trick she has just learned from the bartender). The silliness again disrupts the gaze from capturing her as an object of desire. Though her actions might be read as masculine (playing golf, driving, doing bar tricks), her constant clumsiness "feminizes" her actions. Though she drives the action of the film, her ability to maintain any consistent control of herself or others keeps her from becoming "too masculine," but with a femininity and attractiveness markedly different than the traditional objectified female.

In a thoroughly screwball manner, Susan manages to thoroughly control the story's action. Despite David's best attempts to meet with Mr. Peabody or Miss Swann, Susan keeps managing to divert him. Insisting that she "needs" his help with her pet leopard "Baby," she gets him to her family farm in Connecticut. At this point, Susan's active desire is fully revealed, as is David's body as an object of desire. He is seen without his shirt, peeking through the shower door (rather risqué for the period). When he finds his clothes are gone, he parades around in a flowing woman's robe, answering the door for Susan's aunt, and jumping into the air. He then puts on a skin-tight riding costume, before Susan relents and finds "clothes" for him. She repeatedly calls attention to how much more handsome he is without his glasses; this entire sequence focuses attention on David's body (Susan manages to shower and change clothes without putting herself on display).

With her desire and intentions revealed ("I'm going to marry him!"), Susan continues to make David's life more and more complicated and his escape back to New York and Miss Swann impossible. His anger keeps him from admitting his desire, except for brief moments when she appears vulnerable—while the camera can gaze at David sympathetically and lovingly, it is hard for the spectator to know how to look at Susan. David saves Susan by forcing a dangerous circus leopard (not Baby) into a prison cell—and then he promptly faints. The faint is the only point during the madcap adventure when David actually gives up—though life is thoroughly out of his control, he keeps up the good fight. The anti-hero must not lapse for long into the passive position, but remain an active participant in the heroine's adventures.

But as mentioned before, the screwball heroine generally ends with the upper hand. To win David for certain, Susan must keep pursuing him. After the dust has fallen from David's lost donation, dinosaur bone, and fiancée, Susan finds David at the museum with the brontosaurus skeleton. Though he scrambles up a platform to avoid her, she climbs a ladder to talk to him, presenting him with the lost bone. As she laments that he hates her (and her ladder begins to wobble) David admits that he loves her—a moment that is interrupted by Susan's falling ladder and then the crumbling skeleton. David "saves" Susan, but she immediately takes over with her chattering—"Oh, David. Forgive me. You can. You still love me. You do."—wrapping up the film's narrative. While he incoherently mutters, "I . . . I . . . Susan . . . I . . . Oh, dear," submitting, as in the opening scene, to a woman—but this time to a woman who desires him. While in Teresa de Lauretis's discussion of patriarchal narrative the heroine waits at the end of the hero's journey, the screwball heroine must journey to claim her man. And though Susan's face is obscured throughout this scene by a veil, the dinosaur, or David's shoulder, the beauty of David (no glasses, though back at the museum) remains available to the camera and spectator.

CONCLUSION

An argument could be made that Grant was able to become the spectacle for a masculine gaze because his persona was "feminized," the explanation that Steve Neale presents for Hudson's and Travolta's appearances as spectacles. Grant did often appear "emasculated" in his films: in *Bringing Up Baby* he runs around in a woman's bathrobe; in *Suspicion* he is unable to support his wife and is shown dwarfed in his father-in-law's chairs; in *My Favorite Wife* his physique is unfavorably compared with "he-man" Randolph Scott's; in *North by Northwest* he is a mama's boy who is taken advantage of by other men and then protected by a woman. But Neale's argument does not capture the strength and sexuality of Grant's screen presence.

On one hand, Grant's screen persona, despite these emasculating moves, remained balanced and thoroughly masculine through the eventual recuperations of manliness achieved by his characters, as well as through the many thoroughly macho characters that he played. Despite his constant failures in *Suspicion* to be the man of the house, Grant's character retains enough strength and masculinity for Lina and the audience to think him a murderer. On the other hand, the "feminized" aspect of his appeal seems to provide further support of his body being able to support a bisexual, desiring gaze. While the desiring gaze directed at Cary Grant can offer a female spectator "comfortable" pleasure as a woman, it can offer a male spectator an "uncomfortable" bisexual pleasure, that can be shrugged off as Grant moves into the more "natural" position as active male protagonist at the end of the narrative.

This "discomfort" to the male spectator position can actually work to heighten the enjoyment of Grant's films. The films where Grant is most clearly a passive object of desire, for at least distinct moments in the film, are comedies and suspense films, genres that depend on spectator discomfort for their effect. Grant's prominent position in classic Hollywood cinema demonstrates that spaces did exist for active female desire—as well as covert male bisexual desire.

Though both Grant's Hitchcock films and his romantic comedies allowed space for a desiring, active woman, screwball comedy may have been more significant in the continued development of strong women on screen. Building on the strength and agency of the female character in this genre, the screwball comedy has served as a model to bring female protagonists into the action genre: *Desperately Seeking Susan* (Susan Siedelman, 1983), *Romancing the Stone* (Robert Zemeckis, 1984), and *American Dreamer* (1984), followed by *True Lies* (James Cameron, 1994) and *Speed* (Jan de Bont, 1994). In introducing to mainstream cinema the image of women as creative, courageous, and determined, these hybrid romance/ccomedy/action films made these "new" women palatable—and commercial. If the glorious Cary Grant could love the screwball heroine, why shouldn't we all?

One Good Take:
Frank Sinatra

by Robert Horton

FROM *FILM COMMENT*

L ittle movies: look at the covers of Frank Sinatra's albums and observe the instincts, the aura, that made him an evocative film actor. On both *No One Cares* and *She Shot Me Down* he is the haunted loner, cigarette in hand, contemplating a lost love and a shot of consoling whiskey. On *Songs for Young Lovers* the singer is under his lamppost, the mise-en-scène separating him from the happy couples passing by. For *Swing Easy* Frank leans back, mid-song, suspended by the delight of holding a note. On the painted cover of *In the Wee Small Hours* the man's disenchantment has turned the early-morning world a sickly pale green, his gaze falling off-"camera," the cigarette smoke disappearing into the canvas like hope itself. On these covers, Sinatra creates a mood. He finds a character. He has style. And he never takes his hat off.

Sinatra the actor, that cocked-hat figure of visual style, got a little lost in the obituaries and tributes that followed his death. It was the singing that drew most of the attention, understandably so; he wasn't the movie actor of the century, and it's hard to mourn an acting career that had been dormant for decades. The postmortem talk also focused on the puzzle of Sinatra's mystique and apparent split personality. How could the angelic singer be such a brutal goodfella? How could the Cyrano-sensitive balladeer be such a tireless broad-chaser? How could the soulful loner swing so energetically with the Rat Pack in tow?

These questions—and the answers Sinatra kept secret—are a large part of his interest as a movie actor. Great stars don't give everything away, and for every time Sinatra revealed himself in a song or a movie, he masked himself with swagger. Look at his filmography and you conclude that he lost enthusiasm for acting, while his interest in singing never flagged even after the voice began to fray. In the films following his comeback in *From Here to Eternity*, there is a real actor present, an intriguing personality, part lover, part loser, part punk. His acting in *The Man with the Golden Arm* is as fearless as his singing on *Only the Lonely*: The journey is a descent into the inferno, and Sinatra throws himself into the pit with scarcely a pause to consider the way back.

He didn't always have it, in movies. In the first films that capitalized on Sinatra's bobby-soxer stardom, he looks like an immigrant kid invited to sit at the same table as the sophisticates: happy, likable, not sure which fork to use. While Gene Kelly grins with the kind of confidence Frankie would have a decade later, The Voice is limited to boyishness and sidekick duties. He's surprisingly nonthreatening, considering that he is, for crying out loud, Frank Sinatra. *Anchors Aweigh* (1945), *Take Me Out to the Ball Game* (1949), and *On the Town* (1949) are all fun movies, but they are merely the highball before the serious drinking begins.

When his movies fizzled at the box office and his singing career was seriously slowed, Sinatra made his famous comeback with *From Here to Eternity* (1953), as the skinny little wop Angelo Maggio. The story of Sinatra's resurgence is so captivating that it seems churlish to suggest his performance is less than great, but he relies a bit too much on a Dean Martin–style drunk routine, and does some of the comic relief as though he knew he was providing comic relief. But you love him.

He's so slim, so wiry and juiced up; when he's supposed to be insolent, he really looks insolent, and when he's supposed to be excited, he's on the moon. Marching into the stockade, straight as an arrow with plenty of lip, he finally grows into his screen persona: He needed the tough monkey Maggio to bring the chip out onto his shoulder, where it would remain.

Even as laundered from the James Jones novel, the film's rough view of the military is quite a change from the starched uniforms of *Anchors Aweigh* and *On the Town*. Interesting thing about Sinatra's best years on screen: The timing was such that he often played a World War II soldier or a returning veteran. In *Suddenly* (1954) he essays his most psychopathic variant on the subject, a talkative vet who won the Silver Star (as he keeps reminding people) but did too much "choppin' " in the war. Now a hitman, he takes over a small-town home in order to assassinate the U.S. president. It's still a startling and modern performance, full of sick smiles and direct addresses to the audience; his criticism of former presidential assassins ("Booth? Hah!") sounds like something out of a Kubrick movie.

Sinatra's career changed as his body shape morphed; when he became rounded off in the early Sixties, his film roles softened and he seemed to lose his edge. His weariness is effective, too, by the time of the Tony Rome movies, but a spark is gone. In *Suddenly* the punk is still very much on the loose; he's as angular and angry as Sid Vicious, who would twenty-five years later make such a memorable hash of "My Way." Sinatra keeps his hat on, indoors, until the very last moments of the film, when he hunkers down over a rifle (the film unfortunately predicts not only Sid Vicious but Lee Harvey Oswald); the hat adds the finishing angle to the killer's aggression.

He's another starved, embittered vet in *Young at Heart* (1954), an excellent film. Sinatra-philes ought to refer to this one when they talk about the persona, but it's been neglected. The soap opera story might be a problem, or maybe people blank out when they consider the powerfully perky presence of Doris Day. Director Gordon Douglas builds a portrait of the perfect Fifties family in the first half-hour of the film, then plops disappointed musician Barney Sloan (Sinatra) on their doorstep. Barney (a name he changed from something Italian) slouches into the model home and says, "Figures. Rug on the floor. Piano. Smell of cookin' from the kitchen. It's homes like these that are the backbone of the nation. Where's the spinning wheel?"

This is absolutely the Sinatra of the late-night saloon, the wounded lover the fates have conspired against. (Barney is convinced he will be killed by lightning someday, which would fit his history of lousy luck.) Sinatra's luscious streak of romantic self-pity blossoms into full heady flower here, in his sneering dialogue and the way he escapes into the corners of well-lighted rooms. The movie has its share of album-cover moments; my favorite is Barney, alone in the crowd at a holiday party, sitting in front of a tinsel-draped Christmas tree as he morosely contemplates the merrymakers. Nursing his own failure, and his feelings for sunbeam Doris (she's engaged to marry can-do songwriter Gig Young). Frank gets to wrap himself in the melancholy blankets of "Someone to Watch Over Me" and "One for My Baby," both sung as unappreciative audiences chatter away in second-rate clubs.

I saw Sinatra in concert once, just once, in the cavernous Tacoma Dome in the mid-Eighties. That's about as far as you can get from the New York piano bar of the mind, where Sinatra is always weeping at the keyboard and noodling the opening notes that lead him to sing, "It's quarter to three . . ." The Chairman might have been forgiven for dogging it that night, but he was in terrific voice. At one point in the concert, he brought the lights down, sat on a stool, and waved a (full) wine glass around, explaining the nature and tradition of the saloon song. Then he sang three or four of them in a row, including "One for My Baby," and suddenly this building designed for hockey games and Bon Jovi concerts was narrowed to the confines of an intimate little joint after closing time. You could feel the audience reaching out to the singer, the loser, in a way they did not during the swinging tunes. Sinatra understood that sad things go deeper than happy things.

There has been much speculation about where this streak in Sinatra came from: the longing of a kid staring out at the skyscrapers of Manhattan from the streets of Hoboken, the trauma of a career collapse, the tumultuous marriage to Ava Gardner. Whatever the source, the character had arrived by the time of *Young at Heart,* and would stick. As Sinatra worked feverishly in the mid-Fifties, with the vigor of the resurrected, he would return to the dark outcast as often as he would execute more conventional roles in standard fare such as *Guys and Dolls* (1955) and *High Society* (1956). It's tantalizing to note that Sinatra was cast as the wife-slapping carny Billy Bigelow in *Carousel* but bolted the production because of the time-consuming process of shooting extra takes for both the 70mm and Cinema-Scope prints of the movie (Sinatra became famous for insisting that he had only one good take in him). He might have been extraordinary in that sad, sad musical, bringing out a darkness more fragile than Gordon MacRae's blustery characterization. In so many movies of this period Sinatra looks delicate, almost a little ill, needing the attention of a woman to bring him back to health.

The Man with the Golden Arm (1955) was adventurous and risky, but Sinatra didn't have to be talked into doing it; when Otto Preminger sent the first pages of the script to Sinatra and Marlon Brando, Sinatra committed to the project before another page was written. (He'd already been aced out of the Brando part in *On the Waterfront,* a tale of Hoboken, which may have added to the urgency.)

Actors tend to be overrated for showy roles, and underrated for just being. But Sinatra handles both ends beautifully in *The Man with the Golden Arm;* as the heroin addict Frankie Machine, he's harrowing in the cold turkey scenes, vulnerable when trying to maintain in the real world. He and Kim Novak are very touching together; when he shares his (possibly pathetic) dream of becoming a jazz drummer, she helps him by recalling that, come to think of it, he *was* always good at whistling and beating on tables—and his face shines with gratitude.

Sinatra and Novak don't look like movie stars slumming it in a down-and-out game of dress-up, they look like two people who got left at the side of the road during the postwar boom years. Preminger brings his usual cool eye to depicting their dreams. The audience can decide for themselves whether the department store window diorama of suburban success, into which they gaze wistfully, is worthwhile or chilling.

The Joker Is Wild (1957), the story of Joe E. Lewis, is more of a conventional Hollywood biography, but the scenes of Lewis flopping around in a hotel hallway after his throat is cut, and waking up in the hospital after, are as naked and disturbing as anything Sinatra did on film. The disabling of Lewis's career places Sinatra as the outcast again; at one point the down-on-his-luck Lewis tries to avoid an onstage cast party by sneaking around behind the scrim, so the shadows of the happy people are projected as he walks by. All of this exquisite tough-luck imagery; it's as though Sinatra's mystique fed the ideas of his movies: the actor as auteur. Sometimes this is even true in the jokey sense: There are gags about his weight in those early musicals, in *The Man with the Golden Arm* he wonders if the bobby-soxers will go for his drumming, and in *Pal Joey* (1957) and *Can-Can* (1960) he incorporates his own Vegas lingo into the script. It's an acknowledgment that a Personality this big can even defy temporal and geographical logic; or were the words "ring-a-ding-ding" really heard in nineteenth-century Paris?

Pal Joey does have a lingo all its own—the idiom that came from the Rat Pack by way of jazz (with a little of Bing Crosby's surreal locutions thrown in). When I was in high school, before home video, I would sometimes plunk a tape recorder down in front of the TV and tape movie dialogue; one of the movies I wanted to study was *Pal Joey,* just because Sinatra's slang was so peculiar, so confident and effective. I think I had some idea that such patter might help me in my own life, but for a teenager in the disco era there weren't that many opportunities to wonder, "Who's the mouse with the built?" or announce, "That's what I like—champagne that fights back."

Joey is a nicer version of the John O'Hara character from the Rodgers and Hart stage musical, but he certainly fits the casino breeziness of the emerging Chairman of the Board. Sinatra is so easy in this movie you could overlook just how completely he owns it, wears it around his padded shoulders. The film doesn't bite very deep, preferring comedy and music over the moral iffiness of Joey being "kept" by rich widow Rita Hayworth. She bankrolls the broken-down crooner's own Frisco club, Chez Joey, but he blows it by sticking up for chorus girl Kim Novak (the mouse with the built). In some of the Rat Pack movies, Sinatra's cockiness may seem smug or cartoonish, but he keeps the loser close to the surface here. (Damn, he was good at remembering Hoboken.) When his ship comes in, Joey takes to smoking in bed, reading *Variety*, and wiggling his toes in slippers embroidered with his name. Sinatra doesn't make fun of Joey's foolishness—he knows the delight of a street rat's dreams of making it.

Pal Joey points the way toward *Ocean's Eleven* (1960) and the period of Sinatra shrugging his way through lazy movies. But there were a couple of focused, serious outings left. First came Vincente Minnelli's *Some Came Running* (1958), where Sinatra is another military man in another James Jones novel. Although the story is set in 1948, the film seems like one more critique of Fifties conformity, with Sinatra again slicing through the appalling hypocrisy of a small town. When he rolls into Parkman, Indiana, Dave Hirsh takes the best room in the hotel— he promised himself if he ever returned to his hometown he'd take the best room in the hotel. That seems like a very Sinatra thing to do.

Dave comes to town with tagalong floozy Ginny Moorhead (Shirley MacLaine), but he falls for the literary brainiac Gwen French (Martha Hyer). This time the Sinatra character, a published novelist with massive writer's block, is wary of success—he's seen it, and he doesn't like it. He travels with whiskey and a handful of American classics: Faulkner, Fitzgerald, Wolfe. The scene of him lining up his Viking Portable Library in the hotel room rhymes with Bennett Marco, Sinatra's character in *The Manchurian Candidate* (1962), and his curious habit of reading books at random—his room is filled with hardbacks on whimsically chosen subjects. In *Candidate*, it's as though Bennett were trying to fill his mind with distraction after the agony of his brainwashing in the Korean War, but in both cases the characters seem to be groping for a meaning that the world doesn't otherwise provide for them.

Humphrey Bogart died in 1957. With *Some Came Running*, Sinatra

was qualified to carry on Bogie's world-weary mantle; he even appropriated the Rat Pack from Bogart (it eventually became The Clan),
and he very nearly married Lauren Bacall, Bogie's missus. He might
have become a greater actor than Bogart, had he put more effort into
it. The whole business of only doing one take sounds like a refusal to
commit to the acting muse, although Sinatra certainly commits himself to that one take. It's also a way of deflecting people from letting
him see how hard he works—thus the Rat Pack movies ("See folks?
We can make movies without even trying"). Is Sinatra's one-take approach the reason there are so many long, unbroken master shots in
The Man With the Golden Arm and *Some Came Running* and even *Pal
Joey*? Sinatra moves through demanding scenes like a singer navigating
the complexities of a Cole Porter lyric. In a scene from *Manchurian
Candidate,* he enunciates a series of exotic book titles and then
launches into a passionate defense of his sanity; he uses his breathing
tricks to get through the dialogue, and then covers up a flubbed line
at the end.

He has that musicality in his acting. Obviously this is true in singing
sequences, like "The Lady Is a Tramp" from *Pal Joey*—it just kills.
The director, George Sidney, finds camera angles that look like *Life*
magazine photos from the Fifties, and Frank really dances through the
song. But more than that, Sinatra had the ability to lounge against a
desk or walk down a sidewalk with utter grace. I can't think of Sinatra
looking awkward in a movie after *From Here to Eternity*. There is jazz
in those movements, that patter, those looks.

Like some unique stars—Elvis Presley and Eddie Murphy come to
mind—he stopped participating in movies and settled for making vehicles. The mugging, the jokes, the fanny-slapping of the women in
Ocean's Eleven and *Marriage on the Rocks* (1965) seem designed for
the front row of tables at the Sands, or for the entourage that will
laugh at anything the Chairman says. He's still got style, which is why
the Rat Pack stuff is so often fun. The camera likes confidence. But
the tenderness of his playing with Novak and MacLaine, or the warm
appreciation that plays across his face during Rita Hayworth's "Zip"
strip in *Pal Joey,* is retired.

By 1965, in *Von Ryan's Express,* he looks hungover and bored. He was solid enough as Tony Rome, and after a layoff his twilight stab at a cop vehicle, *The First Deadly Sin* (1980), made him gray and tender. (Strange to think that was the year he attacked "New York, New York" with all the vim of a young tiger, but allowed himself to be movingly old in the movie.)

If John Frankenheimer's *Manchurian Candidate* is the last real Sinatra great one, it's a more than respectable way to go out. Aside from pulling a superb performance from Sinatra, the project reflects his interest in politics and his willingness to try on interesting new collaborators. It has one of the oddest scenes Sinatra ever played, and one of the best: his first encounter on a train with Janet Leigh, taken almost verbatim from Richard Condon's novel. The dialogue is roundabout and peculiar, but Sinatra's presence is astounding: His nightmares have driven him to the brink of a nervous breakdown, as they used to call them in those days, and maybe over the edge. Sweaty, smoking, unable to meet the woman's gaze, Sinatra goes all the way to the bottom, barely speaking his lines, his eyes holding on to some familiar place in the middle distance. No actor's tricks here, not even a barstool to hold on to, and he spilled his drink back in the dining car. No hat.

If he hadn't been "Frank Sinatra," would this guy have been hailed as a great actor? Trained actors have technique to fall back on, but Sinatra gave it everything on the first take. Maybe you can only do that for so long, maybe a decade is enough. That scene on the train is beyond the album covers, beyond the Sinatra image, and as honest as Brando and Clift at their fighting trim. In *Some Came Running,* Dave says that having "a little talent" has the same mocking meaning to a writer as it does to a brain surgeon. So Sinatra put his hat back on and returned to singing, his day job—or should we say his middle-of-the-night job? Anyway, back to being the best.

The Color of War

*John Ford Stormed the Beach at Normandy on D-Day,
Armed with Full-color Film. What Happened to the
Footage He Shot?*

by Douglas Brinkley

FROM *THE NEW YORKER*

Most Americans today think that the Second World War happened in black-and-white. That's how it was filmed for newsreels and government archives; that's mostly how it was photographed
for *Life* and the other great picture magazines of the time. Everything—uniforms and ocean swells, gutted buildings and booming
howitzers, tattered flags and flushed faces—comes in shades of gray,
and it is these images that have become embedded in our collective
consciousness. As a result, D-Day and the Nazi death camps can seem
almost as remote to our eyes as do Lincoln and his Union soldiers in
Mathew Brady's sepiatone daguerreotypes. But the soldiers who fought
on the beaches and battlefields of Europe lived and died amid vivid
colors: blue skies and emerald cropland, billowing purple smoke and
bright-red blood. And soon, thanks to the persistence of three men—

an Army veteran, a historian, and a collector—the rest of us will be able to see the Second World War as it truly looked.

The veteran is Melvyn R. Paisley, an Army Air Forces aviator who became an assistant secretary of the Navy during the Reagan Administration. The historian is Stephen E. Ambrose, whose 1994 best-seller, *D-Day*, noted that John Ford, the celebrated director of such classics as *Stagecoach* and *The Grapes of Wrath*, had been in charge of a camera unit on Omaha Beach on D-Day, June 6, 1944, that filmed the landing—in color. Ambrose's book mentioned a tantalizing clue to the film's whereabouts: In 1964, Ford had told the magazine *American Legion* that it was "in storage in Anacostia near Washington, D.C." But, Ambrose went on, an extensive search had failed to turn up the film. Paisley, reading this at the age of seventy-two, was hooked. He set out at once to find the lost footage.

Paisley knew that Ford's mission had been to record Operation Overload—the landing of a hundred and seventy-six thousand Allied soldiers on the beaches of France—for posterity. The director told *American Legion* twenty years later, "The objective of my outfit was simple, just take movies of everything on Omaha Beach. Simple, but not easy." Ford's own job, as the head of cinematography, was primarily logistical. As he put it, "It was up to me to see that everybody who should have a camera had one." Nevertheless, Ford considered his D-Day work one of his most significant achievements.

Early in 1944, the Office of Strategic Services (the precursor of the CIA) had dispatched Ford to a secret laboratory at London's Denham Studio, where films of the Allied war effort were processed and edited. Upon arriving, Ford announced to the head of the operation, "I'm in command, you're second. I'll take the toughest spot, you take the second-toughest spot." Ford's posturing notwithstanding, what were really the toughest assignments went to Brick Marquard and Junius Stout: They were the lead cameramen whom Ford selected to go ashore with Army Rangers in the invasion's first wave, in order to scout the best camera positions for filming the action to follow.

Even so, Ford opted to reconnoitre the area himself. He fitted certain landing craft with automatic cameras, designed to start rolling as soon as the landing ramps were lowered. Ford said that once he got to the beach "I ran forward and started placing some of my men behind things so they'd have a chance to expose their film." Even under fire, the director stayed focussed on his craft, and he explained later, "I know it doesn't make it blazingly dramatic, but all I could think was that for the most part everything was all so well coordinated, fitted perfectly, went beautifully." Marquard was awarded the Silver Star for his efforts; Stout was killed in Normandy, shortly after the invasion.

Of course, the big picture of June, 1944, was beyond any one participant's frame of vision. "My memories of D-Day come in disconnected takes like unassembled shots to be spliced together afterward in a film," Ford recalled of his own experience. "I was too busy doing what I had to do for a cohesive picture of what I did to register in my mind. . . . I was reminded of that line in *The Red Badge of Courage* about how the soldiers were always busy, always deeply absorbed in their individual combats."

Melvyn Paisley was a fighter pilot in the war, and afterward he never forgot either the shock of crimson blood or the deceivingly peaceful beauty of the skies he had pierced in his silver P-47 Thunderbolt. He could always conjure up memories of the orange fireballs that erupted when a bridge was bombed, the lime-green stretches of fertile Belgian farmland, the red-and-black Nazi flags, and, everywhere, the thick seas of mud.

Paisley's interest in color was reawakened in 1996, a year before he read Ambrose's book, at a reunion of P-47 pilots in Philadelphia, where he and his wife, Vicki, met Lars Andersen, an amateur military historian and a collector of Second World War films. Andersen was there to show the pilots his greatest find: color footage from the Special Film Project originated by Henry (Hap) Arnold, the commander of the Army Air Forces in the Second World War. As early as 1940, in an article for *National Geographic*, Arnold had written enthusiastically of the military uses of aerial color photography. He understood the technology's public-relations value, too: He wanted to make a full-color record, suitable for wide release, of the Army Air Forces' role in defeating the Axis powers. On Arnold's orders, motion-picture cameras were attached to two P-47s to film a massive dive-bombing raid on the Rhine Valley. Now, in Philadelphia, as the images of Arnold's footage lit up the screen, Vicki Paisley suddenly shouted, "Look, Mel! That's you!" And, sure enough, there was her husband, all of twenty years old, as Hap Arnold pinned the Distinguished Service Cross on his chest at a ceremony in Luxembourg in April of 1945. One of the camera-bearing P-47s, of course, had been Paisley's.

"I was flabbergasted," Paisley recalled, "and I formed a partnership with Lars Andersen to turn victory in Europe into color, which is the way it was fought." But, apart from the color reels that Andersen had unearthed, much of them from the National Archives, only a fraction of the American color footage of the war in Western Europe had been brought to light. The best known of this was some five hours' worth—including film of the Nazi death camp at Dachau—that had been shot by George Stevens. The Stevens footage surfaced when the filmmaker's son—George Stevens, Jr., the founding director of the American Film Institute—was cleaning out his father's North Hollywood storeroom after his death, in 1975. "I realized that I was seeing views that had heretofore been seen only by the men who were part of the greatest seaborne invasion in history," George Stevens, Jr., later wrote.

In 1997, when Paisley set out to find Ford's footage, the prospects looked bleak. Every bureaucrat that Paisley got in touch with seemed to think that the film had been ruined in a Potomac River flood. But Paisley wanted to see an official document declaring that a fact. Instead of relying on high-level contacts to get an answer by telephone, he drove to the Navy's archival facility in the Anacostia neighborhood of Washington, D.C., to snoop around. "I ran into an archivist over there who knew me from the Reagan years," Paisley told me recently. When he explained what he was looking for, Paisley continued, "the archivist told me that it wasn't lost in the flood but that it had been kept in waterproof, fireproof vaults until the Nixon era, and then it was shipped to Norton Air Force Base, in California, to be stored with other unusable World War II surplus."

While Paisley was glad to learn that the Ford film hadn't been destroyed by flood, he was disheartened to learn that Norton had been closed in 1994. With more phone calls, and a little detective work, however, Andersen and Paisley picked up the trail again: in December of 1972, they discovered, the film had been shipped from Norton to the National Archives; then, in the early Nineties, it was moved to a facility in College Park, Maryland. If the Ford footage still existed, in other words, it would be inside the Capital Beltway.

Ford had hoped to turn the footage into an epic about the Allied victory; as it happened, a copy of his work was chopped into short segments, passed by censors, and shown in newsreels—in black-and-white. Ford eventually gave up on the project and went back to Hollywood, leaving his color film to molder until Melvyn Paisley came along.

Paisley's deduction was right. In a card catalog in College Park, he finally found a misfiled reference card for John Ford's reels of D-Day in color, haphazardly appended to a list of Coast Guard films and miscellaneous maps. Paisley immediately requested copies of the film. "It was the bonanza I had dreamed of," he told me. The film had been on a roundabout journey. The stock that John Ford had used left no negatives, but, because of the high quality of the dyes in the film, the color prints have retained their brilliance over a half century.

As soon as Paisley had the surviving reels in hand (some are still missing), he was eager for someone to produce a full-color documentary—an epic, he hoped, not unlike the one that Ford had hoped to make. He is now in the process of donating a copy of the film to the Eisenhower Center at the University of New Orleans, of which I am the director. The center, which is the home of the largest oral history of Second World War veterans, is now working with the director Steven Spielberg and others to preserve the color film. (Spielberg's own Second World War epic, *Saving Private Ryan*, is set for release this month.)

The project has grown so much recently that Ford's work constitutes only a fraction of more than 150 hours of color footage that Paisley and Andersen have assembled from other sources—European and Russian, as well as American. Andersen has also tracked down nine cameramen who shot color film in Europe, and the producer Owen Crump, whom Hap Arnold had put in charge of his film project. (On Arnold's orders, Crump's men filmed Buchenwald, so that the Germans could never deny the murder of six million Jews.) Some of the cannisters they found smelled of vinegar, a sign that they had never been opened. A color roll shot by Jack Lieb, a correspondent at the start of the war, shows scenes of the invasion at Utah Beach, of French peasants farming as bombs explode around them, of wounded soldiers being carried to safety on stretchers, of A. J. Liebling and Ernest Hemingway drinking cognac at Mont-Saint-Michel, of seasick soldiers in Higgins boats coming ashore on D-Day, and of Generals Montgomery and Eisenhower in a heated discussion. Paisley and Andersen have also located color film of FDR on his 1936 South American cruise; with visiting European royalty in 1939; and at Casablanca and Yalta. Film of his funeral, in 1945, has also been discovered. The two have acquired footage shot by the German side, including Hitler at his Wolf's Lair headquarters in 1943, and Himmler and Wernher von Braun at the German V-2 rocket tests. It's all in perfect, terrifying color. And, one of these days, it is likely to provide the makings of a war movie like no other.

Of Guts and Glory

by Steven Spielberg

When I was growing up in Scottsdale, Arizona, my father fueled my imagination with war stories. Technical Sgt. Arnold Spielberg fought the war in Burma as a radio operator aboard a Mitchell B-25 bomber. He was a hero to me; his uniform, the leather bomber jacket, his squadron insignia—a screaming skull with two wings sprouting from the ear—his tinted goggles and campaign decorations was the same outfit Robert Montgomery, Spencer Tracy, and Van Johnson always looked good in. Sometimes my father would go to reunions of the Burma Bridge Busters, as they were called. When my parents spoke of the Holocaust, it was with horror and rage, but when my dad told combat stories, they were tunes of glory. Maybe this is why I became such a war-movie fanatic. Maybe this is why the first movies I ever made as a kid were war stories of that period. War is the stuff of great drama. The stakes are never higher, the goals are never clearer. The enemies are evil and remorseless. Obviously, the propaganda machine was still working on me eighteen years after World War II. My little 8-mm home movies were aimed to sell war bonds in living rooms near you.

The American movies of World War II were pretty much one-sided. Triumph in victory, triumph in defeat, triumph through air power, triumph through the fighting spirit of the common foot soldier. Along the American home front there was a naiveté about the war. America was not being told the hard truth about what real combat was like, what World War II was all about. Not only was the mail censored from overseas, but so were newsreel footage and news articles from the front. The office of censorship was inaugurated by President Franklin D. Roosevelt (and became the Office of War Information). Roosevelt feared that graphic combat footage would demoralize the home front. On the other hand, glorifying our victories might instill in Americans a sense of complacency. Much of the war was spoon-fed to the public in measured doses, and as part of the war effort, Hollywood went along with it. This is probably why the most realistic combat films came out after VJ Day.

When I was growing up, I never got to see the great Signal Corps documentaries made by some of Hollywood's finest filmmakers. John Huston contributed two remarkable works, *Report from the Aleutians* in 1943 and in 1945 *The Battle of San Pietro*. William Wyler turned in a sobering Air Force documentary in 1944 called *The Memphis Belle*, and John Ford as a Navy filmmaker produced the first popular documentary of the war, *The Battle of Midway*, in 1942. Ford also hit Omaha Beach in the late-morning hours of June 6, 1944, and collected some rare, albeit never released, combat footage from the third-wave assaults. All that footage, which had been missing for almost fifty-four years, has recently been discovered through the tireless efforts of Melvyn R. Paisley, Stephen E. Ambrose, and Lars Andersen.

These wartime experiences must have profoundly inspired John Ford because he went on to direct what, in my opinion, was the most honorable story to come out of the war-film years, *They Were Expendable*. And Wyler was so moved by his experiences with the crew of the *Memphis Belle* that he went on to direct the greatest coming-home story in the history of American film, *The Best Years of Our Lives*.

The film that most inspired me to want to direct war movies was not *Bataan* or *Wake Island* or *The Fighting Seabees* that reran on Arizona television in the 1960s again and again; it was William Wellman's *Battleground*. It is the story of the Battle of the Bulge, as told by the men of the second squad, third platoon, "I" Company of the 101st Airborne Infantry Division. The *Motion Picture Herald* said about this film: "This is a way without drums and without bugles. This is the way it was. This is how the boy next door, the grocery clerk . . . the broker, the garage mechanic, your own brother, son, or you, yourself saw the war from an infantry foxhole." The balance of personal drama, the abstract boredom of waiting for something to happen, and the sudden terror of fire fights and hand-to-hand combat set me ablaze as a fourteen-year-old to want to make my own war movies.

So at around that same time I made *Escape to Nowhere*, a little forty-minute silent 8-mm movie. It had a cast of eighty kids playing both Germans and Americans. The Germans wore black-dyed T-shirts, the Americans wore their T-shirts dyed tan. We all went to the army surplus store and for about $1.50 bought plastic helmet-liners—they looked pretty real on film. The movie was about a rifle squad taking a heavily fortified outpost. We shot it near Camelback Mountain in Scottsdale. For bullet hits, I put firecrackers in the ground, lit them and ran back to the camera before they went off. For explosions, I dug two holes in the ground and placed a wood plank, like a teetertotter, to bridge the holes: On one end I piled earth, on the other a clump of sage to hide the board, so when the kids ran over it a huge geyser of dirt would explode into the air. There was lots of glory and lots of dying. Kids are very good at acting out dying. The movie even won a prize in a local amateur film contest. But the years of glorifying war were coming to an end, and a new kind of dying was moving our way, uncut and uncensored.

I think that films like *Sands of Iwo Jima* and later in the Sixties and Seventies *The Great Escape, Kelly's Heroes, Where Eagles Dare,* and *The Dirty Dozen* did little to prepare us for Southeast Asia. Those tragic events shattered every Hollywood war stereotype when the casualties from Vietnam stormed into our living rooms seven nights a week for nearly a decade. In the 1940s, realism in war films didn't really matter. After Vietnam, it was all that mattered.

Saving Private Ryan is the first film on World War II I've made since my childhood, but it is the antithesis of the kind of experience I sought as a kid. I didn't need Tom Hanks to be John Wayne. I wanted to make the kind of war film about which a veteran of Omaha Beach might remark, "This is pretty close to what it was like." At least that was my goal. Looking at many of the World War II movies that had inspired me was a first step, but it was those Signal Corps documentaries like Frank Capra's *Why We Fight* (1942–45) that gave me a reason to tell a story that's almost six decades old.

Of course every war movie, good or bad, is an antiwar movie. *Saving Private Ryan* will always be that, but I took a very personal approach in telling this particular war story. The film is based on a number of true stories from the Second World War and even from the Civil War about brothers who have died in combat. Hanks leads a squad of men to retrieve the last surviving brother of four in order to send him back to his grieving mother in Iowa. Matt Damon plays Private Ryan. What first attracted me to the story was its obvious human interest. This was a mission of mercy, not the change up San Juan Hill. At its core, it is also a morality play. I was intrigued with what makes any of these working-class guys heroes. I think when we fight, war is no longer about a greater good but becomes intensely personal. Kids in combat are simply fighting to survive, fighting to save the guys right next to them. So many of the veterans I talked with while making *Saving Private Ryan* didn't feel they were doing anything especially heroic, they just reacted without any thought for their own safety. When they became heroes it wasn't because they wanted to be like John Wayne, it was because they were not thinking at all. They were acting instinctively, from the gut. These dogfaces who freed the world were a bunch of decent guys. It's their stories that now should be told.

Eve's Bayou

Too Good to Be a "Black" Film?

by Mia L. Mask

FROM *CINEASTE*

E ve's Bayou director Kasi Lemmons is a film-industry triple threat.
The young artist, whose acting credits include *Candyman* (1993),
Fear of a Black Hat (1993), and *Til There Was You* (1997), made her
screenwriter-director debut with *Eve's Bayou,* one of the most financially successful independent films released last year. The film was so
successful at the box office, earning over $13 million in only a few
weeks on an investment of $4 million, that it prompted Trimark ex-
ecutives to find out who was going to see the film, leading them to the
surprising discovery that over half of *Bayou*'s moviegoers were white.
Not only was it a major crossover vehicle—playing in art houses and
mainstream theaters alike—it also dominated the NAACP's Image
Awards nominations, beating studio films *Soul Food* (20th Century-
Fox), *Rosewood* (Warner Bros.) and *Amistad* (DreamWorks) for a total of seven nominations. It should come as no surprise, however, that
Lemmons's picture has been successful, since it is a well-made movie
with strong performances, striking cinematography by Amy Vincent,

and an unobtrusively dramatic score from Terence Blanchard. What's at issue—for critics who have piled praise on the film—is whether *Eve's Bayou* is too well made, too universal in its appeal, and too sophisticated in subject matter to be considered a "black" film.

Bayou begins with voice-over narration spoken by Eve Batiste, as she recalls her childhood in a haunting flashback to the tragic summer her family came apart at the seams. Shown from young Eve's perspective, much of the narrative comes from a child's point of view but not so much as to limit the film's dramatic depth or spiritual mysticism. The opening lines set the tone for a story reminiscent of a Toni Morrison or Zora Neale Hurston novel. "Memory is a selection of images," Eve tells us. "Some elusive, others printed indelibly on the brain. The summer I killed my father, I was ten years old." From these chilling and enigmatic first lines, audiences gain an introduction to the Batiste clan, an affluent, Creole family living in backwoods Louisiana during the 1960s.

We learn that the folktale behind the bayou involves miscegenation, land inheritance, and lifesaving witchcraft. According to legend, the Batistes are the descendants of an African slave named Eve and her one-time owner, General Jean-Paul Batiste. That their family history begins with sexual transgression in the form of miscegenation proves ironic. The violation of sexual taboos such as adultery and incest plague the Batiste household, gnawing away at boundaries and bonds between family members, destroying the image they have established and try to maintain for themselves as well as others.

The narrative revolves around Dr. Louis Batiste (Samuel L. Jackson), a prominent small-town doctor, his beautifully elegant wife Roz (Lynn Whitfield), and their three children, fourteen-year-old Cisely (Meagan Good), ten-year-old Eve (Jurnee Smollett), and nine-year old Poe (Jake Smollett). Louis's stalwart mother (Ethel Ayler) and sultry sister, Mozelle (Debbi Morgan), are the nearby extended family. On the surface, Louis is a devoted husband, loving father, and an excellent provider. His wife Roz may have doubts about his fidelity but chooses to keep up appearances and ignore her husband's indiscretions. The facade of bourgeois respectability begins to crumble when Eve accidentally catches her father in the adulterous act, setting off a chain of events that force the family to deal with latent sibling rivalry, repressed jealousy, and incestuous desire.

Eldest daughter Cisely, whose adolescent adoration of her father engenders her own adult self-fashioning, makes a desperate attempt to deny Eve's tearful report she "saw Daddy messin' with Matty Meraux." Cisely's sassy defiance in defense of her father's transgressions escalates until a profound misunderstanding eventually turns her against him. At this crucial moment of misinterpreted desire, Lemmons uses the unreliable narrator to demonstrate how a change in perspective alters the way audiences construe a given scene. Unfortunately, this same scene becomes the reference point for the film's cliché conclusion during which the narrator speaks rapturously about the inaccessibility of truth.

The central focus of *Eve's Bayou* may be prepubescent Eve's relationships with mother, father, and siblings, but equally important to the story's dramatic trajectory is her Aunt Mozelle Batiste-Delacroix, the spiritual center of their world and Eve's emotional anchor during this period of familial discord. Lemmons prompts audiences to notice parallels between Louis and his sister. Both behave selfishly by entertaining passionate extramarital affairs so lengthy in duration that these *affaires d'amour* end in tragic standoffs. Yet Mozelle is depicted as the more sorrowful—and therefore sympathetic—of the two. Her sensitivity and spirituality, which manifest as the "gift of sight," ironically fail to prevent recurring tragedy in her own life, making Mozelle a melancholy albeit introspective woman whom the local voodoo priestess (Diahann Carroll) refers to as "cursed." Morgan, whom audiences will remember from lengthy stints on daytime soaps *All My Children*, *Loving*, and *Generations*, is perfectly natural in *Bayou* as the soulful essence of Creole culture. By contrast, seasoned actress Diahann Carroll, under hokey witchdoctor makeup, stands out like a sore thumb, and her underwritten character amounts to little more than caricature.

Perhaps in an attempt to maintain the momentum of its crossover appeal, veteran film critics have been reluctant to celebrate *Eve's Bayou* as an "African-American" film for fear racial affiliation might frighten off would-be viewers. Andrew Sarris, for example, remarked, "To hail *Eve's Bayou* as the best African-American film ever would be to understate its universal accessibility to anyone on this planet." This statement of unwavering support is also contradictory, implying that ethnic art—in this case African-American cinema—cannot evoke the pathos or poignancy ascribed to mainstream (read: white) cultural products. By extension, the statement reinscribes the hegemony of whiteness as the locus of universal humanism.

As Richard Dyer suggested in his seminal essay, and reiterated more recently in his book *White,* "Black people can be reduced to their bodies and thus to race, but white people are something else that is realized in and yet is not reducible to the corporeal or racial." Implicit in this reviewer's assessment of *Bayou* is that it's too good to be stigmatized as a "black" film. Yet the statement fails to challenge the categories of whiteness and blackness on which the critic's approbation of *Bayou*—and analytical authority—depend. Other critics, who obligingly lauded Lemmons for making a film that wasn't really about race, echoed such comments.

The critical confusion is a result of Lemmons's representation of upper-middleclass black folks rarely depicted in American popular culture (particularly in the post-Cosby Nineties). Just because *Eve's Bayou* provides a picture of the Creole bourgeoisie doesn't mean these people—or this film—cease to represent an African-American experience. Most reviewers remain unaware of how fully entrenched most colored folks are in middle-American values and are therefore more likely to praise such films than critique them for a dependence on generic conventions.

Lemmons's portrait of a rural, affluent, French-speaking black family does threaten essentialist notions (including those held among some African-Americans) of black experience as definitely urban, ghetto-centered, and youth-culture dominated. As a woman filmmaker, Lemmons provides substantive roles for black actresses beyond the treacherous girlfriend, unwieldy bitch, and commonplace 'ho' roles so familiar to audiences from theatrically released black cinema. While there is a precedent for black-directed films in rural settings about women and their daughters, including Julie Dash's *Daughters of the Dust* (1991), Lemmons's *Bayou* further challenges the way a male-defined, urban esthetic (macho ghettocentricity) has come to define New Black Cinema. Parallels between Dash's *Daughters* and Lemmons's *Bayou* stop there.

To hail *Eve's Bayou* is to praise a film that received standing ovations at the Telluride and Toronto festivals and earned Kasi Lemmons the Director's Debut Award from the National Board of Review. It is to recognize as enjoyable the charisma of stars Samuel L. Jackson and Lynn Whitfield. More significantly, to applaud this movie is to acknowledge that the strongest performance comes from child actor Jurnee Smollett, who convincingly portrays Eve, despite the few melodramatic moments scripted for a grown woman rather than a precocious preteen. To hail *Eve's Bayou*, however, as the "best African-American film ever" precisely because it's not African-American is to fail to acknowledge the reasons for its crossover appeal.

Yasujiro Ozu

The Subtly Observant Eye

by Phillip Lopate

FROM *CINEASTE*

The oeuvre of Yasujiro Ozu (1903–1963) tends to provoke a religious hush, making it difficult for the critic to isolate the virtues and defects of individual films. Compounding the problem is Ozu's consistency: On the surface his pictures seem to share so many elements, resembling one another structurally and thematically, that it is not always possible even for an aficionado to disentangle in memory *Late Autumn* from *An Autumn Afternoon*, say. In fact, there was more variation over the course of his long career than the static image we have of an Ozu movie generally suggests: consider the freewheeling camera movements of his silent period, the neorealist (*The Record of a Tenement Gentleman*) or melodrama (*Tokyo Twilight*) anomalies. Still, the charm of diving into Ozu's world is that one knows, more or less, what to expect: the subtly observant eye for family dynamics; the preference for character over plot; the serene acceptance of life's tragic limitations; the restrained cinematic style (camera generally placed low, mood-setting or palette-cleansing "pillow shots" which offer depeopled landscapes and interiors; uninterrupted autonomy of individual scenes).

When so many movies try to take the viewer by storm, Ozu's gently invite you in. Artistically, he is the opposite of the bully. He is patient, alert. As Donald Richie noted in an appreciation of Ozu, "Actually, these films are not slow. They create their own time and clock-time ceases to exist; the audience is drawn into Ozu's world, into a realm of purely psychological time. What would at first appear a world of stillness, of total inaction, is revealed as mere appearance. Beneath this lies the potential violence found in the Japanese family system, and also the quiet heroism of the Japanese faced with his own family." Or the American with his. The major payoff in watching Ozu is that, formalist nuances aside, you are more often than not deeply moved by his characters' struggles, so penetrating is his wisdom about the tension between civilization and its discontents.

I have been going to Ozu movies for more than thirty years now. When the first selective retrospective was mounted at the Museum of Modern Art, in the mid-Sixties, I attended as often as I could. It was something of a revelation, combining the satisfaction of discovering a new cache of Jane Austen novels with a cleansing visit to a Buddhist retreat. Inevitably, there developed a snobbish, cliquey sentiment around Ozu, equivalent to being in the vanguard of Mozart-lovers. Later, the word spread, and there were fuller retrospectives mounted at revival houses and museums, where one could catch up with obscurities like *The Toda Brothers and Sisters*. I remember arranging a first date at *The Only Son*, a rather austere early sound picture by Ozu, shown at the late Gallery of Modern Art on Columbus Circle. It was a test: If the woman liked it, I was infatuated; if not, *sayonara*. She loved it, and though we were incompatible in most other ways, we ended up messily entangled for seven years. I blame Ozu.

Nevertheless, I continued to worship at the shrine. During the Eighties, when an Ozu retrospective again made the rounds, I found myself secretly growing impatient with some of the minor works. But the towering masterpieces, such as *Late Spring* and *Tokyo Story*, seem to me part of our essential culture, able to be revisited as often as *King Lear* or the *St. Matthew Passion.*

Here we have three Ozus from the Fifties, recently reissued on videotape—*Early Summer, Floating Weeds,* and *Good Morning.* The first is a masterwork, just a smidgen below the level of *Late Spring* or *Tokyo Story*; the latter two are intriguing albeit flawed. All three have been handsomely transferred to video, with crisp visuals and clearly legible subtitles. In some ways Ozu films, since he used mostly intimate, interior compositions with shallow depths of field, and stayed away from wide-screen formats, do not suffer as much as the work of other world-class directors from being seen on the small screen. On the other hand, they do suffer precisely because television is a home medium, which treats most comfortably the familial and domestic. Ozu's family tableaux, lacking that larger-than-life projection that ennobled the quotidian and freed moviegoers to choose where to fix their meditative attention, become reduced, annexed as they are to the banal rhythms of the soap opera and the sitcom. Still, we know how to make these adjustments by now, adding a twenty percent quality surtax to the video image. And since Ozu's greatness is more a matter of script and acting than richness of visual field, we continue to have access to the best parts in these tapes.

Early Summer (1951) uses the favored Ozu storyline of a family trying to get their reluctant daughter married. (Often this reluctance has to do with her unselfish understanding that, in marrying, she would be abandoning her parent to a lonely old age.) On one level an ensemble work—distributing its attention judiciously between a set of elderly parents, their grown children and spouses, the grandchildren, relatives, and friends—its core of intensest feeling belongs to the marriageable daughter, played by the incomparable Setsuko Hara. Hara's great gift was to convey complex, thoughtful heroines whose defiance and willfulness hide behind the sunny, acquiescent mask of a Japanese good girl. In the film, she is twenty-eight, appealing but not getting any younger, an office worker helping out the family's finances. Her boss, wondering what her story is, gossips with a girlfriend of hers, who volunteers the information that she used to collect Katharine Hepburn photos. "Is she a lesbian?" he asks baldly. No, comes the answer. We deduce that it is Hepburn's independent, headstrong quality that appeals to her. He admits that sometimes she seems attractive to him, sometimes not. This crystallizes the ambivalence around her and her vulnerability as a marital candidate. Certainly we may find Setsuko Hara fetching enough for any occasion, but the character she plays is meant to be somewhat short of a beauty—and, in any case, too proudly intelligent to avail herself of Pretty Woman privileges.

Early Summer reunites Setsuko Hara with her star from *Late Spring*, Chishu Ryu, the quintessential Ozu character actor. Ryu's specialty was the rigid, stern, scholarly, patriarchal figure, who, in the end, is kind enough to bend. In *Late Spring* they had played father and daughter, this time they are brother and sister. Since the father in *Early Summer* is rather passive, older brother Ryu has become the functioning head of the family. He sets out to find a husband for his sister. But she is too much the modern woman to sit still for an arranged marriage. In the end, she thwarts his strategy by impulsively selecting her brother's friend, a rather unsuccessful widower with a child who is moving to the cold northern countryside to take a job. There is no question of romance either way: She candidly tells a woman friend that she doesn't love him but will feel safe and protected with him.

As for the widower, we are given no indication that he has even thought of his friend's sister previously as a potential mate: The final deal is cooked up between the heroine and the widower's mother, and he merely accepts their agreement with baffled resignation. But her own family is angry that she decided to act alone, without consulting her. This is not the Japanese way. Besides, her mother confesses, she had had high hopes at one time that her daughter would make a good catch, snare a wealthy man, and live in a big house. "When she graduated from high school everyone was talking about her." The disappointment that parents feel in their grown children is characteristic Ozu. As for the brother's anger that she has chosen his friend, this is more psychologically loaded. For all their sibling tensions, there is the suggestion that she worships her brother and is marrying his friend as a surrogate for him.

So we are left with a bittersweet ending. The main goal has been accomplished, the potential "old maid" has been married off, but the family has been broken up in the process, and financially straitened with the loss of her salary. As the bride's elderly father tells her mother, "We shouldn't want too much."

One of Ozu's subtlest moves is to take us close enough to a heroine who so keeps her own counsel by presenting us with varying degrees of candor and reserve. Within the family she is most formal and dishonest, or at least unforthcoming. When an aged uncle drops in and teases her in front of her brother about her unmarried status, she giggles, hides her face, and runs away. In a later scene, alone with the same uncle, she responds to a similar prodding of his by saying, "Find me a man." We see her several times in the company of her women friends, both married and unmarried, who bicker, hilariously and ritualistically, about which side is better off. Alone with her confidante friend, she is utterly unbuttoned, even mimicking satirically the hick accents of the country folk who will be her new neighbors. The film is filled to the brim with sharp character details, showing us once again what superbly economical dialogue writers Ozu and his favorite screenwriting collaborator, Kogo Noda, were. And, contrary to the notion that Ozu never moved his camera in later years, there are some lovely tracking shots.

Good Morning (1959) was intended as a popular comedy. Ozu, one senses, pulled some of his punches and reigned in the darkness to achieve that purpose, and the result was one of his most successful films. It was also Ozu's second color film (the previous year's *Equinox Flower* his first), and the transition from his customarily restrained black and white to the kindergarten-cubby glossy, optimistic brashness of Agfacolor is a little startling, as if he had borrowed Doris Day's cinematographer. But perhaps this Hollywood Fifties comedy look is fitting in a film which revolves around the strain on traditional Japanese society to adapt to American consumerism. In an old, lower-middle-class neighborhood where the housewives without a washing machine enviously eye the neighbor who has one, two little boys covet a television set so that they can watch wrestling and baseball games.

Ozu was a master at handling child actors, and the two brothers come across adorably in their brazen outspokenness. When their stern father (Chishu Ryu, naturally) tells them they are talking too much and should shut up, they go on a silent strike, punishing him by literally enacting his request. Eventually, their father relents and buys a television set, though he has already gone on record as saying TV will produce a nation of idiots. Meanwhile, the neighbors continue to fester with busybody gossip, grudges, and rivalries. What the family was in *Early Summer*—a prison of inescapable pressures to conform—the neighborhood is in *Good Morning*. (The title comes from the little boys' insistence that adults also talk too much, spouting commonplace inanities.)

Good Morning is delightful the first time you see it; it works like a charm. But it doesn't deepen on subsequent viewing, partly because its "fart" jokes become tiresome and partly because its very construction so neatly alternates themes that craft triumphs over complexity. Even the ever-respectful Donald Richie admits in his book that this is Ozu's most "schematic" film. It reworks materials from his earlier, silent masterpiece, *I Was Born, But...* (the two little boys went on a hunger strike in that one), but without the kicker of the boys becoming ashamed of their father for kowtowing to his boss. Here, there is nothing to challenge the father's authority but a mundane, easily satisfied acquisitiveness on his sons' part.

I once asked the knowledgeable Kyoko Hirano, film programmer of the Japan Society, why Japanese films of the prosperous Sony period were not as deep as in the golden age of Mizoguchi, Naruse, Kurosawa, and Ozu. Usually one thinks of culture as following money, yet the Japanese filmmakers of today, talented as they are, seem to lack that profound sense of awareness, the transient sadness of things. Very simple, she said. Japan used to be a poor country, and that poetic sadness was an outgrowth of material sparseness. But now it has become mainly middle-class, and the typical, consumerist Japanese no longer feels that "cherry blossom" poignancy which Westerners had assumed was an ingrained feature of Japanese culture.

Good Morning seems to anticipate at times this Japanese future. Ozu's next motion picture, *Floating Weeds* (1959), looks backward. "Though this is a contemporary film," he said, "in mood it really belongs to the Meill period." A remake of his 1934 silent, *The Story of Floating Weeds,* about a troupe of travelling players, it benefited from the great Japanese cinematographer Kazuo Miyagawa, who had shot Mizogochi's *Ugetsu* and Kurosawa's *Rashomon,* and who brought a lush density of color and compositional perfection to Ozu's dramatic scenes and cutaways. The establishing scenes in the first half are particularly fascinating, as the troupe fans out over the town—the male secondaries trying to make time with the village women while selling tickets to performances, etc. The troupe's leader is a dictatorial, washed-up ham (played with piglet-eyed opacity by Ganjiro Naka-mura, an actor Ozu seemed to favor precisely because of his inexpressiveness) who has steered his company back to this town so that he can look up his old flame and their illegitimate son. The boy, now about to start college, does not know that the visiting actor who has always been presented as his "uncle" is really his father.

The old flame, played by the great character actress Haruko Sugi-mura (the selfish daughter in *Tokyo Story* and the money-lending ex-geisha in Naruse's late *Chrysanthemums*) is unfortunately given little to do as a sweetly patient, forgiving woman who would like the actor to settle down with her in old age. The real fireworks come when the troupe leader's mistress and leading lady (the voluptuously overripe Machiko Kyo) jealously sniffs out his old involvement. She confronts him, in a beautifully shot downpour: He calls her a bitch and an ex-prostitute whom he "saved," while she reminds him of the many times she bailed him out from financial jams by appealing to theater owners. They are two of a kind, both tough, gamy birds, and their crude language will come as a shock to those who associate Ozu with good manners. The old actor wants to distance himself from this seedy vulgarity and settle down with his ex-flame and son. But the young man rejects his father when he learns the truth, and runs away with the troupe's pretty ingenue.

This whole subplot in the second half, involving the young man, is wooden and melodramatic. It reminds us not only how poorly suited Ozu was for melodrama, but also how bland and weakly realized most of his young male characters are. The handsome, youthful male lead, the staple of American movies, seemed an embarrassment to Ozu, who much preferred to concentrate on boys or elderly men—when not depicting his juicily thoughtful heroines. The sound-stage tinniness of these father-son confrontations suggest that, alongside the rich Buddhist emptiness, or *mu,* that Ozu was able to achieve, there were times his later films struck a less profitable emptiness, that came from scraping away too much.

The richness of the first part seems all but kicked away in the second half, as if Ozu had lost interest in his hammy, overemotional characters. The exception is whenever Machiko Kyo appears on the screen; she maintains an operatic presentation of self entirely suitable to the screenplay's theatricality. In the last scene, their troupe dismantled by debts, she and her aged actor-lover go off together in a train to start anew. They belong together, these callous troupers, and she attends to him, pouring him wine with touching forgiveness, in a moment that redeems all the wobbliness of the film's weaker parts. Even in his less inspired films, Ozu was always able to reach into himself and produce such moments of gestural wholeness. In short, it is always a good thing to see an Ozu film, even if not every Ozu is equally good.

Deliverance

*Youth-Crazed Hollywood Relegated Classic Tough-Guy
Directors John Boorman and John Frankenheimer to the Has-
Been Heap Some Time Ago. But Neither is the Retiring Type,
and This Fall Two Career-Reviving Movies Reveal Them to
Be at the Top of Their Game.*

by John Brodie

FROM GQ

One night last spring, a hush fell over the bar at the Palm as the
first few minutes of *The Deep* played on the TV. The princelings
of the entertainment business who were waiting for their tables
stopped schmoozing and fell into a shared reverie. It was so quiet you
could hear ice tinkling in the glasses at the otherwise boisterous Los
Angeles steak house. While Peter Benchley's 1977 follow-up to *Jaws* is
not likely to be taught in film schools anytime soon, the opening sequence is permanently etched in the brains of a certain generation of
guys. The image of Jacqueline Bisset emerging from the blue Carib-
bean in her wet white T-shirt is right up there in the hubba-hubba
pantheon with Catwoman, Jeannie's evil twin, and that Farrah Fawcett
poster. The silence ended abruptly, however, when a Warner Bros.

development executive turned to the gang and asked, "Hey, what movie is this?"

The gaffe was telling, for it is against this limited historical perspective that directors John Boorman and John Frankenheimer have struggled to recapture the attention of an industry that fawned over them, then forgot them, some twenty years ago. There are many Hollywood executives in decision-making positions with scant knowledge of movies made before the late Seventies, when *Star Wars* forever changed the action-adventure genre. Since then the action movie has metastasized from being about ordinary men in extraordinary circumstances to special-effects extravaganzas. In the recent spate of mind-numbing "event movies"—*Godzilla, Armageddon,* and *Lethal Weapon 4*—all semblance of reality gave way to cartoonish mayhem. But as we head into fall and the visceral *Saving Private Ryan* emerges as the film of the summer, these two masters of old-school entertainment are poised for a return to the A-list.

Though neither has won an Oscar, Boorman and Frankenheimer have made major contributions to the regular-guy cinematic canon. Frankenheimer directed *Birdman of Alcatraz, Seven Days in May, The Manchurian Candidate,* and *French Connection II.* Boorman blew Hollywood off its hinges with a double shot of Lee Marvin in *Point Blank* and *Hell in the Pacific.* For his next big trick, he made *Deliverance.* But in a town where one president of production employs what he calls "the ten-year rule" (i.e., any great director without a box-office hit in a decade does not get hired), both Frankenheimer and Boorman have had a hard time getting the plum assignments of late. Neither Boorman's last feature, *Beyond Rangoon,* nor Frankenheimer's, *Year of the Gun,* set any box-office records. Yet rather than go gently into that good night of career retrospectives, the two men have recently gone outside the system to prove themselves. Boorman made a $6 million black-and-white gangster movie whose scale resembles that of a Sundance kid's debut; Frankenheimer swallowed his pride and went to work in cable television, which ultimately led him back to a feature, this month's *Ronin.*

Boorman's film, *The General,* will hit theaters in December to qualify for the Academy Awards, but he is already reaping its benefits. In May this biopic of the cheeky Dublin crime boss Martin Cahill garnered the best-director prize and rave reviews at the Cannes Film Festival. Boorman wrote the script in three weeks, after spending more than a year and a half in development hell at Paramount Pictures.

If *The General* (which is distributed by Sony Pictures Classics) does not make him a hot property again, Boorman will at least be the subject of Hollywood buzz. Next year Mel Gibson will be starring in *Payback,* a new film adaptation of the novel by Donald Westlake (writing as Richard Stark) that spawned the 1967 masterpiece *Point Blank.* At sixty-five Boorman will have the queasy sensation of having lived long enough to see one of his films remade. And audiences will have the opportunity to compare his handiwork with that of freshman director Brian Helgeland, because Sony Pictures Classics will be releasing a refurbished print of Boorman's film as a companion piece to *The General.*

Frankenheimer's stock is also on the rise this fall, thanks to *Ronin,* a gritty heist film shot in Paris and Nice. Made for United Artists, the thriller is the culmination of a long march back into favor for the great American director. Over the past fifteen years, he was left for career dead more times than he would care to count. Rather than give up, Frankenheimer, who had developed a reputation for being difficult and a hard drinker (he has been sober since 1981), made three Emmy Award–winning cable movies, which proved to the powers-that-be that he could bring a picture in on time and on budget. His film about the prison riot at Attica, *Against the Wall;* his Chico Mendes biopic, *The Burning Season*; and his Civil War prison drama, *Andersonville*, all won best-director Emmys. His fourth trip to the cable well, the miniseries *George Wallace,* earned eight Emmy nominations this summer. Early buzz on *Ronin,* which stars Robert De Niro, Jean Reno, and Stellan Skarsgard, has already catapulted the sixty-eight-year-old Frankenheimer into the directing chair of *The Good Shepherd,* MGM's upcoming epic about the formative years of the CIA.

Frankenheimer, like Boorman, remains stoic about his time away from the A-list. But the director's absence speaks volumes about ageism, faddishness, and how action movies have changed. "At the end of the Seventies, when George Lucas and Steven Spielberg revealed that the audience was actually twelve-year-olds, increasingly the good or thoughtful or original movies got pushed into a kind of ghetto, the ghetto of art films," says Boorman.

"When I was in my twenties and a very successful director, I knew who the older directors were and I revered them. Then I came upon a bunch of people that really knew nothing about film history and about anything that was made five years before," says Frankenheimer.

John Boorman's first meeting at MGM, in 1966, set the tone for his subsequent dealings with the Hollywood Beast. MGM's chairman and CEO, Richard O'Brien, sat at one end of the conference table. Boorman sat with Lee Marvin at the other. The actor, who as a marine had received a Purple Heart after being wounded in Saipan, took charge. Exuding menace, Marvin asked O'Brien in his nicotine-scarred baritone, "Do I have script approval and cast approval?"

The head of MGM, a former banker who did not relish conflict, replied, "Yeah."

"Well, I defer these approvals to John," Marvin said, before rising slowly from his chair and leaving the meeting. Marvin had in effect handed the sophomore director unprecedented creative control. The actor and the director had joined forces only a few months before. Boorman had recently graduated from making documentaries for British television to directing the Dave Clark Five in a shagedelic knockoff of *A Hard Day's Night* called *Catch Us If You Can*. Marvin was hot off his Academy Award–winning performance in *Cat Ballou*. The two had met in London when Marvin was there shooting *The Dirty Dozen*. After a long night of drinking at the actor's flat, Marvin agreed to star in the project that became *Point Blank*.

The evening's denouement came when Marvin asked Boorman what he thought of the script and Boorman replied, "It's a piece of shit." Marvin concurred and threw it out the window. ("It fell in the gutter, and apparently Mel Gibson picked it up," Boorman now jokes.) Together with screenwriter Alex Jacobs, the duo went on to improvise a character study of a criminal named Walker who is betrayed by his colleagues, shot at point-blank range, and left for dead. When Walker miraculously survives, he becomes the embodiment of bloody vengeance.

Boorman would need creative control to make a movie that has more in common with postmodern splatterfests like *Reservoir Dogs* than with other popular 1968 releases, such as *Funny Girl* and *The Odd Couple*. The book was originally set in San Francisco, but Boorman deemed that city "too soft." So *Point Blank* became his meditation on Los Angeles's moral vacancy. "[The painter] David Hockney went to L.A. at the same time as I did, and we've often talked about how differently we responded to it," says Boorman of his fellow English expatriate, who paints the city in cheery hues. And even though Boorman had grown up under difficult conditions in London during the blitz (as recounted in the autobiographical film *Hope and Glory*), he was "future shocked" by L.A. In the mid-Seventies, he moved his wife and four children to Ireland, where they bought an old stone mansion outside Dublin in the Wicklow Hills. From then on, Boorman kept Hollywood at arm's length. With the exception of *Deliverance,* made for Warner Bros., he has done his best work free and clear of the studios.

"John really has to have freedom to do good work," says the actor Jon Voight, who plays Inspector Ned Kenny in *The General* and who has remained close to Boorman since they worked on *Deliverance*. The major creative interference Boorman dealt with on the river thriller was not from Warner Bros. but from the author, James Dickey, with whom Boorman disagreed about the meaning of the movie. Dickey saw the river ride in the macho tradition of Ernest Hemingway's and William Faulkner's initiatory rites. Early on in the shoot, the director's differences with Dickey escalated from creative to personal, when the novelist began addressing the actors solely by their characters' names. Says Boorman, "He was drunk all the time, and he was losing his distinction between fact and fantasy. He said to me, 'Everything in that book happened to me.' Well, when I saw him get into a canoe, I realized it wasn't true."

The General's black-and-white photography and leisurely paced scenes give it a dreamlike feel. "John uses very long takes to establish mood, like the scene in *Deliverance* where these backwoods guys come out and take Ned Beatty and me into the woods," says Voight. "There's a lot of cutting in movies today, especially with the techniques that have been created through MTV and commercials, but John's style is from somewhere else—documentary."

John Frankenheimer cut his teeth in live television, directing countless hours of *Playhouse 90, Climax,* and *You Are There.* He left that medium in the Sixties, when TV sets became readily available and the networks began courting the lowest common denominator. He then directed a string of movies that pulsated with the nervy energy of espionage and betrayal. And they felt real. While shooting *The Train,* Frankenheimer wrecked two locomotives and Burt Lancaster learned to drive one. He was never put off by grit or grime. It is impossible to imagine a present-day studio executive allowing a sequel to turn on the notion of the hero's being abducted by an evil drug lord, imprisoned in an SRO hotel, and made into a heroine addict. But that was precisely the premise of *French Connection II.* The scenes of Charnier's men shoving needles into Popeye Doyle's track marks would be unthinkable in anything with Will Smith or Harrison Ford.

"Action has to come out of story," says Frankenheimer. "And in most of today's movies, it doesn't. I think you have to involve the audience with a character and then put the character in jeopardy. But that's only my theory. It's just a different way of making movies." Frankenheimer is relaxing in his Hollywood Hills home after doing some final polishing on *Ronin.* The director and his wife of more than thirty years, the actress Evans Evans, have fled L.A. more than once. Reminders of their sojourns abroad fill the house: Toulouse-Lautrec prints hang in the living room, totems of their years in Paris. His wife's

Rolls Royce Silver Shadow is parked in the garage, recalling their stint in the Belgravia section of London. A complete set of leather Louis Vuitton luggage lines the garage wall, ready for the next job on location.

Frankenheimer is tall and lean; he still exudes the alpha-male confidence of the tournament tennis player he was as a boy in Queens, New York, and during his college years. He has his own court and plays six times a week. While he may not be able to give you a shot-by-shot description of every one of his films, he can tell you the score of every championship match he played.

The Cold War and the politics of the Sixties cast a long shadow over Frankenheimer's work. While at Williams College, he was recruited for the CIA. (He declined.) And in the late Sixties he became deeply involved in the presidential campaign of Robert Kennedy. The senator spent his final afternoon at Frankenheimer's house in Malibu, and the director drove him to the Ambassador Hotel the night Kennedy was assassinated. (Frankenheimer heard the news on his car radio. Critics have often pointed to this event as a turning point in Frankenheimer's career, citing early Seventies films like the dreadful Richard Harris comedy *99 and 44/100 Per Cent Dead* as the work of a director who had given up.

For Frankenheimer the professional *annus horribilus* was 1977, the year Paramount was touting *Black Sunday* as potentially the highest-grossing film of all time. *Black Sunday,* a thriller about a terrorist attack during the Super Bowl, was going to be bigger than *Jaws,* according to the studio hype. And for less than $8 million, Frankenheimer achieved a series of logistical feats: He got permission from the NFL to shoot in the Orange Bowl during the Pittsburgh vs. Dallas Super Bowl; he convinced Goodyear to let its blimp be the villain; and he was able to shoot Robert Shaw running across the fifty yard line during the actual game. "I tried not to believe all the hype," says Frankenheimer. "But it wasn't the big hit everybody thought it was going to be. It really undermined my confidence. And what happened was, I started drinking. It starts off with Mouton-Rothschild, and it ends up with Smirnoff. And before I knew it, I was a full-blown alcoholic."

While Frankenheimer was drinking, he burned a lot of bridges and was no longer offered the best material. So after getting sober in 1981, he spent the remainder of the decade shooting pedestrian adaptations of novels by Robert Ludlum (*The Holcroft Covenant*) and Elmore Leonard (*52 Pick-up*). The director soon found himself at a fork in his career. He had the choice of directing a Dolph Lundgren shoot-'em-up or telling the story of the Attica prison riot for HBO. "I called a friend of mine and said, 'I've been offered this wonderful script, but there's no money and it's for television, and I think I ought to turn it down,' " says Frankenheimer. "And my friend said, 'You should turn it down. And then you should sit by the phone, wait for it to ring, and think about the good old days.' "

There was trepidation at HBO as well. "I was worried he would be resentful that his career had taken him back to television," remembers Bob Cooper, who was then senior vice president at HBO Pictures. "But he came into the first meeting and said, 'Look, I need to prove myself.' He was hungry, and he was invested in what *Against the Wall* could mean for him. It was amazing to watch him—he was nervous as a little kid at the Emmys," The $5 million telefilm, shot in twenty-nine days, won the prize that had eluded Frankenheimer during his *Playhouse 90* years.

After that Emmy, it would take two more trips to the podium—and a final bit of hazing—before he rejoined the A-list.

In 1995 New Line Cinema had begun shooting what would turn out to be a jinxed remake of *The Island of Dr. Moreau*. The film's two stars, Marlon Brando and Val Kilmer, were the kind of actors most directors approach with a whip and a chair. After the film's first director was fired abruptly, New Line Productions president Mike De Luca called Frankenheimer about coming out of the bull pen to save the production.

Undaunted, Frankenheimer took the job "for the money," he says. "I realized that if I got through that experience, I could get through anything." He is loath to discuss the shoot except to say that Brando, who made a reel-to-reel tape recording of their first meeting, was not the only problem. Kilmer, too, seemed unimpressed he was working with a director who had coaxed prize-winning performances from the likes of Kirk Douglas, Frank Sinatra, Paul Scofield, Jack Lemmon, Laurence Harvey, and Gene Hackman. "I told Kilmer, 'You don't have the credentials to argue with me,' " says Frankenheimer. "But the list doesn't do you any good in that situation."

For every actor who's blasé about the list—or for every junior executive who does not know his film history—there are one or two key decision makers around town who have either studied the work of Frankenheimer and Boorman in school or who are film buff enough to champion the sexagenarians. (The directors share a thirty-seven-year-old agent at International Creative Management, Ken Kamins, whose office is jokingly referred to as "the cryogenics lab.") Besides De Luca, United Artists president of production Lindsay Doran has been an advocate of directors of a certain vintage. She had no qualms about turning *Ronin* over to Frankenheimer—especially when she discovered he was bilingual and had worked with French crews.

As a result of Frankenheimer's years abroad, *Ronin* has a decidedly European feel. The title refers to samurai warriors whose master has died in battle, but the term has been updated here to refer to KGB-, IRA-, and CIA-trained operatives making their way in a post–Cold War world. The film boasts two spectacular car chases—one through the streets of Nice, the other along the banks of the Seine, including a tunnel sequence that eerily recalls Princess Diana's death. Chases are one of his strong suits, and *Ronin's* look refreshingly low-tech.

Frankenheimer's retro aesthetic would seem diametrically opposed to the aesthetic of today's event-movie directors. His fuddy-duddyism took on an ironic cast this past summer, when he again had to confront an old rumor linking him with his stylistic antithesis, Michael Bay, the director of *Armageddon*. In June, Bay, who is adopted, gave an interview to *Entertainment Weekly,* stating that he had tracked down his natural father. Bay wouldn't name him, but he did offer a tantalizing bit of information: His birth father was a famous director. Bay has told friends he believes Frankenheimer to be his father, and some years after blood tests were performed, the two discussed the matter at a Directors Guild of America dinner. Bay declined to comment for this article. All Frankenheimer would say is, "There were tests done at UCLA Medical Center in 1987 involving him, his [birth] mother and myself. And those tests conclusively proved that I am not his father." However, a decade ago, blood tests seldom yielded definitive results.

Intrigued by the rumor of the Frankenheimer-Bay connection, and the odds against anyone's breaking into the movie business, let alone becoming an A-list action director, guests at industry dinner tables have made the two directors the focus of a nature vs. nurture debate. New fuel was added to the fire when *Daily Variety* coincidentally ran separate front-page stories with photos of the two men. Friends of Bay's cited the cover as an example of how much the two look alike, while friends of Frankenheimer's saw no resemblance at all.

As Frankenheimer heads into production on *The Good Shepherd*, Hollywood's most coveted actors are lining up for roles. The film, a kind of "Waspfather," follows a brilliant young Yalie from his time in Skull and Bones through the formative days of the OSS and on to the Bay of Pigs. The narrative jump-cuts through the American century as the hero loses his soul in the fun house of international espionage. "We're getting the kinds of calls from actors on this that remind me of the interest people had to work with Robert Altman on *Short Cuts*," says producer Frank Mancuso, Jr.

Like John Huston, who triumphed with *Prizzi's Honor* at a time when the town had dismissed him, Frankenheimer is ready to play for the trophy that has eluded him his entire career—the Oscar. "There is this misconception that talent runs out, and there are certain careers where that is true," says Lindsay Doran. "But you spend any time with John and you feel like he could wrestle a lion." Indeed, as Frankenheimer bids me farewell one summer night after we have shared a bowl of pasta, his grip is fierce. It is the grip of a champion who is ready to play on the grass at Forest Hills once again.

Touch of Evil Retouched

*In 1957, After His Film Noir Classic Had Been Hijacked and
Recut by the Studio, Orson Welles Wrote a Fifty-eight-Page
Memo Detailing How* Touch of Evil *Could Be Saved. Forty-
one Years Later, Someone Listened.*

by Jonathan Rosenbaum

O rson Welles had final cut in Hollywood just once: on his debut
feature, *Citizen Kane.* And only one of his features, the relatively
impersonal *The Stranger,* ever turned a profit on first release. By the
1950s, the only feature work he could get in the United States was as
an actor; directorial efforts such as *Othello* and *Mr. Arkadin* were made
overseas, with European financing, under conditions that were trying,
to say the least. In late 1956 Welles was invited to play the villain in a
routine Universal Pictures crime thriller. Thanks to the efforts of
Charlton Heston, who was playing the lead in the picture, Welles was
soon promoted to director. *Touch of Evil* was his first Hollywood-
produced film since 1948's *Macbeth.*

Welles's script rewrites and the six-week shoot both went smoothly.
His dealings with Universal began to falter only after a screening of

his rough cut, which studio executives found difficult to follow. A second editor was brought in, and three weeks later, miffed at his loss of control, Welles left for Mexico to start work on an independent effort, *Don Quixote*. When he returned two months later; the studio would not let Welles direct the new footage, and a third editor was assigned to whip the film into shape. Welles saw the results once, in early December 1957. In an honest effort at an appeasing response, Welles composed fifty-eight pages of notes, addressed to studio head Edward Muhl. After all his frustration with studios in the recutting of *The Magnificent Ambersons*, *The Stranger*, *The Lady From Shanghai*, and *Macbeth*, he was determined to make a final attempt to get what he wanted. Welles's memo pleaded for changes in the sound and editing, and though some of his suggestions were followed prior to the film's release, many were not. *Touch of Evil* was his last Hollywood picture.

Thirty-three years later, while editing Welles and Peter Bogdanovich's book, *This Is Orson Welles*, I came across the edited version of the memo, which was then part of the manuscript. Welles's notes offer a rare glimpse into the strategies and motivations of a master filmmaker. But HarperCollins cut the memo due to lack of space. (This past spring, Da Capo Press included the edited memo in the second edition of *This Is Orson Welles*.)

A few years later, producer Rick Schmidlin concocted a wild scheme: to follow all of the memo's instructions for the first time and put together the *Touch of Evil* Welles had had in mind. After Schmidlin showed Universal an edited sample of one of Welles's suggestions, the studio saw a way to get more value out of an old chestnut. With the studio's approval, Schmidlin enlisted me as a consultant and hired Walter Murch—the celebrated editor of *The Conversation*, *Apocalypse Now*, and *The English Patient*—to carry out the editing.

Murch describes the editing as analogous to performing a skin graft using only skin from the same body; because none of the work entailed restoring lost footage, it was a matter of different placements and configurations of existing shots, sound, and music. Truly, no work of this kind has ever been done before—work that is neither a restoration nor a "director's cut" in any ordinary sense, but a delicate revamping based on the execution of instructions that were drafted some forty years earlier.

Originally released in a ninety-three-minute version, *Touch of Evil* enjoyed a brief second life when a 108-minute preview version was discovered in the mid-Seventies. Containing more of both Welles's footage and footage shot by contract director Harry Keller during postproduction, the longer cut, which some have erroneously labeled as the director's cut, has subsequently become the only one available (the home-video version incorporates parts of both). While Murch's revamping comes closer to Welles's creative intentions, the most any posthumous cut can hope to achieve is an interpretation of what Welles had wanted at only one stage.

Aptly labeled "film noir's epitaph" by Paul Schrader, *Touch of Evil* describes the dark events of one twenty-four-hour period in a sleazy Mexican border town after a local businessman and his stripper girlfriend are blown apart by a time bomb planted in the trunk of their car. The plot focuses on the battle of wills between Mexican by-the-book cop Vargas (Heston) and crooked, evidence-planting American cop Quinlan (Welles). Sucked into the conflict are Vargas's wife, Susan (Janet Leigh); Quinlan's partner, Menzies (Joseph Calleia); a local gangster (Akim Tamiroff); and a madam (Marlene Dietrich).

Welles's celebrated opening crane shot weaves an intricate crisscrossing pattern between the honeymoon couple on foot and the doomed couple in the car, as all four characters cross the border. In all previous versions, this dazzling shot is accompanied by Henry Mancini's suspenseful score and overlaid by the film's credits. In the new edit, per Welles's specifications, there are no credits over this shot, and the only music comes from the various clubs and from a car radio.

Though the suspense is lessened, the physical density and atmosphere are heightened, altering one's sense of the picture's personality from the outset.

In the first reel, Murch says, he used more crosscutting between different parts of the story. "It's better now because the opening reel is more like the rest of the film." In a few cases the soundtrack has become more densely layered. Gone is a patch of dialogue in a hotel lobby between Heston and Leigh, which Welles neither wrote nor directed. A few frames are pulled from a frightening close-up of a strangled corpse, making its impact more subliminal. Ending the pianola music halfway through Welles's first scene with Marlene Dietrich makes the second half of their dialogue play differently; lines that had teetered on the edge of camp mannerism suddenly come across as straight.

Eventually, a clearer understanding of Welles's design for the film emerged: a more fluid narrative; more opportunities for certain atmospheric elements to register; and even a sharper sense of why Menzies switches his allegiance—because of his moral principles, not through any collapse of willpower.

"The changes have made the film more consistent with itself," Murch says. "That's odd, because a film that has been admitted into the gallery of the most memorable films of the twentieth century was a hybrid of what Welles and the studio wanted. So people who know the film have accepted its stylistic contradictions. Now that they are gone, it'll be a shock, because those who know the original film have gotten used to it the other way. It's like when you jump on somebody else's bicycle: It just feels different."

You Ain't Heard Nothin' Yet

by *Andrew Sarris*

FROM *YOU AIN'T HEARD NOTHIN' YET: THE AMERICAN
TALKING FILM, HISTORY AND MEMORY, 1927–1949*,
OXFORD UNIVERSITY PRESS

The first lesson one learns almost immediately after undertaking
to write a comprehensive and critically weighed history of the
American sound film is that one can never finish; one can only stop.
After many years I have decided to stop, at least as far as the period
between 1927 and 1949 is concerned. I could work until the next
millennium sifting the endless trivia for clues to the tantalizing mysteries of the medium, but my marvelously patient editor has urged me
to cease and desist, and I do so with a sense of relief.

Mine is more a macrocosmic than a microcosmic treatment in that
I have chosen to focus on stylistic and thematic configurations rather
than on minutely detailed descriptions. Having written regularly on
film for more than forty years, and having taught film as an art and
as one of the humanities for over thirty, I have been compelled to
maintain an aesthetic lifeline between the past and the present. By
contrast, archival specialists tend to develop so much of a rooting
interest in their excavations that they discount the onset of the new,

whereas journalist novelty-seekers keep trying to cut the umbilical cord that still links us to Lumière and Griffith. My own view of the talking picture from the twenties to the present is that it remains alive and well, but that it never seems to yield up all its meanings and beauties and associations the first time around. Ideally, film scholarship should have evolved as a cooperative enterprise by which each contribution could provide a foundation for its successor. Instead, recent decades of "discussion" have been characterized by an enormous amount of fiercely polemical writing that seems to have pulverized the subject beyond repair. The result is that every study has to start from scratch, despite the maddening repetitiousness of the process.

My own purpose, however, is not to exhume any ancient conflicts, but rather to chart some of the changing ways we have thought about film from period to period. What were once perishable memories are now preserved artifacts. With the spread of television, videotape, videocassette, and laser disc technology, the cinematic past is now a palpable presence in our cultural lives. Memories can be refreshed; judgments can be revaluated. Movies themselves can be shown to pass beyond the parameters of any methodology of the moment, be it sociology or semiotics, technology or stylistics, dramatic narrative or symbolic iconography. In this way a historical context can be reconstructed: This, in short, is the purpose of this book, and, I confess, its own controlling methodology.

Unfortunately, the problem of quantity alone seems virtually insurmountable with respect to the American sound film. There are so many movies, literally thousands and thousands of them, and it is very difficult to discuss a few without involving the rest. Literary historians, for example, have a much easier time in that relatively few trees from the forest of fiction are logged for the stately mansions of literature. Literary character types do not "cross over" from good books to bad books to the extent screen icons "cross over" from good movies to bad movies, a cultural phenomenon designated in the arcane methodology of the semiologists as "intertextual references." One thus does not have to become a print freak to function as a literary person.

Besides, the burden of cultural guilt falls more heavily on the casual reader than on the casual moviegoer. The reader who has not perused the "right" books according to the canonical tastes of his age must study literary history and criticism in order to repair the defect in his sensibility. By contrast, the moviegoer who has not seen the "right" movies according to the comparatively permissive and yet too often contentious Film Academy will argue up and down that the movies he has chanced to see are fully as relevant to the total subject as any others. The badgered film historian is thus obliged to fill in on all the possible movie encounters of his potential readers, and this can be a very tedious and soul-destroying process. Unfortunately, the most available alternative—cribbing a film history from faded news clippings and microfilm—is even worse.

Then, also, there are so many dreamlike associations in the memories of millions of moviegoers, more than a few of whom insist on writing their own books on the subject. Star-gazing, for example, can be said to constitute one of the mass religions of our time. The Garbo and Sullavan cults have become as ritualized as their equivalents long ago for Isis and Osiris, except that the mass of star-worshippers have not formally accepted or authorized any high priests of criticism to mediate between the true believers and their deities. In this realm of abject reverence the illuminated icons demand incantations rather than insights. I, like most of my colleagues in the modest craft of movie-reviewing, cannot claim infallibility in these matters. We all have our blind spots and aesthetic afflictions, I suppose, and it is probably more advisable to acknowledge them frankly and openly than to let them fester in pseudo-objective phraseology about art and truth and beauty.

It is in this spirit of contrition that I relate an episode in the writing of my first book, *The Films of Josef von Sternberg*. Myron Gladstone, my very capable copy editor on that occasion, complained about my incessant repetition of proper names, suggesting instead "Marlene Dietrich" first time, "Miss," "Ms.," or just plain "Dietrich" the second, and "she" or "her" the third. Stubbornly, I resisted my editor's very sound advice. Against even my own better judgment, I felt the compulsion to type out "Marlene Dietrich" in full again and again as if that were the only way to invoke her image. Once her full name perished in a pronoun, her face seemed to fade away as well into a figure of speech. Whereas my editor was concerned with my inefficient use of language as information, I was obsessed with my emphatic use of language as incantation. It was thought versus feeling, logic versus magic. But even monotony, I felt, was not too high a price to pay for the power of summoning Marlene Dietrich's glowing presence from the silver screen to the printed page.

At the time of my contretemps with my copy editor, I was reminded of parental scoldings in my childhood for referring to my mother as "she" in her presence. The mere use of the pronoun implied disrespect for the magical role of maternity expressed in the noun. Friends, acquaintances, and students have reported similar episodes in their own childhoods, and thus the noun-into-pronoun taboo must be a fairly universal phenomenon. It marks also another link between cinema and psychoanalysis, two dream-oriented flowerings that have co-existed and cross-pollinated from the very beginning.

The problem persists: How *does* one write about moving pictures with words that won't budge from their syntactical sequence? By taking the more efficient path of linguistic expression one tends to reduce the cinema to thematic synopses and bloodless categories. By taking the more expressive path one tends to supplant the cinema's sensibility with that of belles-lettres. I would hasten to add that there is absolutely nothing wrong with the practice of belles-lettres in the writing of film history as long as belles-lettres contents itself with commenting on cinema, and does not presume to impersonate it. The gap between movies and the words used to describe them must always be understood in any transaction between the writer and the reader. And it must be understood also that there can be no equivalent in even the most illuminating literary fireworks for the *son et lumière* that makes up the essential experience of the sound film.

Of course, there is and always has been a considerable literary component in the cinema. Too much, in fact, for most film scholars up through the 1950s. The novels and plays that were pillaged by studio story departments constituted an allegedly alien influence on what was purportedly a visual medium. The fact that most people went to the movies to see photoplays focused on stars rather than moving pictures shaped by images only confirmed the catchpenny vulgarity of the motion picture industry. Consequently, as long as the "purity" of the medium was at stake, it was relatively simple to dismiss most movies, and especially most Hollywood movies, as poisonously impure. Film histories could be written very easily in this snobbish atmosphere. One did not even have to go very often to the movies to qualify as an expert on the subject. A familiarity with a handful of silent film classics was sufficient preparation for scholarly scolding of the pernicious talkies, often sight unseen. Indeed, the American sound film was born in a state of original sin for having caused the death of the silent film with all the latter's poetic pantomime and metaphorical montage.

Perhaps the most literate summation of this general attitude was provided by Dwight MacDonald in 1942 in the course of a harsh critique of Sergei Eisenstein's *Film Sense* as a stylistic recantation on the stake of the Stalinist Inquisition:

Was it only a dozen years ago that, with pious excitement, we went to "little" movie houses—the very term has disappeared—to see the new films from Russia? Is it so short a time since many of us were writing on the cinema as *the* great modern art form, the machine art whose technique was most in harmony with the dynamism of the machine age, the art that most powerfully affected such peculiarly modern areas as Freud's subconscious and Pavlov's reflexes, the only art that could sometimes bridge the gap between serious creation and mass taste, so that [*The*] *Birth of a Nation,* Chaplin's comedies, *Potemkin,* and a few other films might be said to have been the only works of our time that have seemed both popular and great? Our enthusiasm was not misplaced, our theories were not unfounded. And yet the wonderful possibilities that lay before the cinema ten years ago have withered into the slick banality of Hollywood and the crude banality of post-1930 Soviet cinema. The potentialities, which really existed, which, for that matter, still exist and in even richer profusion, simply were not realized, and the cinema gave up its own idiom and technique to become once more what it was before Griffith: a mechanical device for recording stage plays. Like so much else in the past decade, it crept back into the womb, into the unconscious. It has been many years now since anywhere in the world, a film has been made which, aesthetically speaking, is cinema at all.

So much for the few thousand sound films made between 1929 and 1942, a period later hailed by many auteurist, genre, and otherwise revisionist film historians of the Sixties, Seventies, and right into the Nineties as a Golden Age in its own right. The American sound film has reached its seventieth year, and it and its audiences are endowed with (perhaps even encumbered by) a more extensive historical consciousness than was ever before possible or feasible. The Theory of Progress which animated the socially conscious film histories of Lewis Jacobs, John Grierson, Siegfried Kracauer, Paul Rotha, Richard Griffith, Jay Leyda, Georges Sadoul, et al. has been supplanted by a vague, aimless nostalgia for the Good Old Days. With the past having become infinitely more promising than the future there is a tendency to suspend all judgments of old movies. The motives may range from the most awe-struck admiration to the campiest condescension, but the result is the same: to make the very subject of old movies the occasion for mindless "fun." I think that this attitude is both mistaken and short-sighted. The time has come for evaluation to walk side by side with elucidation, and not to loiter six paces behind. As a practicing polemicist on this issue for the past three decades, I am well aware of my own role in returning old Hollywood movies to the realm of serious study. But I never intended to foreclose the future behind a body of rigid dogma. We are all hostages to history, and we always shall be. Moreover, if we are to make any progress as film historians, we must learn to incorporate the opinions of the past into a valid context for the present. Methodology is no substitute for history. That I am widely regarded as a registered New York–based auteurist of the Sixites, Seventies, Eighties, and Nineties serves only to place my own writing in a historical context for future reference. I write without the slightest presumption that my own words shall be or should be the last words on the subject. *Pace* my Marxist-Progressive predecessors, I am merely one antithesis to your many theses, and I find now that I must explain your positions before I can fully expound my own.

This particular film history is motivated also by the conviction that film studies have become a legitimate part of the liberal arts curriculum. My conviction is not universally shared in academe, and so this book is addressed almost as much to the doubters as to the devotees. After more than forty years of published missionary work on the movies, I sense that I have reached the point of consolidation and summation with a subject that has been lurking luminously in the darkness for as long as I can remember. The American sound film is like an aged parent, whose own childhood I have researched in order to understand my cultural heredity. But I am always aware of the young people in my classes. And the eternal skepticism in their eyes makes me all the more eager to explain what has been so interesting and so edifying in the American cinema since the bawling, squawking birth of the talkies.

* * *

On New Year's Eve, 1929, it was raining in New York, but the streets were still full. The theaters were packed as if there had never been a depression; the memories of 1929 and of the big slump were fading. People who had once preferred to stay home were coming out, filling the hotels and smart restaurants.

On Broadway, one could see Alfred Lunt and Lynn Fontanne in their newest drama, or *Bitter Sweet,* a play by the latest rage, Noel Coward. For those not able to afford the price of a theater seat, there were movies now, including Helen Morgan in *Applause.* With sound a commonplace now, and color, the simple two-color Technicolor that enlivened sequences of many musicals widely used, the movies were better than ever.

John Baxter, *Hollywood in the Thirties*

The two preceding paragraphs, which open John Baxter's study of Thirties' talkies, reflect the irresistible temptation of many film historians to correlate sociological history with movie history. The bulk of Baxter's book is not sociologically oriented, but he feels obliged nonetheless to usher in the decade with references to "a depression" and "the big slump." The point of view expressed is that of fun-seeking New Yorkers on New Year's Eve, 1929, deluded by the false hope of a new decade to fill up the hotels, smart restaurants, theaters, and movie houses on Broadway's Gay White Way. A sprinkling of still legendary celebrities—Alfred Lunt and Lynn Fontanne and Noel Coward on stage, and Helen Morgan on the screen—suggests that the glitter and frivolity of the carefree Twenties may linger briefly into the Thirties. Unfortunately, Baxter's sense of history is somewhat askew. An awareness of a great and irreversible economic depression did not overwhelm most people's minds with the stock market crash in October 1929. We have seen so many movies in which an entire era ends in the tumult on the floor of the New York Stock Exchange on Black Thursday, October 24, 1929, that we have come to believe in this fateful day as a kind of economic Pearl Harbor. Indeed, the Thirties in America have often been defined as the period between the Crash and Pearl Harbor, despite the resultant encroachment on the Twenties and Forties. (For that matter the "movie" Thirties can be said to extend technologically and stylistically from *The Jazz Singer* [1927] to *Citizen Kane* [1941], but there is no need in this particular study to stretch the point.)

The "Crash," however, was not an instant disaster like the explosion of the *Hindenberg* on May 6, 1937. After Black Thursday, October 24, 1929, there was a brief rally before Black Tuesday, October 29, 1929. The market then continued to fall until November 13, by which time $30 billion in capital values had been liquidated. Yet, as John Kenneth Galbraith has noted in *The Great Crash 1929*, the Depression that followed the Crash took a relatively long time to take full hold.

In January, February, and March of 1930 the stock market showed a substantial recovery. Then in April the recovery lost momentum, and in June there was another large drop. Thereafter, with few exceptions the market dropped week by week, month by month, and year by year through June of 1932. The position when it finally halted made the worst level during the crash seem memorable by contrast. On November 13, 1929, it may be recalled, the *Times* industrials closed at 224. On July 8, 1932, they were 58. This value was not much more than the net by which they dropped on the single day of October 28, 1929. Standard Oil of New Jersey, which the Rockefellers were believed to have pegged at 50 on November 13, 1929, dropped below 20 in April 1932. On July 8 it was 24. U.S. Steel on July 8 reached a low of 22. On September 3, 1929, it had sold as high as 262. General Motors was a bargain at 8 on July 8, down from 73 on September 3, 1929. Montgomery Ward was 4, down from 138. Tel and Tel was 72, and on September 3, 1929, it had sold at 304. Anaconda sold at 4 on July 8.

No one any longer suggested that business was sound, fundamental or otherwise. During the week of July 8, 1932, *Iron Age* announced that steel operations had reached 12 per cent of capacity. This was thought of its sort to be a record. Pig iron output was the lowest since 1896.

Galbraith makes only two references to movies in his account of the Crash, but both are provocative though peripheral. The first deals with the rickety financial structure of the film industry:

On August 17, the *Leviathan* and the *Ile de France* left port fully equipped for speculation on the high seas. Business on the *Ile* the opening day was described as brisk. One of the first transactions was by Irving Berlin, who sold 1000 shares of Paramount-Famous-Lasky at 72. (It was a shrewd move. The stock later went more or less to nothing and the company into bankruptcy.)

The economic misfortunes in the Thirties of such studios as Fox, Paramount, RKO, and Universal were not the stuff of which popular scenarios were made. Nor could economic disaster be necessarily equated with aesthetic deficiencies. Many of the most interesting movies came off the most inefficient and most quixotic assembly lines. Nonetheless, Hollywood was part and parcel of the most speculative apparatus of the capitalistic system. Its moguls had much in common with the robber barons of oil, steel, railroads, automobiles, and pyramiding trusts generally. From its beginnings the film industry was plagued by patent wars, boycotts, double-entry bookkeeping, and endless litigation. Yet remarkably few movies provided any insight into corporate power struggles over film or any other product. No genre could explain the Crash or the Depression that eventually rippled out from the financial wreckage on Wall Street.

In addition, a great many movies were set neither in the immediate present, nor in the United States. Josef von Sternberg's *Morocco* and Ernst Lubitsch's *Monte Carlo* were two of the most memorably innovative sound films of 1930, and two of the least appropriate models for sociological analysis. Lewis Milestone's *All Quiet on the Western Front* dealt in fraternal and pacifistic terms with a war of some two decades earlier recounted from the point of view of German soldiers in the trenches. Howard Hawks's *The Dawn Patrol* and Howard Hughes's *Hell's Angels* provided chivalric gloss for the aerial conflict above the trenches of the Great War of 1914–18. George Hill's *The Big House* and Mervyn LeRoy's *Little Caesar* were closer to the here and now in 1930, but both films dealt with romanticized criminal elements considered much too raffish to serve as "realistic" characters. King Vidor's *Billy the Kid* and Raoul Walsh's *The Big Trail*, two of the more ambitious Westerns of the year, remained impervious to the troubles in the concrete canyons on Wall Street. One could go on and on through the entire roster of 1930 releases in a vain search for the cutting edge that snipped off the Twenties from the Thirties.

That movies for a time affected more people than any other art form led many influential Marxist critics to infer that Hollywood was grinding out frivolous entertainments as a deliberately counter-revolutionary service for the capitalistic system. On the other hand, a very large number of early talkies (as well as late silents) were grubbier and more sordid than one would expect "propaganda" movies to be.

For every upper-class drawing room there was a lower-class barroom. For every Ronald Colman there was a James Cagney. Indeed, the very persuasive Scottish documentarian and critic John Grierson explicitly warned Hollywood not to "Colmanize its Cagneys." Hollywood, at least on the surface, could be low-down even when it was not hard-boiled.

Galbraith's second reference to movies addresses itself with scathing irony to the frequently proposed mission of Hollywood during the Great Depression:

> The failure of the bankers did not leave the community entirely without constructive leadership. There was [New York's] Mayor James J. Walker. Appearing before a meeting of motion picture exhibitors on that Tuesday, he appealed to them to "show pictures which will reinstate courage and hope in the hearts of the people."

Mayor Walker was not to be alone in his exhortations. After the inauguration of President Franklin Delano Roosevelt in 1933, the advent soon after of the New Deal, and the subsequent passage of the ill-fated National Recovery Act with its NRA eagle emblazoned on the nation's screens, Hollywood was virtually mobilized to "fight" the Depression by accentuating the positive in whatever nook and cranny it could be found. This was as sure-fire a prescription for "escapism" as any. What is unclear is the extent to which movie escapism varied from 1929 to 1930. Had Mayor Walker and his contemporaries been depressed by movies before the Crash? Or, as is more likely, had the Crash itself transformed movies into potential morale-boosters?

In this context John Baxter's notion that movies were considered better than ever in 1929 seems bizarre. To be sure, the public was enthralled by sound for a time. Nonetheless, most film historians have considered 1929 the worst year artistically in the history of the American cinema.

What has occurred is a shift from one extreme to another. The standard film histories written before 1950 treat sound as a catastrophe from which the cinema never fully recovered. A book like Baxter's (published in 1968) absorbed the revisionism of the New Criticism while trying to deny it. Hence, according to Baxter:

> Among the first points to strike any researcher into the American cinema of the Thirties is the inability of modern critical theory to cope with the bulk and nature of the material. There is no inflexible rule for allocating measures of blame and praise in films of the period, but the presence in Hollywood of hundreds of major film artists, most of whom contributed to many films other than those they directed, argues against the applicability of the *auteur* theory or any variation of it.

Having dissociated himself from the presumed spirit of auteurism, Baxter then crawls back to the practical application of *auteurism*: "But while films have been grouped throughout the book under directors, this system has been adopted as much for convenience as for any other reason."

Aye, there's the rub. How does a historian cope with the vast amount of material to research without some system of priorities. Also, Baxter seems oblivious to the fact that, if it were not for the revised perspectives of what he calls "modern critical theory," the Hollywood movies of the Thirties would not be considered worthy of study and re-study at all. A revolution in taste has overthrown traditional condescension, but it is not sufficient simply to celebrate this revolution. We must track down the old movies to their own time, when they were taken much less seriously than they are today.

Still, film history can never be synchronized with so-called real history. In addition to the omissions, the distortions, and the oversimplifications, there is the inevitable factor of cultural lag. F. Scott Fitzgerald was particularly perceptive on this point in his essay, "Echoes of the Jazz Age," published in November 1931:

> Contrary to popular opinion, the movies of the Jazz Age had no effect upon its morals. The social attitude of the producers was timid, behind the times and banal—for example, no picture mir-

rored even faintly the younger generation until 1923, when magazines had already been started to celebrate it and it had long ceased
to be news. There were a few feeble splutters and then Clara Bow
in *Flaming Youth*: promptly the Hollywood hacks ran the theme
into its cinematographic grave. Throughout the Jazz Age the movies
got no further than Mrs. Jiggs, keeping up with its most blatant
superficialities. This was no doubt due to the censorship as well as
to innate conditions in the industry.

Fitzgerald continued his love-hate relationship with the movies to
his death in 1940. Hollywood never ceased to disappoint him with its
timidity and banality, and yet he was always attracted to the medium
for its magical properties that he considered largely unfulfilled. Unlike
Hollywood's puritanically leftist critics, who wanted to abolish the
pleasure principle altogether, Fitzgerald preached a voluptuously he-
donistic doctrine, but one more observant and more audacious than
the censors would allow. In this respect, Fitzgerald was mercifully free
of the moralistic cant spouted by so many of his colleagues. He was
therefore taken less seriously than he should have been in the sancti-
monious Hollywood of the Thirties. One wonders what kind of movies
he would have made if he had attained the power of a Mayer or a
Warner. It is very possible that he would have eventually found himself
at the head of a bankrupt studio. It is possible also that he might have
had a shot at filming the Jazz Age in action just about the time sound
came in, and not much later. The only period of film that came close
to recording the Roaring Twenties ran from about 1927 through about
1932 or 1933. For that matter, the Thirties dissolved into World War
II before the darker corners of the Depression had been illuminated.
And the ambiguities and absurdities of World War II did not begin
to surface until the Fifties and Sixties. Hence, to demand instant top-
icality of the cinema is to reduce the medium to a news broadcast.
One would never expect such haste from a supposedly serious and
reflective art-form.

What fascinates me the most in Fitzgerald's observation is its sub-
stantiation of my own inability to find much trace on the screen of

the supposedly optimistic "Roaring Twenties" that came crashing down on Black Tuesday, October 29, 1929, prompting the famous *Variety* headline of Wednesday, October 30: "Wall St. Lays an Egg." In the invaluable The American Film Institute Catalogue for feature films made between 1921 and 1930, there are fifty-some-odd references to "brokers," "stock brokers," and "the stock market" in movies of that decade. Yet, most of the synopses treat the stock market as an always precarious and often dishonest enterprise. People are being "ruined" on the screen all through the Twenties, and some of the adapted literary properties date back to the Crash of 1893. The stereotype of the crooked, mustache-twirling Wall Street stock promoter pops up repeatedly in Westerns and in a variety of honest, country-bumpkin melodramas. Indeed, D. W. Griffith had taken after the avaricious grain speculator in *A Corner in Wheat* as early as 1909. Of course, the melodramatic tendencies of movies attracted them to financial disasters as well as to every other kind, but there were also in American movies strong anti-urban and anti-speculative tendencies. Furthermore, Hollywood has always been comparatively vague and squeamish about the subject of money in the context of the "spiritual" values propounded on the screen.

Were the Thirties, then, such an abrupt break from the Twenties as we have imagined? If we are to think of the Twenties as a giddy, carefree decade, we have to banish from our minds the infamous red-hunting Palmer Raids, which, in retrospect, made Joe McCarthy look like a parlor pink, or the convulsive Sacco-Vanzetti affair, which caused riots around the world. The enormous power of Protestant temperance groups and the Ku Klux Klan in this era somehow comes into conflict with the overly facile image of the flapper in the speakeasy as all-pervasive. Around the world, chaos and instability were the rule rather than the exception. Inflation demoralized Weimar Germany, and massive unemployment hobbled Britain years before Black Tuesday. (Even a 1982 valentine to the snobbery and sportsmanship of the Twenties, namely the Oscar-winning *Chariots of Fire*, shows restless crowds of the troubled and unemployed in Britain.) Also, from the middle Twenties the filmmakers picked up from the poets and novelists the laments for all the slaughtered victims of a pointless world war.

It might be noted that even so perceptive an observer as Fitzgerald failed to detect the New Woman on the Hollywood screen because he was following the sociologist's habit of looking only at American actresses and contemporary "Americana" in Hollywood movies. One had to look for the New Woman not in Clara Bow or Joan Crawford, but in Greta Garbo, Pola Negri, Marlene Dietrich, and the Louise Brooks of such G. W. Pabst classics as *The Lost One* and *Pandora's Box*. The same mistake is made when sociologists confront the films of the Thirties. It would never occur to them that Ernst Lubitsch's *Trouble in Paradise* (1932) (with a very pointedly egalitarian screenplay by Samson Raphaelson) had as much to say about the Depression as did King Vidor's *Our Daily Bread* (1933). Similarly, William Dieterle's *The Life of Emile Zola* is as much a rebuke to Hitler as it is a belated defense of Dreyfus.

If the Twenties were not simply a succession of F. Scott Fitzgerald's wild parties, the Thirties were not simply an album of Walker Evans's "poor folks" photographs. There were plenty of poor folks in the Twenties, and plenty of wild parties in the Thirties. There were few Hollywood films in the Thirties as grim and pessimistic as Erich von Stroheim's *Greed* and King Vidor's *The Crowd* from the Twenties. Actually, many of the changes between decades for movies had more to do with the coming of sound and the tightening of censorship than with worldwide economic convulsions. Because the motion picture industry weathered the Depression better than most other industries, a mixture of pride and guilt contributed to a lack of rhetorical urgency on the screen.

Most Hollywood movies were oriented toward a middle-class vision of life even in the Thirties. The occasional bread line here, and the occasional chain gang there, were isolated occurrences in semireligious light shows built around the rituals of family and courtship. But were the Walker Evans photographs any more "real" or "typical"? The issues of ideological Expressionism aside, the fact remains that though twenty-four percent of the work force was unemployed in the depths of the Depression, seventy-six percent was employed, and that a considerable portion of that seventy-six percent derived a certain satisfaction from the plight of the twenty-four percent. I write this from my own observations as a child of the dispossessed twenty-four percent. I would not argue that the middle-class smugness and self-satisfaction one finds too often in Hollywood movies of the Thirties is admirable, but I *would* argue also that it is not necessarily a misrepresentation of the popular mood. It is for this reason that I find Hollywood movies, for all their flaws and puerilities, more truthful than the nobly angled portraits of the poor in collective poses reeking of the sanctimoniousness of "charity" drives. What I find more interesting in newsreel footage are the accidental revelations around the periphery of the ideologically imposed imagery. Willard Van Dyke's ill-advised diatribe against urban life and in favor of suburban sprawl in *The City* is undercut by the heart-stopping images of New Yorkers surging across Fifth Avenue and 42nd Street on a sunny day in the Thirties. Every face, every article of clothing, conveys a precious message from the sweet, dead past. This is the ultimate thrill generated by the time machine for almost all old movies.

For most of Hollywood's history as a center of movie-making, the studio system has often been blamed for the lack of individual creativity. The very word "studio" lost its traditional connotation of an artist's workplace, and suggested instead an enclosed factory and a ruthless assembly line. Occasionally, a director, a writer, a player, even a producer, might beat the "system," but the system itself was deemed too pernicious and too pervasive to be defied on any large scale. Hence, most movies were not merely inept, but completely mechanical and impersonal: This was the standard line of critics, scholars, and historians.

"When the movie industry was young," the late Hollywood director George Stevens once recalled, "the filmmaker was its core and the man who handled the business details his partner. . . . When the filmmaker finally looked around, he found his partner's name on the door. Thus the filmmaker became the employee, and the man who had the time to attend to the business details became the head of the studio." There is in this archetypical anecdote the evocation of an era, when movie-making was more individual, less industrial. It is now impossible to prove that there was ever an era of artistic enlightenment inasmuch as most silent movies have disintegrated into dust. Nonetheless, D. W. Griffith remains to this day the ghost at all Hollywood banquets, though many of the idiosyncrasies of his personal vision made him eminently unfashionable even with the sternest critics of the corporate structures that eventually stifled his one-man enterprises. The exact date the cinema lost its soul to commerce is difficult to determine. Many film historians have testified to the existence of a Golden Age simply to create a context for the familiar rhetoric of decline and fall. The gold may have turned to brass before 1925 or 1920 or 1915, but certainly by 1929 the studio system had become stabilized to such an extent that critics hostile to the new talkies had a supply of contemptuous catch-phrases close at hand.

There were two particularly deplorable aspects of the studio system as far as its detractors were concerned: one, that it substituted committee approval for individual choice, and two, that the committee in question was capitalistically oriented, both in terms of making profits off screen and of promoting its ideology. Thus, there were two contrasting, if not conflicting, images of the artist against which Hollywood was counterposed. One was that of the romantic, anarchic, alienated outcast in the ivory tower, accountable to no one, least of all the mass audience. The second was that of the responsible, concerned, constructive muse of the masses as those groundlings surged over the barricades to claim equality and justice. There is no need to debate these simplistic propositions at this late stage of revisionist film history. The only point to be made is that the studios were blamed for the faults of Hollywood movies for so long that when the virtues of these same movies were belatedly discovered by the auteurists in the Fifties and Sixties, a strong body of anti-auteurist opinion arose to champion the notion of studio as auteur. There arose a certain tension between the auteurist hypothesis that certain directorial auteurists overcame the limitations of the studio system, and the anti-auteurist hypothesis that the studio system itself was the source of much supposedly individual inspiration. The nature of the evidence—i.e., the movies—shifted also from clues in solving a crime to signs in identifying a creation. It was no longer a question of who was to blame for Hollywood movies but rather, who was to get credit for them.

The principle of studio authorship has certain practical benefits for the opportunistic film historian. The property rights and physical possession of prints vested in the studios gives them powerful leverage with scholars, museums, and cinemathèques. Jean Renoir, for illustrious example, once told me that he did not own outright a single print of any of his films, not even for his personal use. Ergo, the many museum tributes to Zukor at Paramount, Zanuck at 20th Century-Fox, L. B. Mayer and Irving Thalberg (but not Samuel Goldwyn) at Metro-Goldwyn-Mayer, Uncle Carl Laemmle at Universal, Horrible Harry Cohn at Columbia, the worrisome Warner Brothers, David O. Selznick, and even ultra-nouveau Joe Levine. What is one Papal tribute more or less when the Sistine Ceiling is at stake?

Nonetheless, there is something more to the theory of the studio as auteur than there would be, say, to ludicrously marginal inquiries into the influence of publishers on novelists. Studios and their reigning producers, with or without portfolio, seem to have been something more than mere fiduciary agents, though something less than flowering artists. And at certain levels, movies did seem to bear the unmistakable imprint of a studio signature, be it in a neat hand or in a sloppy scrawl. As it happened, I grew up in the Thirties and Forties with a keen awareness of studio identities. By some quirk, I always lived closer to Loew's theaters, which showed Metro, Paramount, Columbia, and Universal releases, than to RKO theaters, which showed RKO, Warners, and Fox features, and I became aware very early in my moviegoing life of an imbalance in my screen diet. Studios *did* make a difference, but even now, with the benefit of much hindsight, the exact contribution of studios to the art of the cinema is difficult to determine. The separation of cause from coincidence must thus remain a very speculative venture. At the very least, however, the Hollywood studios can be said to have functioned for decades as a society within a society for American filmmakers. That these studios were located on the Pacific coast rather than on the culturally more influential Atlantic coast has much to do with the tone, content, and reputation of Hollywood's output. Therefore, an adequately sociological study of the American cinema can hardly ignore the territorial imperatives of the monster-moguls ensconced in Southern California. Theirs was the power, if not necessarily the glory; the initiative, if not necessarily the inspiration; the bottom line of production, though not necessarily the higher spheres of creation. Fortunately, the studios were never a monolithic bloc of crass commercialism, but rather many raging torrents of conflicting tastes and aspirations. The official religion of the studios upheld collective craftsmanship over personal artistry, as did many of the practical requirements of the motion picture medium. At some point, however, craft lifted itself up into art, and an individual personality here and there found its own inimitable voice in the group-sing of studio filmmaking.

The quantitative challenge to any comprehensive study of the studio system is formidable indeed. Between 1929 and 1949 the major studios were credited with 6,848 features out of a total of 11,886 features released in America in that period. This would average out to be about 342 major studio movies each year out of a total of 594 American releases. The average number of foreign films imported to the United States each year in this period comes to about 150. We tend to assume that the great bulk of these movies, both domestic and imported, are of little serious interest, and our assumptions are probably correct, and yet we cannot be entirely sure that there are not still some archival treasures buried in the studio vaults. It would be simpler for film historians if most of the talkies had suffered the same fate that befell most of the silents. For the most part, however, the talkies have lived to tell their tales firsthand, and the critical sifting has not yet been concluded. It would be, therefore, premature to evaluate the studios on the basis of each year's ten-best, twenty-best, or even fifty-best and one hundred-best lists. Nor can we assume that all the films from so-called major studios qualified as major attractions, or that all the films from minor studios or independent producers were necessarily small-scale either commercially or aesthetically. The numbers and even the credits do not even begin to tell the whole story of the studio mystique.

It must be remembered first of all that most of the motion picture moguls entered the industry as theater owners. Thus, in many instances, exhibition was the tail that wagged the dog of production. The task of a studio was to turn out enough product to satisfy the needs of a theater. This meant not only feature-length films, but cartoons, short subjects, travelogues, and newsreels. Mickey Mouse and the other denizens of Disneyland generally worked under the aegis of RKO, Popeye was at Paramount, Bugs Bunny at Warner, Tom and Jerry at MGM, and, on a lower level, Mighty Mouse at 20th Century-Fox. Yet, now that we know more about the creative backgrounds of the various animators we can see that studio affiliations were marginal factors in the evolution of the style and content of the various cartoon figures. Similarly, the fact that there was a different trademark for each studio's newsreel operation as there was for each studio itself did not produce any discernible distinctions in the ideological treatment of the news. *The March of Time,* however, did project a more aggressive approach to news subjects, an approach associated with the Luce publications. Nonetheless, an infrastructure was set up in each studio to supply all the necessary ingredients for an evening at the movies. A composer here, a set designer there, could go a long way in imposing a particular motif on a studio. It is in the nature of sociological criticism to disregard these motifs as extraneous ornamentation, but it is out of this ornamentation that the stylistic nuances of Hollywood movies begin to emerge.

The growing popularity of double features and animated cartoons in the Thirties caused the decline of the two-reel live-action comedies that survived most conspicuously and most creatively from the silents in the idiosyncratic works of Laurel and Hardy. Conversely, many "feature-length" films in the era of double features were barely an hour long. The whole subject of running time has more to do with the economics of moviemaking than with its aesthetics. The average shot length, or A.S.L. as it is abbreviated in scholarly film journals, is another factor that may be more fiscal than formal. As much as André Bazin has written about the evolution of the long take and deep focus as a sign of stylistic maturity, the fact remains that the cheapest westerns tend to park the camera in front of a saloon set and let the leads and a horde of extras cavort within the frame of the lens (and, ultimately, of the screen) without any close-ups, change of angle, or crosscutting. Thus, the average shot length of a poverty row production may compare favorably in duration with that of a well-rehearsed William Wyler superproduction like *The Best Years of Our Lives* (1946). Consequently, there is no statistical shortcut to the critical task of sifting through thousands of studio productions for the comparatively few films that transcend the studio-imposed limits of custom and commerce.

Nonetheless, the mythology of the omnipresent, if not omnipotent, mogul persists to this day, largely because the moguls themselves cooperated so avidly in even the ego-bashing publicity that proclaimed their power. In an era when assimilation was considered the better part of valor, the moguls made little effort to conceal their humble immigrant origins and lack of education. Their virtual illiteracy only added spice to their success stories, and their ostentatious Jewishness only confirmed the legend of their shrewdness. Of course, the myth of the mogul was fabricated long before the Holocaust added a frisson of horror to even the most casual caricature of allegedly Jewish acquisitiveness and *nouveaux-riches* affections. Nonetheless, a post-Holocaust reader may be somewhat startled to discover in the published Description of Characters for Moss Hart and George S. Kaufman's *Once in a Lifetime*, a famous 1930 satire of Hollywood in the midst of the talkie trauma, the following entry for Glogauer: "A good-natured, nervous, energetic little Jewish picture magnate. Aged 50."

The fact that Hart and Kaufman and many of their cohorts in the Algonquin Circle were Jewish also does not eliminate a tinge of facile anti-Semitism in the pose of cultural superiority toward the déclassé dream merchants on the opposite coast. Not that these merchants laid any great claims to intellectual aspirations. For one thing, they did not want to alienate the uneducated, uncultivated multitudes that attended movies. For another, they seemed to enjoy poking fun at themselves. Carl Laemmle, the president of Universal Studios, signed his name to a short foreword preceding the screen version of *Once in a Lifetime* to the effect that people in Hollywood did not mind a good laugh at their own expense. Laemmle himself never denied the story that he had forced Erich von Stroheim to change the title of his epic of mountain-climbing adultery from *The Pinnacle* to *Blind Husbands* because no one would want to pay money to see a movie about a card game. Similarly, Adolph Zukor was widely credited with changing the title of Cecil B. De Mille's adaptation of James Barrie's *The Admirable Crichton* to *Male and Female* because the paying customers might be misled into thinking they were going to see a film about the navy! Samuel Goldwyn, the acknowledged master of Malibu malapropism, employed an army of press agents led by Lynn Farnol to coin classic gaffes of self-contradiction as "Include me out" and "A verbal agreement isn't worth the paper it's written on."

The legend of the culturally moronic mogul became so pervasive in the industry that when a college-educated producer popped up in the front office, his intellectual pretensions were still good for a laugh, as in the caricature of a Walter Wanger–like arriviste in Sam and Bella Spewack's *Boy Meets Girl*, which, like *Once in a Lifetime*, went from stage to screen with most of its anti-Hollywood satiric conceits intact. For a long time this apparent ability to take a joke was not recognized as a defense reaction against deep feelings of insecurity and self-hatred. The contempt for movies within the movie industry itself has never been properly chronicled. It is not surprising that many Hollywood magnates ended up being prouder of the art collections on their walls than of the treasures in their film archives. Yet, their very benign neglect of their bread-and-butter occupation for the sake of the high-art snobberies in New York and Europe enabled many of their dedicated crafts employees to work creatively within the margins of dissent and irreverence.

My Stardust Memories

by William Zinsser

FROM *THE AMERICAN SCHOLAR*

Every time a new Woody Allen movie comes along I can't help thinking back to one of his earlier films, *Stardust Memories.* That's the one that gave me my movie career.

The year was 1980, and I was sitting at my typewriter in New York, plying my writer's trade. When the phone rang I had no great expectations: Freelance writers answering the phone tend to be braced for negative news.

"Bill, honey?" said a young woman's voice. "This is Sandra from Woody Allen's office. Woody wondered if you'd like to be in his new movie."

That was something new in phone calls. I had never done any acting or dreamed any theatrical dreams. But who didn't want to be in a Woody Allen movie? I knew that he often cast ordinary people in small roles. What small plum did he have for me? I hesitated for a decently modest moment and then told Sandra I'd like to do it.

"Good," she said. "Woody will be very pleased." She said that someone else would be calling me with further details.

A half-hour later the phone rang again. "Bill, honey," a voice said, "this is Stephanie from Woody Allen's office." How wonderful, I thought, to be in a line of work where I was called "Bill, honey." Stephanie said she was calling to get my measurements. Measurements! I caught a whiff of greasepaint over the telephone line. She needed my jacket size, my waist size, my trouser length, my inseam, and my collar size, and I gave them to her gladly. I would have told her anything. I wanted to ask what role I was being measured for, but she was gone. I called my wife to tell her I was in show business.

The next day the phone rang again. "Bill, honey," another voice said, "this is Jill from Woody's office." Jill explained that my scene was going to be shot on Friday morning at a film studio in uptown Manhattan. I should get there by nine o'clock and check with the wardrobe people about my costume. Meanwhile I should also report to the movie's casting agent to have my picture taken and to fill out some forms.

The agent's office was on Central Park West, and the next day I went to see her. She explained that she specialized in casting extras, and her walls were lined with photographs of extraneous-looking people. She was a woman who had seen a lot of faces, and as she stood me against a wall and peered into her Polaroid camera. I thought I heard a small sigh.

"Where did Woody find *you?*" she asked.

In the winter of 1963 I got a call from an editor at the *Saturday Evening Post*. The magazine wanted an article about a hot new comic who was playing at a club in Greenwich Village: Everyone said he was going to be the next big talent. Sure, sure, I thought: Great new comics come along every day and are never heard from again. I asked what the comic's name was. His name was Woody Allen. That didn't sound promising either. But I agreed to write the piece, and a few nights later my wife and I turned up at the Village Gate.

It was an enormous barn, depressingly dark and empty; not many people had come out to catch the hot new comic. But suddenly I became came aware that an amazing jazz pianist was at work. Through the gloom I made out a pallid man in dark glasses, curled intently over the keyboard, caressing harmonies out of it that were highly cerebral but also highly emotional. "The comic's not going to be any good," I said to my wife, "but at least I've found a great piano player." It was Bill Evans, who would become the most influential jazz pianist of his generation.

The comic, however, was no less an original artist. A frail and seemingly terrified young man, blinking out at the audience through black-framed glasses, Woody Allen at twenty-seven was already a veteran of writing sketches for Sid Caesar and other giants of television's golden age of comedy. But as a performer of his own material he was still a novice; at his first gigs his manager had had to push him trembling onto the stage.

Allen's monologue consisted of telling the story of his life. It was the life of a chronic loser, told in a rapid salvo of jokes: "As a boy I was ashamed to wear glasses. I memorized the eye chart and then on the test they asked essay questions." "I won two weeks at an interfaith camp, where I was sadistically beaten by boys of all races." The jokes, though simple, were unfailingly funny, and beneath the humor they were doing serious work as autobiography. This was a champion nebbish, one that every underdog in America could—and soon would—identify with. Allen had invented a perfect formula for an anxious new age: therapy made hilarious. A few days later I interviewed him to learn the details of the life I had heard refracted in the jokes—"my father and mother were called to school so often that my friends still recognize them in the street," he told me—and my article was the first long piece to take note of his arrival as America's resident neurotic.

In 1970 I moved to New Haven to teach writing at Yale. During those years Allen not only came of age as a movie writer and director, with *Sleeper, Love and Death, Annie Hall, Interiors,* and *Manhattan.* He emerged in full bloom as an essayist, contributing to *The New Yorker* almost fifty pieces that raised literary humor to new altitudes. He was obviously the true descendant of his hero, S. J. Perelman, and I used his work in my teaching.

I knew from following Woody's career that he had been a pioneer wearer of sneakers in fashion-proud Manhattan. At Yale I had also gone casual and was seldom out of sneakers myself. But I was prepared to kick the habit when I returned to New York in the summer of 1979; I wasn't going to disgrace my native city or myself with rube behavior. What I hadn't known was that during my decade away from New York its sartorial codes would disintegrate. People now appeared to be walking around in little more than their underwear, and when the fall theater season opened I was surprised to see men attending Broadway plays in sweaters. I continued to wear a coat and tie, but sneakers were on my feet more often than my upbringing would have thought proper.

One Saturday in the spring of 1980 I was walking down Madison Avenue. Suddenly my eyes fixed on a pair of sneakers walking toward me, and the wearer of those sneakers seemed to fix on mine. It was as if the sneakers recognized each other. We both stopped, and I saw that it was Woody Allen. We stood for a few minutes and talked about our work and about writers and writing. Then we went our separate ways and I didn't give it any further thought. In Allen's brain, however, one last neuron must have fired, for it was a week later that Sandra called to ask whether I would like to be in Woody's new movie.

Promptly at nine on Friday morning, I showed up at the movie studio and was sent upstairs to a wardrobe room and given my costume. It was the habit of a Catholic priest. I thought of all my Protestant forebears; they would just have to understand that I was doing this for my art. The somber black robe fit me well, its white clerical collar snug around my neck, and I went back down feeling holy enough to administer a sacrament. Woody Allen was standing on the set, which was the interior of a shabby passenger train.

"Do I look spiritual enough for you?" I asked him.

"Those aren't spiritual glasses," he said. The director of the visually impeccable *Interiors* wasn't going to have a Catholic priest caught wearing the horn-rimmed spectacles of an Ivy League WASP. He called for a prop woman, who came with a cardboard box full of glasses.

Picking fastidiously among them, he fished out exactly the pair that would be worn by a blue-collar parish priest in Queens. They were made of chrome, they had wide side pieces, and they were ugly. I put them on and looked at myself in a mirror. There was no sign of the kindly face that normally gazed back at me. The man in the mirror was an unforgiving man of God.

What was being filmed was part of the opening sequence of *Stardust Memories,* which served as a prologue to the movie itself. It took the form of a surrealist fantasy. Two trains are proceeding on parallel tracks. One is full of beautiful people and one is full of ugly people. Woody Allen is trapped on the ugly people's train, and he looks with longing at the people on the other train: handsome Edwardian men in white flannels and boaters with tennis racquets and croquet mallets, laughing women in long white dresses and Gibson Girl hats, twirling parasols.

Frantic to get off the losers' train, Allen begins by pulling on the bell cord. In his hands it's a comic prop fit for Harold Lloyd, and his efforts to stop the train lead only to entanglement. Next he appeals to the conductor, showing him his ticket and pointing to the adjacent train. The conductor studies the ticket impassively and hands it back. Desperate, Allen scans the rows of ugly passengers and sees one last hope of salvation: a Catholic priest. That was my moment.

The sequence took all morning to film. There was the usual quest for perfection: the fussing with lights and angles and sound, the re-shooting of scenes that didn't satisfy Allen or his cinematographer, Gordon Willis. Finally it was time for my scene, and Allen gave me my instructions. I was to show no emotion when he approached me as a supplicant. It was the best possible directing advice for someone who has no idea how to act and would ruin a scene by trying to. I'm a person who doesn't photograph well; if a photographer asks me to smile I contort my cheeks in a weird simulacrum of mirth. But to show *no* emotion is easy; anyone can keep his face blank. It's also the perfect response dramatically—the ultimate nightmare for any petitioner seeking help.

Without boasting, I can say that I gave Allen no glimmer of hope when he came pleading. No matter how many takes were required to solve Gordon Willis's technical problems, some of which were related to a jouncing mechanism under the seat that made the train appear to be moving, my performance was steely in its discipline, and when it was over—all six seconds of it—I turned in my ecclesiastical garb and left. I had the rest of my life to look back on my movie career.

But it wasn't over. Several months later the phone rang and a familiar voice said, "Bill, honey, this is Sandra at Woody Allen's office. We need you for another scene."

Sandra explained that the final destination of the ugly people's train is a city dump, where everyone is discharged to wander over acres of garbage. The scene had been filmed the previous fall at a dump in New Jersey, but the weather was cold and everyone's breath was showing. Allen wanted to shoot it again, this time at the main New York City dump next to Jamaica Bay, near Kennedy airport, the biggest dump in the world. As a new addition to the cast of train passengers, I was needed among the dump walkers. Sandra said the bus would leave from Vesey Street, in lower Manhattan, at 5:30 A.M. the following Tuesday. Could I be there?

"I'll be there," I said. "What about my costume?"

"Not to worry," she said.

On Tuesday morning, earlier than I've reported for any task since basic training in World War II, I found a large bus parked in the predawn darkness of Vesey Street. Most of the ugly people were already on it; extras are so dependent on their occasional day's work, one of them told me, that they take no chance of being late. Their aspiration is to graduate to a "five-liner," the next higher union job, which calls for five lines of dialogue. During our long day together, with its endless waiting around, also reminiscent of the army, I found them to be men and women of deep resignation and good cheer.

Our bus took us across the East River and through the lightening streets to a senior citizens' center in outer Queens, near Far Rockaway, where, in a recreation room, our costumes were neatly hanging on coatracks. Seeing my priest's habit and my chrome glasses waiting for me, I understood that in film production, as in baseball, it's not over till it's over; costumes stay rented for the duration. I changed into my holy attire and several of the extras called me "Father" and asked for a blessing. The sun finally came up.

Back on the bus, we proceeded to the dump, a vast range of hills made entirely of garbage. Sanitation trucks kept arriving with garbage from all over the city and seagulls came screaming down to meet them. It was an ideal landscape for a surrealistic movie; a place at the end of the world, alien and desolate. We were told that Woody Allen had visited the dump the previous day to decide where he wanted to shoot our walk. He chose a spot where the garbage was piled in a configuration that pleased his artistic eye, and that's where our bus now arrived to meet him and the crew. But Allen had forgotten that garbage doesn't hold still. Monday's picturesque formations had been compacted under new truckloads of trash, and the panorama that greeted him on Monday wouldn't do. Shooting would be delayed until he got the garbage rearranged.

The Sanitation Department had evidently been told to cooperate with the filmmakers, for soon we saw trucks with new garbage making their way up the mountain. Galvanized by their approach, Allen turned into Toscanini, conducting each driver to where he wanted the load dumped, until at last a high wall of garbage had risen not far from where we were standing. The air was scented with the refuse and unfinished meals of seven million New Yorkers, and new gulls descended in noisy armadas. Woody was satisfied.

Our assignment as outcasts from the ugly people's train was to trudge aimlessly across the garbage, looking dazed and forlorn. It wasn't hard to feel like a lost soul; we were in a land of lunar strangeness. Underfoot, the terrain was damp and fetid, grabbing at our shoes. Allen placed his camera so that we would be framed against his wall of garbage. It loomed behind us like a mountaineer's cliff, sealing us off.

So began what would stretch into hours of walking on the dump. On one level it was one of the most interesting days I ever spent, wholly outside the normal experience of a lifetime. Cinematically, however, it was tedious work. The skies were gray, and the sporadic sun reflected off the garbage unevenly. Allen and Willis wanted to make sure that whatever sequences they shot would match one another in quality of light and density of seagull. They shot us from a distance, straggling across the tundra, and they shot us in close-up when we came near, our faces etched with loathing at our fate. But perfection eluded them, and at midday we were sent off for a break.

When we returned after lunch the unthinkable had happened: Our seagulls were gone. Fleets of sanitation trucks were dumping new loads about one hundred yards away, and our gulls had flown over to get a fresher meal. We needed new gulls so that the afternoon scenes would match the morning scenes. Word went out, trucks arrived with new garbage to top off our old garbage, and the gulls came screaming back. Shooting resumed, and in midafternoon, on a peak in Queens, my movie career really did come to an end.

Stardust Memories opened in September, and a few days before the premiere my phone rang. "Bill, honey," a voice said, "this is Beverly at Woody Allen's office. There's going to be a screening tomorrow night at the Coronet Theater for everyone connected with the picture. You're welcome to come and bring any guests." I called my wife and children, and the next night we all went to the Coronet to see Daddy in the movies.

Around me I recognized quite a few of my fellow uglies from the train and the dump. But they weren't the only freaks in the theater. Uglies were everywhere! It was as if we had all been sprinkled with some mutational dust coming through the lobby. To my relief, the lights went down and the movie began. I was nervous—would my debut be a success?—but soon the worst was over. My face, enormous on the screen, was cold enough to scare even a venial sinner, and when it later reappeared in a close-up at the dump I was proud to see that it was still unleavened by the quality of mercy. I could relax and enjoy the rest of the film.

Actually it was a querulous movie, not all that enjoyable. Allen plays a celebrity comedy writer who yearns to be allowed to make a serious picture and to be taken seriously as an artist. Instead he is hounded by his adoring fans at a film festival in the Catskills and at other public appearances, the resentful prisoner of his fame. Like its prologue, the movie took an owlish view of humanity. All those fans swarming over Allen—the Hieronymus Bosch school of filmmaking—were as ugly as the passengers on the train and at the dump. Now I understand who all the men and women around me in the theater were; the casting agent had done her job well. When the movie ended and the audience spilled out onto the sidewalk, passersby strolling up Third Avenue stopped in wonderment at so much genetic disarray.

After the film was released, I heard from some of my former students at Yale. As master of one of Yale's large residential colleges, I had known many undergraduates. But when I handed them their diplomas they had every right to expect that I would no longer keep popping into their lives as an authority figure. It was their bad luck, however, to be Woody Allen's natural constituency, and as soon as *Stardust Memories* opened, they flocked to see it. When my stern clerical visage jumped out of the giant screen, I was told, startled cries went up from various parts of the theater. It was the sound of Mother Yale's sons and daughters regressing to the womb. They hadn't graduated after all.

I was sorry to have caused them such a traumatizing moment. But as I look back on my movie career I have a larger regret. I never got called "Bill, honey" again.

Oh, Kay! You're OK with Me

by Rex Reed

FROM *THE NEW YORK OBSERVER*

Kay Thompson, one of the most uniquely fascinating women in New York, passed away on July 2. Roy Rogers got more space, but Kay Thompson got more tears. None of the obituaries got it right and *The New York Times* didn't even try. Yes, she was best known as the creator of Eloise, the precocious six-year-old who poured Perrier down the mail chute at the Plaza Hotel in the first of four children's books that have sold more than a million copies, and the blazing star, with Fred Astaire and Audrey Hepburn, of the classic 1957 movie musical *Funny Face*. But she was so much more than that.

Stylish, elegant, supersophisticated and fun to experience, Kay was an accomplished singer, dancer, actress, composer, pianist, arranger, author, satirist, and businesswoman who was ahead of her time for nine decades—awesomely professional and never dull. She would have been ninety-six on November 9, but she was younger than anyone I know. She was hooked on life. There will never be anyone else like her. She invented the word "bazazz" and she had plenty of it. She gave me the last formal interview she ever granted, and we were friends and fellow mischief-makers for twenty-six years. I first met her on a windy autumn day in 1972 when I interviewed her for *Harper's Bazaar*. "Bobbledy Boo Bop do Boo Bop do Bobbledy Bop!" she scatted, popping her fingers as she time-stepped her way to a corner table in the Oak Room of the stuffy old Plaza Hotel like a magic ray from a voodoo moon. She wore chamois pants by Halston with a black-ribbed Italian scoop-neck sweater, a black belt with a big silver Pilgrim buckle, no makeup, and sunglasses on her head as she folded her frame (five feet five inches that seemed more like seven feet) into a leather chair like crushed chiffon. She looked like a cross between Georgia O'Keeffe and a syncopated condor and spoke with talons for teeth.

"This isn't going to be one of those 'And then I wrote' pieces, is it? I don't like looking back. Let's keep it crisp as lettuce." She liked the result and sent me a dozen peonies in an old ice bucket with a note: "Bobbledy Boo Bop do Boo Bop do Bobbledy Bop . . . It's Great— Love, Kay." She never spoke to the press again.

Kay didn't give a fig about the past, but to explain why she was in a class by herself, a bit of background is necessary. The facts are not important because, like Diana Vreeland, she made them up as she went along. We do know she started playing jazz piano at the age of four and at the age of fifteen performed Franz Liszt's "Hungarian Fantasy" with the St. Louis Symphony, tripping over a potted palm on her way off the stage. At seventeen, she moved to California, changed her name from Kitty Fink, got a severe nose job, and invented Kay Thompson.

"KAY, I THINK YOU'VE GOT AN ACT"

She sang with Bing Crosby and the Mills Brothers, got fired from every job on radio, and ended up in a pre-Broadway tour of *Hooray for What*, a political revue with songs by Harold Arlen and Yip Harburg, choreography by Agnes De Mille, and direction by Vincente Minnelli. She sang a wistful song called "Poor Whippoorwill" and got sacked in Philadelphia. Years later, Harburg told me she was rotten. All I know is the humiliation hounded her throughout her life. She never trusted anyone again and never returned to the stage. Instead, she made one screen appearance in a 1937 Republic potboiler called *Manhattan Merry-Go-Round,* which, to quote Kay's favorite one-line review, "chased its own tail on a one-way ride to oblivion." She didn't appear on the screen again for twenty years.

In the mid-Forties, as a vocal coach in the Rolls-Royce Arthur Freed Unit at MGM, she changed the sound of movie musicals. Frank Sinatra credited her with teaching him everything he knew about singing. She put the sob in Judy Garland's voice. She made Lena Horne growl. In legendary musicals like *Ziegfeld Follies, Good News,* and *The Harvey Girls,* she revolutionized the whole concept of group singing, incorporating bebop and jazz. Listen to the harmonies in "The Trolley Song" in *Meet Me in St. Louis.* Pure Kay Thompson magic. Everything she did was original. She influenced vocal groups like the Hi-Los. Nelson Riddle copied her harmonics in his orchestrations for Sinatra and Peggy Lee. In Judy Garland's historic "Madame Crematon" number in *Ziegfeld Follies,* she introduced the first rap song, forty years before Harlem did.

After work, she compiled special material for parties that everybody at MGM still remembers with awe. One night at a birthday party for her colleague Roger Edens, she created a breakneck tempo extravaganza called "Jubilee Time," performed by Garland, Cyd Charisse, Peter Lawford, and songwriter Ralph Blane, all dressed in costumes from *Show Boat,* and choreographer Robert Alton said, "Kay, I think you've got an act." "What's an act?" The world soon found out.

"After MGM, I had a headache for two years," she said. "So I dragged in Andy Williams and his three brothers and we went on the road." Walter Winchell called it the greatest nightclub act in history. On opening night at Le Directoire in New York, Constance Talmadge and William Randolph Hearst turned to Maurice Chevalier and asked him what he thought. "I don't know," he said, stunned. "I've never seen anything like it." She rode the crest of success in posh watering holes like the Café de Paris in London and the Persian Room in New York. Then she got bored and another phase of her polka-dot career began.

"I'M GOING TO WIPE THE FLOOR WITH THAT MAN."

In 1955, the first of four Eloise books was born after fashion editor D. D. Ryan introduced her to illustrator Hilary Knight. The books were a sensation. The rumor that the precocious moppet left alone in the Plaza Hotel to fend for herself ("And charge it, please") was based on Kay's goddaughter, Liza Minnelli, is pure caca. Eloise was Kay herself, with an uncanny way of tapping into the kid in every grown-up.

As Eloise's adventures spread to Paris, Moscow, and Christmastime, Kay, restless again, abandoned the books and teamed up with her old friends at the Freed Unit, who moved to Paramount for one final fling at Hollywood's golden age. *Funny Face,* now a milestone in musicals, had problems. Kay hated Fred Astaire. She also hated Edith Head's clothes. Audrey Hepburn was wearing Givenchy. Kay wanted something equally special, so she persuaded Roger Edens to call the egomaniacal, implacable Edith Head while she listened on the extension phone.

"Kay is playing a fashion editor based on Diana Vreeland," he said, "so we need a wardrobe that is Coco Chanel." Dead silence, followed by "Roger, go fuck yourself." Kay said, "Don't worry, I'll do my own clothes," and she did. When it came time for the "Clap Yo Hands" number with Astair, she told Audrey, "I'm going to wipe the floor with that man," and she did. In the film she made history with the flamboyant production number "Think Pink," which was based on her own personal fashionoid philosophy.

When anyone asks what made Kay so special, Liza Minnelli says, "Once upon a time there was this amazing woman who could do anything, and once you saw her do it, it was too late to analyze what it was she did because she had already changed your life forever." Her musical genius can be heard in the early Garland musicals, but rent *Funny Face* and you can see it.

"Bobbledy Boo Bop do Boo Bop do Bobbledy Bop!" Shunning her triumph on the screen at last, she fled to a palazzo in Rome where she constructed a fake fireplace out of cardboard pinned together with zebra sheets from Porthault and lacquered her coffee tables with a case of nail polish. A cache of unfinished manuscripts, when last seen, was stored in a latrine in the garden. Back in New York, she established squatter's rights at the Plaza Hotel and stayed for seven years without a bill. When the new management under Donald Trump kicked her out, the Eloise painting and Eloise postcards went, too. Now they're back—a living testimonial for kids of all ages, to Kay more than to her six-year-old alter ego. The day Judy Garland died, she took charge of Liza Minnelli's life and apartment at 300 East 57th Street, where she sawed off the legs of the grand piano and covered it in red vinyl. Eccentric to the end, she spent the past ten years in Liza's penthouse on East 69th Street in a wheelchair, but her individuality and spirit were undiminished.

One Christmas, when we were both stranded in the city, we decided to dine together at my apartment. She never showed up, but sent over the entire dinner instead. At five minutes to midnight, she phoned to announce, with a sigh of relief, "Well, we got through that one, didn't we?"

Kay on style was like Brooke Astor on manners. She staged Halston's first fasion show in Europe in the Hall of Mirrors at Versailles and taught Prince Albert of Monaco how to "sell" a song for a charity benefit. He told her he envisioned himself a singing bartender in a Third Avenue saloon and auditioned the tune. She listened and said, "I see. Remember the Hotel de Paris in Monte Carlo? That balcony overlooking the curve during the Grand Prix? You're wearing a white tuxedo and a scarf. A silver jag pulls up and out comes the most beautiful woman you have ever seen in a multicolored chiffon gown with a gardenia in her hair." Prince Alert said he could see it perfectly. "Now sing it again."

Her favorite costume was a prison uniform with four yards of red scarf wrapped around her neck. Sometimes she stopped traffic on Fifth Avenue wearing bones and turkey feathers. She rarely went out, but worked out at home with two one-pound dumbbells colored "hot titty pink." Looking more like Louise Nevelson in her declining days, her beauty regimen was restricted to a pale light powder from Kenneth, Chinese lily pink lipstick and Ivory soap. Nutritionally, she fought the "monotony that has no place in a creative mind" with many sugar-free nibbles throughout the day—in the A.M., an egg and a slice of orange, then two hours later, two ounces of Gorgonzola and some cold roast beef with a chunk of grapefruit—"nothing much after nine P.M. Maybe a peach before bed. Nothing heavy before sleep unless you want to dream about dock strikes." In the end, she was living on nothing but Coca-Cola, but there was still a trumpet in her heart. She would forget the oddest things, like the name of Louis B. Mayer's secretary at MGM, but she never lost her humor. Singer Jim Caruso remembers her leaving a message on his answering machine. After the part about how to leave a fax, her basso profundo responds impatiently: "You can likely be faxed, but can you be fixed?" The last thing she said to Liza was "Take care of Eloise." The last thing she said to Mr. Caruso before she died was "See you in the movies."

She left behind a future fortune in Eloise royalties, a cult of movie fans who still sing "Think Pink" aloud during reruns of *Funny Face,* forty pairs of shoes, and a treasure of unpublished work including *Darling Baby Boy,* about her lavishly overindulged pet pug, whom we all suspect she killed by feeding him a diet of lime Chuckles, chocolate-covered cherries, and braised livers in Marsala wine sauce. You couldn't tell her, though. She would throw her hands in the air, shout "The drapes are on fire!" and leave the room.

"The best thing my mother ever gave me was Kay," says a broken-hearted Liza Minnelli. "I thought she'd be around forever." Bobbledy Boo Bop do Boo Bop do Bobbledy Bop! She was, but it wasn't long enough.

The Devil Beats His Wife

*Small Moments and Big Statements in the Films
of Charles Burnett*

by Cliff Thompson

FROM *CINEASTE*

Maybe it's just part of being a successful artist: You're proud of the work that made your reputation, but, being an artist, you want to put it behind you and move on to something new. Trouble is, your fans don't want to let you. If you're Sting, they sit in the back of the concert hall year after year and holler, "Roxanne!" If you're Woody Allen, they buy tickets for each new film hoping it will be a remake of *Annie Hall*.

As frustrating as that kind of response must be for an artist, it could be forgiven in the case of the filmmaker Charles Burnett, whose early movies *Killer of Sheep* (1973) and *My Brother's Wedding* (1983), share a subtlety largely missing in much of his more recent work. *Sheep* and *Wedding* managed the not inconsiderable feat of showing black families and communities with their uniqueness intact, and yet not allowing that uniqueness to devolve into the kind of stereotype that overshadows character. The people in those films and in Burnett's masterpiece, *To Sleep with Anger* (1990), come across as black and human, not necessarily in that order. (This is all the more amazing in the case of the first two films—and is a testament to Burnett's skill as a director—since the budgets for *Sheep* and *Wedding* did not even allow for professional actors.)

In *Killer of Sheep*, set in an impoverished neighborhood in South-Central Los Angeles, the main character is Stan, played by Henry Gayle Saunders. In the daytime Stan works in a slaughterhouse, surrounded by sheep, poor creatures neither responsible for nor aware of the hideousness of their surroundings; nights and weekends, he hangs out with their human counterparts, friends and acquaintances too busy struggling to reflect on why they must struggle so. But Stan reflects; at least he has plenty of time to, since his frustration with the monotony and dreariness of his life has—in addition to making him emotionally distant from his wife and two children—turned him into an insomniac. (The film's joke is that in the daytime Stan kills sheep, and at night he counts them.)

Killer of Sheep is virtually plotless, which bothered some reviewers upon its release but which actually goes along with the sleeping/waking theme. Stan's true problem is not that he can't get to sleep but that he seems to be in one long, tiresome dream from which he can't rouse himself; episodes in the film, as in a dream, don't conclude so much as blend into different episodes. In some Stan is a participant, in some an observer, in some not present at all. What ties them all together is the meanness of the characters' lives, whether they are in the middle of a domestic dispute, on their way to put money on a horse, or in the process of cooking up a shady deal.

It is a blessing, given the period in which this film was made, that the idea for it did not enter the mind of a blaxploitation-film director (one of the creators of *Hell Up in Harlem*, *Across 110th Street*, and all the rest). If it had, Stan would surely get together with a couple of equally disgruntled buddies, buy some Saturday Night Specials, and take what was rightfully his from The Man. As it is, Stan has his temptations. A couple of thugs want him to go in on a job; a female liquor-store owner, not particularly attractive but certainly available, comes on to him. What makes Stan interesting and admirable is that, in an environment where decency is barely noticed, let alone rewarded, he passes up these little diversions.

And what saves *Killer of Sheep* from being a condescending, bleeding-heart little message of a movie ("Look at how these poor black people have to live! Isn't it AWFUL?") is Stan's persistence, for all his moodiness, in finding small, simple things to appreciate. Sometimes even this backfires. Having coffee with a friend, he holds his mug to his cheek and says, "This remind you of anything?" After putting the mug to his own face, the friend says, "Nothing." Stan then explains, in a wistful tone, that the heat on his cheek makes him think of the hot forehead of a woman with whom he is making love. "I don't go for women with malaria," the friend says, then proceeds to laugh derisively.

Sometimes, though, the little pleasures come through. When Stan's young daughter looks out the door of their house at a sudden downpour and asks, "What makes it rain, Daddy?" Stan answers, "The Devil's beating his wife." They both smile at this black Southernism, a saying used when the sun shines during a rainstorm—a lovely event in the midst of dreariness, one that should be savored while it lasts. It is a moment that perfectly captures the spirit of *Killer of Sheep*, a small, quiet gem of a movie.

My Brother's Wedding focuses on Pierce (Everett Silas), a thirty-something man who lives with his parents and works in their dry cleaning store while he tries to "find" himself. His parents (like Burnett's) have Southern origins and values, which include a strong work ethic. Pierce is both scornful and a little jealous of his brother and sister-in-law for their career success. *My Brother's Wedding* deftly explores the irony of the generation gap as it applies to black people: while Southernness (whether in cuisine, speech, or attitude) has traditionally been associated with blackness, the work ethic that goes with it is seen as Uncle Tom–ism by many younger blacks, who scoff at their peers' attempts to make it in the "white" world—and who assume that any black who does succeed has sold out. If, as the saying goes, there is a crime behind every great fortune, then in the view of black people like Pierce, there is a lack of integrity behind every successful African-American. Like *Killer of Sheep*, *Wedding* is subtly evocative of a particular aspect of black life, and it has something *Sheep* doesn't have—an immediate conflict. When Pierce's best friend is released from prison, Pierce is forced to choose, finally, between his upright family and his friend's criminal ways.

While *Wedding* has a more identifiable conflict and a firmer grounding in black Southern culture than *Sheep*, with *To Sleep with Anger* Burnett again outdid himself on both fronts, while making progress on a third—the enlistment of professional actors. *To Sleep with Anger* is the story of Suzie (Mary Alice) and Gideon (Paul Butler), a middle-class couple getting on in years. They have raised their grown sons (Carl Lumbly and Richard Brooks) in California, but they themselves are unaltered products of the South where they grew up. So deeply ingrained are their old traditions that Gideon confides to Suzie early in the film that he has misplaced his Toby, or personal good-luck piece. Coincidentally—or maybe not—the disappearance of the Toby is followed shortly by the appearance of Harry (Danny Glover), an acquaintance from Suzie and Gideon's youth, who has come for a visit of indefinite length. Here begin the troubles.

To Sleep with Anger is a marvel of characterization and subtlety. Early on, Gideon tells a story to his young grandson, and at its conclusion the boy asks for another. "You tell me a story," Gideon responds. The boy starts out, "Once upon a time . . ." and is cut short by the sound of the doorbell and Harry's arrival. Touches like this can slip easily past the viewer, who understands them only in retrospect; the same relationship exists between Harry's actions and Suzie, Gideon, and their family. Danny Glover's Harry is a human version of Southern Comfort—he's smooth and sweet, he puts you in a good mood, and Lord help you once the mood has passed. His manipulations come close to tearing the family apart.

So smooth is Harry—and so understated is this film—that the viewer who misses some key bits of dialogue may miss altogether Harry's purpose. But at one point, when Harry waxes personal to Suzie and then cannot resist pulling out a snapshot of his dead sons, he tips his hand: He has come to take away one of Suzie's sons to replace his own. As it happens, one of them is ripe for the taking. The younger son, played by Richard Brooks, is a study in discontent. On the one hand, he bristles at the responsibilities that come with marriage and fatherhood; on the other, he resents the family in which he, as a grown man still called Babe Brother and even "boy," is not always treated as an adult. Babe Brother's every gesture is tinged with unhappiness, none more so than his smile, which serves only to put the grim cast of the rest of his features in relief. Babe Brother's unhappiness and Harry's exploitation of it are the building blocks for a fascinating, tension-filled story.

Adding nuance is Burnett's visual style. This does not seem at first to be the case: With the exception of one sequence, for which the filmmaker is indebted to *The Godfather* (shots of a baptism are intercut with shots of Harry entering devious mode), *To Sleep with Anger* is typical Burnett, in that the shots are very straightforward. But they are, in fact, emphatically so, as if to underscore the difference between what you see and what you get: While the camera looks straight at Harry, Harry is anything but straight, answering with a riddle every question put to him. Here, visually speaking, Burnett goes the simplicity of, say, *Killer of Sheep* one better. The camera looks foursquare at everything and everyone, as if setting up still photographs. For that matter, the camera, when not focusing on actual family photos, puts every character in a frame of a different sort—be it a doorway, a car window, the window of a house, the branches of a tree, or a shock of white hair. Everyone is made to look ready to be photographed, prepared for public viewing. Tension is thus created between appearance and reality. Visually as well as thematically, *To Sleep with Anger* is a powerful piece of filmmaking.

Unfortunately, it was also a box-office disappointment. If Burnett felt frustrated by that, then perhaps—understandably—he set out to snare with his next film a wider audience than his critically acclaimed but ill-attended earlier movies had drawn. Or maybe he had another aim. "There's something unique about different peoples and what they've experienced," Burnett told *The Christian Science Monitor* in

1990. "The thing is to not reduce it, not trivialize it, but show what it is, and show its universality." To be sure, Burnett's first three films had achieved this goal as far as black people were concerned. He had shown, for those who didn't already know it, that black people do indeed have something unique—a culture, in other words. He had shown many blacks' rootedness in Southern ways, and laced his films with jazz and blues tunes. Particularly in the case of *Killer of Sheep*, he had shed light on the tendency of blacks, as an oppressed people, to snatch joy from desperate situations—to improvise, a skill at the heart of jazz and blues, the music created by blacks. But maybe, after *To Sleep with Anger*, Burnett felt that this approach had run its course—that he had taken subtlety and understatement as far as he could, that it was time to make statements about black people, and race in general, in bolder terms.

Either reason, or both together, could logically have been behind Burnett's 1995 film, *The Glass Shield*. This is a story about the Los Angeles County Sheriff's office. But it is also a Charles Burnett film, and so the standard equipment of Hollywood cop movies—gore, steamy sex, high-speed chases, and more gore—are refreshingly absent. What takes their place is a statement about institutionalized corruption and racism and the need to maintain one's integrity in the face of them. It is a statement that, while not novel, is well worth making, as it never hurts to be reminded of these things. As for making the statement in the form of a movie, that is not necessarily a bad thing, either. Drama and political message can dance well together, provided drama leads. Here, it struggles in vain to keep up.

Shield's central character is J. J. Johnson (Michael Boatman), a wet-behind-the-ears graduate of the Sheriff's Academy and the first black deputy to join the sheriff's office. When he pulls into the parking lot on the morning of his first day, not yet wearing his uniform, another deputy tells him that the space he's pulled into is for employees only. Flashing his badge and a smile, J. J. says, "I am an employee." The look on the white deputy's face is one of alarm. The viewer sees this, but J. J. doesn't—he has already rounded the corner and is off to begin his career of defending the citizenry. And so it goes: While the bright-eyed J. J. dreams of one day having the precinct named after him, signs of prejudice and worse proliferate around him. Before long J. J. is sucked into it. A racist white deputy stops a driver simply because he is black and behind the wheel of a nice car; J. J., as the deputy's backup, finds a gun in the driver's glove compartment; the gun is soon linked, rather conveniently, to a recent killing.

Later, as the driver faces a murder charge, J. J. perjures himself by saying that the driver was stopped for a legitimate reason, because of an illegal turn. He tells this lie for what he believes is the greater good, not knowing—as the viewer cannot help but know—that the black driver has been victimized from the start. And so it is necessary to wait for J. J. to discover, and the plot to confirm, what the tone of the film has suggested to us all along. We do not follow the story; it follows us. Michael Boatman, currently a gay mayoral aide on the sitcom *Spin City*, is an immensely appealing actor, and it is because of this that J. J. is not merely irritating. (Not to mention unbelievable. A black man in 1990s Los Angeles who joins the police force and is surprised by the racism he encounters?) One reacts to Boatman's J. J. as to a good friend who is clueless on a particular issue. But Boatman's performance is not enough to make *The Glass Shield* compelling.

Burnett managed a bit more dramatic power in *Nightjohn*, released late in 1996. Set in the antebellum South, this is the story of Sarny (Allison Jones), a twelve-year-old slave on the plantation of Clel Waller (Beau Bridges). Chiefly, it concerns Sarny's relationship with John (Carl Lumbly, the older son in *To Sleep with Anger*)—a black man who has escaped slavery but has decided to become a slave again for the sake of teaching to read the other slaves he encounters. As with *The Glass Shield*, the message here—that literacy equals power for black people—is a worthy one, and the fact that the film was released in the middle of the recent Ebonics debate is, to say the least, interesting. But the message is hardly new, and in delivering it Burnett, maybe for the first time, stumbles into cliché: the conflict between the young, headstrong slave who wants freedom for himself and others, and the older one who warns that all this freedom talk will just get somebody killed.

Still, there is some of the old Burnett magic at work here. Clel Waller discovers that someone has forged passes to help two slaves escape; then a Bible, thought to have been merely misplaced, turns up in the slaves' quarters. Waller reasons that whichever slave stole the Bible must be able to read and must therefore have forged the passes. The slave must be whipped as an example, and when Waller finds who he thinks is the guilty party, he gives the disciplinary assignment to his son, a young man not as progressive as he believes himself to be. When the son hesitates with the whip, the accused slave (Lorraine Toussaint) analyzes the reason why: He is torn, she says, between not wanting to displease his father and not wanting to end up like him. Hearing this, Clel Waller tells his son, "She's readin' you pretty good, boy." There, from the mouth of this trader and mutilator of human beings, comes the sharp, Burnett-style observation: that as important as literacy is, intelligence should not be measured solely by the ability to interpret words on paper, that there are many ways of analyzing what is in front of us, many ways of "reading."

It is this kind of quietly powerful insight that is Charles Burnett's real strength—not the brand of halfway-thought-out hollering best left to others (Oliver Stone and Spike Lee come to mind). Or, if it is the bold message that Burnett is now bent on sending, one hopes that he will continue to bolster it with the small, perfect moments that characterize his best work.

Cruel to Be Kind

by Chris Chang

FROM *FILM COMMENT*

Humans who are cruel to humans, as the preeminent pragmatist Richard Rorty points out, are far easier to stomach than, say, New Yorkers who are cruel to New Yorkers. Why? "[Because] our sense of solidarity is strongest when those with whom solidarity is expressed are thought of as 'one of us,' where 'us' means something smaller and more local than the human race. That is why 'because she is a human being' is a weak, unconvincing explanation of a generous action." If we side with Rorty, in what is admittedly a not very Christian position, we are far more likely to identify with local rather than global pain. (Which explains nothing about why we identify more closely with cruelty to animals; but we'll leave that to ASPCA theorists.)

New Yorkers, in the opinion of many, get what they deserve. Director Todd Solondz, currently a Gotham resident, has used New York City as a primary location in only *Fear, Anxiety and Depression* (1989), the first of his three films. His cinematic psyche is clearly directed away from the metropolis toward the pathos of suburbia or the pathology of New Jersey. One of the more outspoken critics at the 1998 Cannes Film Festival press conference for his most recent film, *Happiness,* was a representative from the New Jersey Film Commission. Sidestepping the film's topics—pedophilia, genital mutilation, suicide, etc.—she was apparently most offended by Solondz's decision to situate said events in New Jersey. The Garden State, forever in the shadow of its media-savvy neighbor, has long suffered from negative publicity, the majority of which perhaps stems from extreme population densities living within easy proximity to the toxic horizons of fire-belching industrial sites. (Or is it the hair?) What was once a suburban dreamscape has become synonymous, correctly or not, with a landscape of failure; and there's nothing like failure as breeding ground for cynicism. Is Solondz situating acts of cruelty within New Jersey because he detests it? Or is he using cruelty and New Jersey to achieve grander (global?) cinematic aims?

To understand the gravity of Solondz's third feature requires a recap of the first two. Solondz, I assume, would be the first to admit *Fear* as his least successful film. It goes overboard in a cliché representation of the soul of the "tortured artist" and derives much of its obvious style from the work of another filmmaker. The story begins in the bedroom of Ira Ellis, a supergeek playwright so crippled by nerdiness he can't even close his perpetually sniveling lips. He writes a fan letter to Samuel Beckett expressing his admiration and identification with the dark master's work, and hopes they will someday collaborate. It is, of course, pathetic. To make the obvious echo of patently Woody Allen–style neurosis ring true, Ira is played with an overabundance of self-deprecation by Solondz himself. If one considers the fact that Woody Allen is the *ne plus ultra* parody of the neurotic, you'd have to have a paradoxically highminded conception of self to pull off a parody of Woody Allen. Solondz gives it a go, and basically cancels himself out in the realm of meta-parody. But it's actually humorous to watch. The preliminary wonder of asking "Where did they find this guy?" gives way to the even more bewildering "Where did he find himself?" If anything, you have to give him credit for radically exposing his own image in such a way.

The lesson Ira learns after desperate attempts at relationships with women who are distinctly not right is simple: You can't see how good you have it until it's gone. He already had the perfect girl; his eyes happened to be elsewhere. He comes to the realization too late, of course, and is left to dwell alone in cartoon ineptitude. Artistic perseverance, in this equation, equals solitude. A telling sequence occurs in a subway station early in the film. Ira and the "good" girlfriend, i.e., the one he cannot see, walk down a platform toward the camera. Ira walks forward as her monologue about her childhood molestation fades into the background. A voiceover seizes the soundtrack and commands Ira to suffer for his art. As he hears the internal rally call to aesthetic arms, he looks upward in blind dumbstruck inspiration, and remains oblivious to the two thugs raping his companion in the background. Cut to a scene of friends discussing the sophomoric quality of his latest play, *Despair*.

This is probably the first time you'll see rape used as art direction. It's also the first example of Solondz's willingness to use cruelty as a way of exploring depths—and voids—within the human condition. The sequence is shot in a way that conveys no compassion for the victim and only a mildly humorous contempt for the foregrounded idiot. A horrible crime has been overpowered and trivialized by the comedy of a foolish ego. It's an example of a maliciously contrived scene that creates nervous laughter—a practice that becomes more pronounced as Solondz gets closer to true (local?) human pain.

With *Welcome to the Dollhouse* cruelty is given a much more fertile breeding ground—the pubescent terror-dome of a suburban junior high school. The opening shot quickly introduces the center of the film's world, the incomparably awkward Dawn Weiner. (A name beyond analysis.) She stands in a school cafeteria clutching her lunch tray like a life raft. She needs a place to sit, but the only spot available is directly opposite the sultry-eyed Lolita—clearly the institutional bad seed. Lolita is quick to point out that someone recently barfed in the chair; Dawn, her character firmly established, can commence with her lunch.

Dawn is brought to life by a remarkably overexposed performance by Heather Matarazzo. With Matarazzo, Solondz finds a far better analogue for his own locus of insecurity. She's an actor possessing all the elements of panic embodied in Ira Ellis, with the far superior dramatic quality of not being a completely formed adult. Rather than Freudian speculation of events of formative damage (Ira/Solondz), we get to witness the damage itself (Dawn/Solondz).

An obvious affinity the two characters share, and an element that will become iconic in the opening frames of *Happiness*, is faces contorted in direct relation to their inability to cope with the surrounding environment. Solondz is following a common aesthetic practice. In the classical world the eyes are viewed as windows of the soul. In his updated version the lips, perpetually open and exposing the teeth within, are the windows of angst. There is an ancient subtradition in art history beginning at least as far back as the famed 2nd century B.C. statue of Laocoön—a marble vision of a man and his two sons grimacing in fear of their own impending doom. The statue was much admired and emulated by Michelangelo, whose influence throughout the ages on subsequent artists cannot be underestimated. Whether he is acknowledging the art-historical debt consciously or not, Solondz is obviously aware of the powerful visual possibilities the tactic evokes.

The corridors of a suburban public school allow deeper levels of cruelty for Solondz to explore. It's interesting to consider the balance the director establishes between atrocity and comedy as he progresses from film to film. With *Fear,* comedy effectively preempts most of the serious existential pain of the proceedings. Again, this is why the film is the most forgettable. In *Dollhouse* things are balanced with greater precision. Words to describe characters like "paralysis," "crippled," "damaged," etc., come forth naturally; but in *Dollhouse* an actual physical handicap comes into play. (And it's still a comedy.) Dawn, practicing the standard wrong-guy-at-the-wrong-time romancing scheme, enrages Brandon (Brendan Sexton III) by casually using the word "retarded." As it so happens, Brandon's brother suffers from a related disability. His anger is a vivid counterpoint to Dawn's perpetual befuddlement. He's cold, malicious, spiteful, and has promised Dawn he will rape her. He's the first to bark vicious insults, as well as the first to offer Dawn a bit of solace from her heartless school and uncaring family. At this point in her nascent autonomy, rape is an acceptable option.

The mythology of the metropolis allows for richness, complexity,

186 ★ Chris Chang

and fame. No one ever sang a song about "making it" in East Orange. But that's what ultimately makes Dawn a complex character. The simplicity of suburbia, if there is such a thing, reveals simplicity of emotions far more real, and moving, than the pathetic artistic rigmarole of what, for example, the people in *Fear, Anxiety and Depression* had to deal with. It's not that people live simpler lives in suburbia; it's that when those lives break down, the acuteness of suffering becomes more prominently foregrounded against the seemingly simplified backdrop. New York City tends to (simply) swallow stuff up with its monstrous background noise. In barbecueville, by contrast, everyone can hear you scream. If Dawn can make it there she can make it anywhere (even if she won't ever leave); and given the fact she's permanently embedded in the repeatable temporality of celluloid, she can't. Sorry, Dawn.

Between the 2nd century B.C. and the advent of *Happiness,* cultural history took a brief dip into the exact same traumas of suburban angst and familial pain Solondz is currently wallowing in. The TV sitcom, somewhat akin to the image of suburbia itself, has developed from its initial depictions of make-believe idealism to the heartbreak realities of hardcore nihilism. *Ozzie and Harriet,* by way of *All in the Family,* paved the way for *Married with Children.* Obviously dear to Solondz's heart is a certain nadir of televised deprecation that appeared briefly in the late Seventies. It was called *Mary Hartman, Mary Hartman* and, as far as existential dread as an inherent quality of the suburban landscape goes, it remains the touchstone that all who venerate the suicidal lawnscape must aspire to. Unlike other directors who attempt to pass off paeans to TV sitcoms as art films (for example, Paul Thomas Anderson's much overrated *Boogie Nights*), Solondz embraces the TV prototype up front. Make no mistake about it; he's doing everything in his power to recapture the intense Sartrean nausea Louise Lasser first foisted on an unsuspecting public, and he will go to any means, including casting her in his own film, to achieve it. Some may not remember her face or show, but you'll be hard-pressed not to feel the same sensations reinvoked as she reaches into the medicine chest for her Valium, or complains to the husband who wants to leave her (a painfully stoic Ben Gazzara) that she really wishes he would have told her sooner because now she'll have to get "another fucking facelift!" Gazzara, not so incidentally, delivers one of the most painfully stoic lines in *Happiness*. After a brief and uncomfortable attempt at extramarital sex, his lover, sensing something deeply wrong in his unresponsiveness, tells him not to feel guilty. Gazzara responds, as if he were an alien lifeforce somehow thrust into a completely unfamiliar human form: "I don't." And then the kicker: "I don't feel anything." The pain, if you fall for it, is exquisite.

Happiness begins with the image of faces in the throes of extreme discomfort and impending doom. Joy (the magnificently disheveled Jane Adams) has just informed the man she's dating that things aren't working out; she prefers to end it before they go too far. He asks the standard "Is it someone else?" She replies with a classic Solondzism, "No. It's just you." He pretends to take it like a man but finally breaks down into infantilia: "Until the day you die you will always be shit." Cut to black. Roll opening title. One word: HAPPINESS.

The film is loosely bounded by the triangle of Jane and her two sisters, Trish (Cynthia Stevenson) and Helen (Lara Flynn Boyle). Trish is the seemingly perfect homemaker who will constantly remind anyone within earshot that she "has it all." What she doesn't realize, of course, is that having it all includes a husband (Dylan Baker) who prefers to rape small boys. Helen is a beautiful and talented writer of sensational poems with titles like "Rape at 11," "Rape at 12," etc. Her secret is she hasn't been raped—she pines for the "authenticity" she believes actual rape will bring to her life and work. (*Happiness* was originally scheduled for release by October Films, but because of cold-footed discussions with the parent company, Seagram by way of Universal, the decision was made for distribution to be handled by the film's production team, Good Machine.) Lasser and Gazzara play Mom and Dad to the three daughters; and the uniformly excellent cast is rounded out by the presence of Philip Seymour Hoffman as Allen, a telephone sex stalker, and Jared Harris as Vlad, a sexual predator/con artist from Russia. Which is not to mention Marla Maples! She pulls off a coup of a cameo as a real estate broker who, in an attempt to alleviate some of Lasser's suffering, delivers the line, "Divorce was the best thing that ever happened to me." Go, girl.

The singular focus of *Dollhouse* gives way in *Happiness* to a much broader and far darker canvas. *Dollhouse,* in terms of actual sex crime, is all talk and almost no action. (Dawn's little sister is kidnapped and briefly held captive in a basement chamber by a neighbor, but the only transgression is photographs taken in her signature pink tutu.) Solondz, realizing the power and efficacy of using taboo to chastise audiences, has gone out on a pretty thin limb for *Happiness.* Not only is one of the main characters a pedophile, he's played in a sympathetic light by Dylan Baker. Is it shocking? You could travel backward in time about seven decades and ask yourself the same question about Peter Lorre's character in *M:* the perfect prototype of a monster you can sympathize with. But with all due respect, Fritz Lang's strong point was not comedy. Solondz is trying to get at different pathologies, and they take place not so much on-screen as off. Both times I watched *Happiness* I was not so much shocked by the subject matter as by how and when people reacted to it. At first I snobbishly attributed my disgust to being somehow above the sadistic cretins (colleagues) cackling away at inappropriate moments. But what was actually going on, in retrospect, is Solondz purposefully juggling audience expectations. He's deliberately loading graphic moral terror into his films as manipulative subterfuge. Once he establishes the rhythm of comedy with the various syntax of the genre—and given his actual sense of humor—he can make us behave like trained seals. (With a guilt complex.) Comedy catches us off guard and allows *Happiness* to hit with alternating punches of humor and cruelty. Dazed by the blows, we sometimes can't tell the difference.

The terrors of domestic comfort, patently candy-colored in *Dollhouse,* start to fester in deviant, almost Altmanesque ways with *Happiness.* If there's anything you want to see in the next generation of young American filmmakers, it's ambition and riskiness. Solondz has both, but what perhaps makes *Dollhouse* the more successful film, at least to this viewer, is the almost blanket ambiguity of *Happiness.* Pedophile, rapist, ax murderer, whatever—why can't we all just get along? I'm not okay; you're obviously worse. Fine. Moral standards should always be under scrutiny, and the best way to scrutinize is to test them. Solondz has the right idea, but *Happiness* backs off from some of the truly despondent depths he appears to be looking for. In particular, the scenes between Daddy pedophile and his son Billy (Rufus Read) are clearly meant to be the most unnerving in the film, but on a dramatic level they fall somewhat flat. Why? I believe it's Solondz's insistence on ambiguity. After the horrible crimes of the father have been made public, little Billy asks Dad if he's going to commit them again and, more importantly, whether he would ever attempt anything like it on Billy. Good question. He'll do it again, but he'd rather jerk off before he'd touch his own son. Bad answer? Apparently. Little Billy bursts into tears; and we're never sure if it's because he, who has spent the majority of the film dwelling on his own eleven-year-old sense of sexual inadequacy, feels simply terrible about the terrible events or, even more horrific, feels jealous because his own father won't "play" with him. If you're going to go to dark places you might as well go all the way. (Tell that to the New Jersey Film Commission.)

Ambiguous waffling notwithstanding, *Happiness* is a startling film. Solondz clearly has a vision, and whether it's the kind of perspective you want in your own home is not particularly relevant. We would be foolish to pretend the things he displays do not exist, as we would be foolish to accuse him of either glorifying, belittling, or simply exploiting them. What he's managed to create could be called a healthy attitude toward disease. (Cloaked in the guise of comedy.) People will always manage to be unnecessarily cruel to each other for their own idiosyncratic reasons. But rather than a blanket condemnation, temporary sympathy with atrocity, at least in the movie theater, may be the best way to take a look around and see who we are. As far as local pain and cruelty, the filmgoing audience might be the last constituency we can actually talk about. Either you've seen *Happiness*, and we can discuss it, or not. And although it would be possible to imagine Solondz addressing these questions within an urban environment, suburbia not only made him, it's made for him.

Riskinesque

How Robert Riskin Spoke Through Frank Capra
and Vice Versa

by Joseph McBride

FROM *WRITTEN BY*

F rank Capra once told me, in a fit of pique, that Robert Riskin was "a lousy writer." That astonishing statement was a measure of the depth of the great director's bitterness over having to share the glory for his films with somebody else. The tremendous acclaim Capra received in his later years could not remove that thorn from his side. In a classic example of a dig masquerading as a compliment, Capra wrote that Riskin was "a giant among screenwriters—at least when he worked with me." The director whose credo was "one man, one film" and who titled his autobiography *The Name Above the Title* was obsessed with the issue of credit.

Riskin wrote the screenplays of nine Capra movies, including such classics as *Lady for a Day, It Happened One Night, Mr. Deeds Goes to Town, Lost Horizon,* and *You Can't Take It With You,* as well as providing the source material for four others (two of them remakes). You'd think there would have been plenty of glory to go around in that brilliant working relationship, but Capra always seemed to regard credit as a zero-sum game. Sharing the spotlight with his most prominent writer would have meant to Capra that his own credit was diminished.

The conflicts between Capra and Riskin became a cause célèbre after the director vented some of his feelings about their relationship in *The Name Above the Title* (1971). Riskin, who died in 1955 at the age of fifty-eight after suffering a paralyzing stroke five years earlier, unfortunately wasn't around to take part in the debate with Capra, who had the advantage of living thirty-six years longer, ample time to burnish his own legend. Riskin's consciousness that others tried to usurp credit from writers in Hollywood was always acute—he was a founder of the Screen Writers Guild (predecessor of the Writers Guild of America) and an activist during the Guild's fight for recognition—but he never allowed himself to be consumed with bitterness over his power struggle with Capra.

So friendly and harmonious when they were turning out their greatest work together in the 1930s, Riskin's relationship with Capra began to founder over the director's growing tendency to give interviews claiming virtually all the credit for their films. He and Capra fell out for a time over the High Lama scenes in *Lost Horizon* (1937), which Sidney Buchman rewrote according to Capra's wishes. The final straw for Riskin was Capra's refusal to allow his name in the title of the jointly owned production company they formed to make *Meet John Doe* (1941): Frank Capra Productions. "Riskin brought to Capra a slangy, down-to-earth humor, almost a cracker-barrel philosophy, which worked well with Capra's style," Buchman said. "But Bob was a soloist—neither [fellow screenwriter] Jo Swerling nor he could take the fact that Capra was boss. Bob finally wanted to get out and be a celebrity on his own."

There's a lot to be said for the improbably symbiotic kind of writer-director relationship Riskin and Capra had during the ten most productive years of their lives. Buchman wryly described Riskin as "the exact opposite of Capra: Imagine a very cultivated, nonchalant playboy, and you will have an idea of their rapport." Yet Capra and Riskin made the perfect team by complementing and highlighting each other's unique qualities. "Frank provided the schmaltz and Bob provided the acid," said Riskin's friend and fellow screenwriter Philip

Dunne. "It was an unbeatable combination. What they had together was better than *either* of them had separately."

Riskin's fertile but ultimately troubled collaboration with Capra offers a case study of the writer-director relationship in Hollywood. The venom Capra spewed toward Riskin in later years (and toward writers in general: When asked in an American Film Institute seminar how writers felt about the changes he made in their scripts, Capra replied, "I don't give a damn how the writer feels") was a product of his profound insecurity over the nature of the director's creative role. Capra had turned to directing only after failing in his own early attempts at screenwriting, and despite his championing of the auteur theory, he never could convince himself that a director truly deserved to be considered a creator. "One of the things I've noticed is that certain pictures will live forever, and they're beyond you," he told me late in his life. "I look at 'em and they don't seem to be mine. It's difficult for me to understand." That nagging doubt robbed Capra of much of the pleasure he should have taken in his rich body of work.

An urbane, witty man who always preferred a subtle jibe to a frontal assault, Riskin probably would have been more amused than outraged by Capra's intemperate outbursts. He would have deflected them with deftly pointed remarks, such as this excerpt from an article he wrote at the time of *Meet John Doe*: "A singular experience for a writer is to see his characters come to life on the screen in their true and unmarred form. This, Frank Capra accomplishes for you in his masterful and individual way—and generally, just for good measure, throws in some little tidbit of his own, to heighten and clarify your original conception."

The most famous story about Riskin and Capra probably is apocryphal. The story goes that during the 1930s, Riskin became angered by all the talk about "The Capra Touch." He marched into Capra's office, dropped 120 pages of blank paper on the director's desk, and demanded, "Here! Give *that* 'The Capra Touch'!" According to Dunne, that story was spread by Riskin's producer brother Everett but was denied by Riskin himself. Capra insisted that "Bob was too much of a gentleman to come up with that corny scene."

It nevertheless carries a metaphorical truth, one that every screenwriter will recognize. For as Dunne pointed out, the themes and style that have come to be known as "Capraesque" can just as well be called "Riskinesque."

RISKIN WITHOUT CAPRA

"Poor guy, he's just a series of fractions.
He ought to stop acting like a human being."
Magic Town

There has been no biography of this true giant among screenwriters, although I wrote at length about the Riskin-Capra relationship in my 1992 biography *Frank Capra: The Catastrophe of Sucess* (Simon & Schuster) and Patrick McGilligan edited *Six Screenplays by Robert Riskin* (1997, University of California Press). It's Riskin's curse, but also his claim on cinematic immortality, that he is remembered almost entirely as Capra's writer; all six scripts in the Riskin anthology are for Capra films.

Most of the other films Riskin wrote are less recognized today, partly because he rarely worked for other directors of a stature comparable to Capra's. The unsuccessful romantic comedy *When You're in Love* (1937) was directed by Riskin himself, and he was unhappy with his own rambling, fuzzily conceived screenplay. The shooting script in Riskin's papers at the University of Southern California is covered with many more penciled changes than Capra customarily made in the beautifully crafted scripts for the films they made together.

One sparkling exception to Riskin's general run of bad luck with other directors is *The Whole Town's Talking* (1935), a taut, sardonic gangster comedy starring Edward G. Robinson and Jean Arthur, which Swerling and Riskin wrote from a story by W. R. Burnett. This strange but captivating hybrid of genres was expertly, if somewhat impersonally, directed by John Ford. Arthur's tough-talking, softhearted working girl is notable as the prototype of the character she developed to perfection in the Riskin-Capra film *Mr. Deeds Goes to Town* (1936).

The scripts Riskin wrote for Columbia before the imposition of the Production Code in 1933 treat sexual relationships with an audacity and sophistication that seems downright startling in retrospect. If anything, the American screen has seriously regressed in maturity since 1932, when Riskin wrote (in collaboration) such lively programmers as *Virtue,* a caustic melodrama about a reformed prostitute who tries to keep her new taxi-driver husband from discovering her past, and *Three Wise Girls,* a raucous comedy-drama about working girls combating sexual harassment in New York City. Columbia's 1931 Stanwyck vehicle *Illicit* was based on a play by Edith Fitzgerald and Riskin about a young woman who believes that the regimentation of marriage can only threaten the workability of a committed relationship. There's a refreshing sexual candor in all these scripts, a lack of cant, a compassionate understanding of the way men and women really deal with each other. But the films suffer from run-of-the-mill direction by journeymen who failed to infuse Riskin's screenplays with Capraesque vitality and emotional force.

Some of the feeling of artificiality in these movies also stems from Riskin's as yet incomplete grasp of how to blend social commentary with character observation, a quality that did not fully blossom in his work until he began collaborating with Capra. Although Riskin's early screenplays keenly depict the class conflicts of American society and the ordinary person's constant, grinding struggle to earn a living, the broader implications of these themes are left implicit. Ironically, it was by foregrounding the issues of the Depression in the films he wrote for Capra, anchoring them more firmly in their time and place, that Riskin began crafting timeless works of art. *American Madness* (1932), an original screenplay he wrote before Capra was assigned as director, was their first film to face the country's economic problems straight on, a ripped-from-the headlines story of panicked investors causing a run on a bank. Such Riskin-Capra films as *Lady for a Day, It Happened One Night,* and *Mr. Deeds Goes to Town* are among the most vivid depictions of the tumultuous New Deal era.

William A. Wellman was the director Riskin hired for his own venture into independent production, *Magic Town* (1947), which tried to recapture the magical blend of sentimental comedy and social commentary that characterized Riskin's best work with Capra. But in trying to carve out a postwar career independently of the director, Riskin made a fatal mistake in turning over his satire of a perfectly "normal" small town to such a hardboiled cynic as Wellman. Wellman took all the puff out of the soufflé by directing *Magic Town* as if it were a film noir. Just as the treaclier portions of Capra's 1946 *It's a Wonderful Life* could have benefited from Riskin's asperity, Capra's schmaltzy touch was sorely missing in *Magic Town*.

RHYTHMS OF EVERYDAY LIFE
"I'm never conversational before coffee."

Lost Horizon

The first work of Riskin's to be directed by Capra was *The Miracle Woman* (1931), an adaptation of *Bless You, Sister*, a 1927 play by John Meehan and Riskin about a crooked female evangelist. Although the screenplay by Swerling and Dorothy Howell represents a considerable improvement over the play, *Bless You, Sister* was responsible for introducing several of the major themes Riskin and Capra would continue to explore throughout their collaboration, such as the conflict between fakery and idealism in the hearts of social leaders, their betrayal of the public's trust, and the fickleness of the mob. Barbara Stanwyck was incandescent in the title role of *The Miracle Woman*, which film historian Richard Koszarski calls "one of those wonderful films of the early thirties which attacked all the rotten, sacred things the studios could think of."

"*Dialogue by* ROBERT RISKIN" was his credit on the first screenplay he wrote for Capra, *Platinum Blonde*. The 1931 romantic comedy about a raffish newspaper reporter (Robert Williams) who falls in love with a hoity-toity society dame (Jean Harlow) introduced many of the themes that would be developed in later Riskin-Capra films. Like Gary Cooper's Longfellow Deeds, Williams's Stew Smith becomes known as "The Cinderella Man" because of his abrupt immersion into the world of the wealthy. And like Deeds, Stew revolts against the phoniness of high society, ultimately preferring the simplicity of his former egalitarian existence. "Well, if you'll notice," Riskin said of his work, "the chief character is always full of something he's trying to express; he has just one idea he's trying to get over. In *Mr. Deeds*, for instance, there was a country boy given $20 million that he didn't want, and he was always trying to express his distaste for it."

The ambivalence toward wealth that Riskin, the son of Russian Jewish immigrants, shared with his proletarian characters made him the quintessential American screenwriter during the Great Depression, just as Capra, an Italian immigrant, was the quintessential American director of the 1930s. But while many critics have assumed that Riskin and Capra must have shared common political views, that was far from the case. Riskin was a liberal Democrat, an active supporter of Franklin D. Roosevelt's New Deal, while Capra was a lifelong Republican and fervent opponent of the New Deal. Capra took pride in having risen above his immigrant background; Riskin never lost his affinity with the underprivileged. But both men shared a streetwise knowledge of what life was like for the common man and woman on the front lines of the nation's economic crisis. While the sociopolitical tensions between Riskin and Capra help account for their films' political contradictions, those conflicts also were a source of vital energy and gave the films a lifelike complexity.

Riskin's crisp, unpretentious, slangy dialogue struck an immediate chord with movie audiences, for his style represented a quantum jump in verisimilitude over the hammy dialogue in most of the early talking pictures. Riskin's characters talk with the edgy, nervous, overlapping rhythms of everyday life, stylized almost to the point of poetry.

In an exchange from *Platinum Blonde* between Williams and Loretta Young—the reporter named Gallagher who quietly loves him—they talk about Harlow's title character, but they're really expressing the all-too-human misunderstandings about romantic love that animate so much of Riskin's work:

STEW
Oh Gallagher, you've got to meet her. She's it—

GALLAGHER
—and that—

STEW

(enthusing)
—and those and them.

GALLAGHER

Well, I've seen her pictures, and I don't think she's so hot.

STEW

(disparaging gesture)
Ah, you don't appreciate it. Her pictures don't do her
justice. Why, Gallagher, she's queenly—she is queenly—
and I know queens! And oh, has she got herself a nose—
and I know noses too. That little snozzle of hers is the
berries, I tell you. And is it cute when she throws that
little snozzle to the high heavens.

GALLAGHER

Of course I haven't got a nose.
(She gives Stew a hurt look.)

STEW

Sure, sure. You've got a nose, Gallagher. You've got a
nose. But that's different. Women are different, Gallagher.
You know, like brewery horses and thoroughbreds.

GALLAGHER

(deliberately misunderstanding)
Oh now, Stew, I wouldn't be too hard on her. I wouldn't
call her a brewery horse.

HEADLINES AND BREADLINES
"It seems a good artist is just naturally higgledy-piggledy. Maybe that's
why he's a good artist—or maybe it's reversed."

The Thin Man Goes Home

As *Platinum Blonde* so breezily demonstrates, Riskin was a master
of subtext. His dialogue resembled a dazzling game of pool with the
words intricately careening around the screen to arrive at a subtle
point. What gives such depth to Riskin's banter, lifting it above mere
cleverness, is its oblique expression of feeling. A celebrated example of
this kind of love scene appears in Riskin's Oscar-winning screenplay
for *It Happened One Night* (1934). Clark Gable's brash reporter, Peter
Warne, tries to teach some humility to Claudette Colbert's snooty
heiress, Ellen Andrews, by showing her how to dunk a doughnut in a
cup of coffee. The subtext is their sexual attraction and Peter's frustration over Ellie's distance from his way of life:

PETER
Say, where did you learn to dunk, in finishing school?

ELLIE

(indignantly)
Aw, now, don't you start telling me I shouldn't dunk.

PETER

Of course you shouldn't. You don't know how to do it.
Dunking's an art. Don't let it soak so long. A dip and
plop, into your mouth. If you let it soak so long, it'll get
soft and fall off. It's all a matter of timing. I ought to
write a book about it.

ELLIE

Thanks, professor.

PETER

Just goes to show you. Twenty millions and you don't
know how to dunk.

ELLIE

I'd change places with a plumber's daughter any day.

Underneath the wisecracks, the writer's social attitude, his sympathy for "the little fella" over the stuffed shirts and pompous windbags
of the world, runs as clear as a mountain stream. The role reversal of
a proletarian hero teaching an heiress how to survive life on the run
was hugely appealing to the mass audience. Riskin's writing abounds
in expressions of his deep-seated belief that simplicity always trumps
sophistication, that the decent values of ordinary people will always
put to shame the slickness of big-city hustlers. Though this theme still
retains a visceral impact with movie audiences today, there is a reactionary element to it that helps account for the difficulty both Riskin
and Capra had with post–World War II audiences, who were becoming impatient with such a sentimental view of small-town values.
Those two big-city boys from New York's Lower East Side and the
mean streets of East Los Angeles never lost their yearning for what
Richard Hofstadter defined as "the agrarian myth . . . a kind of homage
that Americans have paid to the fancied innocence of their origins . . .
[which] perhaps relieved some residual feelings of guilt at having de-
serted parental homes and childhood attachments."

During the Depression, with the clash between urban and agrarian
values reaching a flash point, such old-fashioned yearnings carried
tremendous emotional weight. To some extent, Capra's wealth and

Republican allegiances were temporarily neutralized by the power of Riskin's social convictions, which allowed the director to tap back into the emotions of the ragged newsboy he once had been. Nowhere is this social impact seen more forcefully than in *Mr. Deeds,* when a deranged, dispossessed farmer (John Wray) bursts into the mansion of Longfellow Deeds, threatening to shoot him for displaying such a lack of compassion for the underclass:

FARMER

How did you feel feeding doughnuts to a horse? Get a kick out of it, huh? Got a big laugh? Did you ever think of feeding doughnuts to human beings! No!

WALTER (the valet)

Shall I call the police, sir?

LONGFELLOW

No! (to man) What do *you* want?

FARMER

Yeah—that's all that's worrying you. What do I want? A chance to feed a wife and kids! I'm a farmer. A job! That's what I want! ...
(pulls a gun)
You're about to get some more publicity, Mr. Deeds! You're about to get on the front page again! See how you're going to like it this time! See what good your money's going to do when you're six feet underground. You never thought of that, did you? No! All you ever thought of was pinching pennies—you money-grabbing hick! You never gave a thought to all of those starving people standing in the breadlines..

After this outburst, the farmer drops his gun, collapses in a chair, and apologizes to Mr. Deeds: "I'm glad I didn't hurt nobody. Excuse me. Crazy. You get all kinds of crazy ideas." But his disruption of Deeds's comfortable existence is what galvanizes the multimillionaire to start giving away most of his money to buy land for poor farmers, providing a symbolic solution to the Depression, a cinematic metaphor for the New Deal. The farmer's shocking intrusion into the frothy world of romantic comedy was also the decisive turning point for Riskin and Capra, the moment when they started devoting their artistic talents to didactic filmmaking.

Some have identified this development in their careers as the moment that signaled the beginning of their decline, which Alistair Cooke, in his review of *Lost Horizon,* blamed on Capra's growing tendency "to make movies about themes instead of about people." But the farmer's confrontation with Mr. Deeds was the moment when Riskin and Capra began to speak urgently and directly for the common men and women in their audience, earning these films an indelible place in American culture.

CREATIVE SYNERGY

"I saw the same kind of crowds night after night, from here to Texas—maybe a lot of damn fools—but it got me. There are so many of them looking for something."

Bless You, Sister

The preaching in the Riskin-Capra films would not have worked if it had not been sincere, at least on the part of the man who wrote the words, and if the director had not been so susceptible to the writer's inspiration. And these films would not continue to delight and move audiences today if their themes were not presented with a leavening wit, a joyous and humane sense of comedic balance. Riskin brought to all his scripts a sardonic understanding of human foibles and a hopeful sense that even the most venal human being was capable of improvement. Capra brought to his direction what Graham Greene called "a kinship with his audience, a sense of common life, a morality."

Neither man's career ever recovered from the trauma of their breakup, although Riskin's creative decline was even more precipitous than Capra's. He never wrote a truly memorable feature after the ambitious but uneven *Meet John Doe,* which he and Capra produced shortly before both went off to service as U.S. government filmmakers in World War II. Capra, however, made two of his best films apart from his former screenwriter, *Mr. Smith Goes to Washington* (1939, screenplay by Sidney Buchman, story by Lewis R. Foster; contribution to screenplay by Myles Connolly) and *It's a Wonderful Life* (screenplay by Frances Goodrich, Albert Hackett, and Frank Capra, based on "The Greatest Gift," a short story by Philip Van Doren Stern; contribution to screenplay by Michael Wilson and Jo Swerling).

The fact that those classics were written by people other than Riskin was seized upon by Capra and his partisans as final proof that Capra was always the true auteur of his pictures. What such arguments overlook is that both *Mr. Smith* and *Wonderful Life* were heavily indebted to what Capra called his "formula," the story and character patterns established in his earlier work *with Riskin*. And, indeed, many of those "Capraesque" elements originated with the writer, who pointedly observed in a 1937 interview: "So little is known of the contribution that the screenwriter makes to the original story. He puts so much into it, blows up a slim idea into a finished product, and then is dismissed with the ignominious credit line—'dialogue writer.'"

The remarkable creative synergy between Capra and Riskin makes their inability to stay together particularly unfortunate, for the truth is that neither was the sole auteur of their films. They were joint auteurs who could not function at full creative capacity without each other. Perhaps there's a lesson in this for everyone who works in the movies, a truly collaborative art form that reaches its highest peaks only when a writer and a director, rather than wasting their creative energies in antagonism, are able to find common ground and bring out the best in each other's talents.

Leo McCarey and "Family Values"

by Robin Wood

FROM *SEXUAL POLITICS AND NARRATIVE FILM:*
HOLLYWOOD AND BEYOND

"GIVE IT BACK TO THE INDIANS"

R ally *'Round the Flag, Boys!* is one of many films that seems stuck with the reputation it acquired on its first release: It is somehow mysteriously "known" to be a failure, so there can be no reason to reassess or even see it. Even Leland Poague, in one of the very few extended and sympathetic studies of McCarey (in *The Hollywood Professionals*, vol. 7), ignores it, neglecting to include it in his list of McCarey's "family" films (it seems to me, with *Make Way for Tomorrow*, one of the two "key" ones); but this may be because it consorts somewhat awkwardly (to put it mildly) with Poague's extremely conservative reading of McCarey.

The commonest line of attack is to regard the film as "disappointing" as an adaptation of Max Shulman's then very popular novel (does anyone still read it?). To me this verdict is not merely unacceptable but incomprehensible. The novel's satire is at once too "obvious" and too smugly self-congratulatory, and its attitude is thoroughly mean-minded, falling right into that common would-be-satirist's trap of having constantly to alert the reader to the author's superiority to his characters. McCarey's film manages to be simultaneously more radical and more generous, and all the best things in it (including, remarkably, the sequence of the Thanksgiving Day pageant, toward which the entire film moves) are not to be found in the novel.

I think there was another reason for the film's initial failure. It came out, in 1958, right on the cusp of drastic change: Censorship was about to break down, yet the Hays code was still firmly in place, including its rigid stipulation that adultery was not a subject for comedy. Hence a certain awkwardness at certain climactic moments in the treatment of the film's sexual themes. The hilarious sequence of the Paul Newman/Joan Collins mutual seduction had to (but couldn't) end with them having sex, since alcohol has by then removed all restraint. When Newman abruptly and illogically puts on his coat and leaves, the audience (who certainly want them to "go all the way") must have felt a bit cheated; still constrained by the conventions of 1930s and 1940s screwball comedy, the film must have appeared a bit old-fashioned. Today, surely, we can understand and forgive.

But if the film's logic is occasionally thwarted by censorship on one level, on another it evades it triumphantly. One can suggest a partial analogy (I am aware that it can't be pressed very far) between "entertainment" and dreams. According to Freud, dreams express unconscious desires—desires so socially unacceptable that our conscious minds cannot accept that we do indeed wish them. When we fall asleep the censor that stands guard over our unconscious dozes off too, and these shameful wishes, after donning disguises that may make them difficult for the dreamer to recognize, can slip by him (the censor, representing the "Law of the Father," is emphatically male). The notion of "entertainment" (by definition, that which is not to be taken seriously) functions as a kind of sleep, and the "censor" is lulled: "censor" here to be understood on various levels—the external censor (e.g., the Hays Office code), the precensor (in the form of producers, financiers, and studio heads), the internal censor within the filmmaker. It is important to stress this last: Hawks and McCarey, for example, habitually discussed their films on the level of plot, action, characters (the "entertainment" level) rather than on the level of thematic or ideological content, and there is no reason to suspect them of disingenuousness. It is unlikely that in making *Rally 'Round the Flag Boys!* McCarey was aware that he was expressing a wish that America (not merely as a nation, but its social structures, values, and ideology) had never existed, and there seems to have been no one around to explain it to him. He saw himself as making a comedy about "people," and followed his "instinct" for what he found (and hoped audiences would find) funny.

Obviously, comedy occupies (at least potentially) a privileged position within this concept of entertainment: It is a truism that one of the functions of jokes is to say what one means in a way that suggests one doesn't really mean it, and which allows the joker to believe this. Here we have the "Catch-22" of entertainment—one can make the most radically disruptive statements provided one makes them in a form that ensures that no one (including perhaps oneself) takes them seriously.

I want here (as I did with *Ruggles of Red Gap*, though in a somewhat different way) to have *Drums Along the Mohawk* present as a point of reference. *Rally* is to *Drums* the ideal complement and contradiction— one of the greatest Westerns answered by one of the greatest Hollywood comedies. I am following tradition in classifying Drums as a Western (on the grounds of thematic content: settlers versus Indians), but it clearly isn't, in the geographical sense: The Mohawk valley is in New York State, which is also the location of *Rally*'s small town cum garden suburb. It is not far-fetched to suggest that the log cabin of *Drums* becomes inevitably (given the developing social structures— capitalism, private ownership, the nuclear family, monogamy, the division of labor, cultural concepts of "masculinity" and "femininity") the suburban home of *Rally* a century and a half later. Both are emblems of white settling/imperialism, the Putnam's Landing of *Rally* associated explicitly, at the film's opening, with the arrival of the Pilgrim Fathers. Ford's celebration, in 1939, of the founding of America is answered, almost two decades later, by McCarey's wish-fulfillment of its un-founding.

In the interests of clarity, I shall discuss the four major components of *Rally 'Round the Flag Boys!* (the family, sexuality, the Tuesday Weld subplot, the missile base) before considering the climax (the pageant, where all the threads come together) and anticlimax (the "happy ending" obligatory in a comedy, with its perfunctory restoration of an order the film has by then thoroughly discredited).

THE FAMILY

If the film has nothing exactly new to say about the patriarchal nuclear family, it says it with remarkable force, economy, and clarity, and with a refusal of compromise made possible by the adoption of the comic mode. We are given:

The home. Putnam's Landing (where, in anticipation of the film's climax, Samuel Putnam was scalped as soon as he landed) has become the "ideal" garden suburb, seventy minutes from New York by commuter train, each house a neat, immaculate, well-appointed family prison.

The division of labor. If the home is a prison, the wife is its chief prisoner. Ford's convincing celebration of monogamy/family in *Drums Along the Mohawk* depended on the film's being set in a particular, and very early, phase of American history, specifically a phase when the family was self-supporting and (to a degree, backed by a strong sense of community) self-sufficient: husband and wife could work side by side in the fields in nonalienated labor that was directly productive, its fruits directly enjoyed. In *Rally,* Harry Bannerman (Paul Newman) commutes while his wife Grace (Joanne Woodward) manages the house and the children; the husband arrives home in a state of exhaustion and frustration, wanting nothing but alcohol, to confront a preoccupied wife and two alienated children. The gender division of *Drums* (the man works to build civilization for the woman who embodies and perpetuates its finer values) has here reached its culmination; the civilization initiated by the building of the cabin and the subjugation of the Indians has developed to a point where it is characterized by overwhelming and continuous repression and frustration, the couple separated for most of their lives as breadwinner and nurturer respectively, and engaged in uncreative and unfulfilling labor.

Oedipus in the suburbs. The children (both boys), as a direct result of this total division of labor, are consistently in their mother's charge, the father an intruder who drops in every evening just before bedtime. The film anticipates a perception now common in post-Freudian thinking that the Oedipus complex is not some "natural" process every child in every culture must pass through, but a product of our specific social/sexual arrangements. The father's return from alienated labor (in one of its extreme forms—"public relations") is "greeted" by a series of unconscious/"accidental" responses: the two boys (a) completely ignore him in favor of television, (b) spill his drink (the last of the whiskey), (c) defy his authority. Indeed, all the marital/familial relationships in the film (aside from that of Comfort Goodpasture and her resignedly tolerant father) are characterized by tension, ambivalence, and mutual hostility: Harry's comment on his firstborn is "I love him as if he was human." Characteristically, McCarey manages through all this to communicate his affection for human beings (as distinct from the social institutions in which they are trapped) and to suggest, beneath the frustrations, the continuing mutual affection of the couple.

Escape and sublimation. Harry escapes, Grace sublimates. The film is clear that all that makes Harry's life tolerable is the combination of alcohol (the whiskey he is deprived of, first on the train, then in the home) and sexual fantasy (the exotic "movies" he projects on his eyelids simply by closing his eyes). Grace, on the other hand, sublimates her sexual energies into civic "duty," the efficaciousness of which the film thoroughly undercuts: her obsessive committee work (including the "Committee for the Preservation of Unknown Landmarks," a title that beautifully encapsulates the phantasmal nature of the benefits to society).

It will be noticed that so far I have not made the film sound particularly hilarious. This is intentional. On the level of thematic/ideological concerns, the raw material of *Rally* could easily be inflected toward melodrama (*There's Always Tomorrow*) or the horror film (*The Shining*). Suffice it to say here that the comedy of *Rally*'s exposition is built entirely upon the conformity/resistance tension, and that there are moments when the exchanges between the two stars irresistibly evoke Laurel and Hardy. As for auteurship, the key moment of this opening section eloquently repeats the "unmarrying" motif from *Make Way for Tomorrow*. "We had more home life *before* we were married, Grace Oglethorpe."

SEXUALITY

A female friend who wishes not to be named remarked to me once in conversation, "There is nothing so desexualizing as monogamy": a pithy way of putting Freud's perception that the monogamous union on which the nuclear family is based (monogamy, at least for the wife, and in theory for the husband) requires the repression or sublimation of enormous quantities of "excess" sexual energy. In *Drums Along the Mohawk,* the degree of necessary repression is relatively low, and the possibility of successful (i.e., satisfying) sublimation strong: husband and wife live, work, play, and fight the enemy side by side, and are members of a close-knit and highly motivated community that at times (in the childbirth sequence, the Halloween dance, and especially in the person of Mrs. McClennan) takes on the character of an extended family. In *Rally,* all such potentialities have disappeared. It is particularly necessary (for the guarantee of the patriarchal lineage) that the women be desexualized. The unhappy consequence of this is that, if the process is really successful, the wife may no longer feel sexual desires for anyone, including her husband; hence the sexual frustration of Harry, a dutifully monogamous male whose wife prefers committees. The primary motivation of his fantasy movies is clearly the desire to resexualize Grace: she functions in them as an exotic Arabian seductress. The embodiment of unrepressed sexuality in the film is Angela Harper (Joan Collins) (unhappily married—consciously and explicitly so, in contrast to Harry's overinsistent protestations of his "happiness"—childless, and with no interest in committees). Angela's campaign to seduce Harry (who reveals repeatedly, if inadvertently, that he wants to be tempted) provides the main impetus of the film's first half, producing a series of magnificent comic setpieces: the car ride from the station; the scene in Angela's home where she gets him drunk, and a logical progress of depression that links the film directly to the screwball comedies of the 1930s culminates in his swinging from a chandelier; the showdown in the New York hotel. This last—besides providing Newman with an elaborate Oliver Hardy routine involving his trousers—has as its climax the moment when Grace, turning up to surprise her husband, confronts Angela emerging from the bedroom performing an exotic (ambiguously Arabian/Indian) dance in a bedspread. The ambiguity of the dance's ethnicity allows us to connect it both to Grace's seductions in Harry's fantasies and to Angela's Indian dance in the pageant, the erotic (banished from the home) returning as the exotic. As usual with McCarey, all the performances in *Rally* are superb, every scene animated by continual inventions of mine and body language; but one senses that he was particularly drawn to Joan Collins, who realizes here a comic potential that one would hardly have guessed at and that was never repeated. It is striking that the character, against all generic expectations and requirements, is never put down or punished, and is actually permitted to intrude briefly into the final scene of martial reconciliation. (In Shulman's novel, she is meted out the worst punishment imaginable: She ends up married to Captain Hoxie.) As the embodiment (on the level of family/monogamy) of anarchy, she is in some respects the film's true center, a point well understood in France—the French title was *La Brune Brûlante*, inspired no doubt by Angela's pageant persona, Princess Flaming Teepee.

BOYS AND "BOOJUMS": THE NEW GENERATION

The film's other potentially subversive figure is Comfort Goodpasture (Tuesday Weld). The conflicting connotations of her name (erotic/ Puritan) sum up the ambiguity of her role. Insofar as she embodies teenage rebellion (in her spiritedness, her energy, her slangy vocabulary, her readiness to abandon an unwanted but persistent and presumptuous suitor in the middle of a lake), it is a rebellion that can easily be contained. I have not been able to ascertain whether the term "boojum" was in current usage in the 1950s or was invented for the film (perhaps by McCarey himself; the hilarious song, "Seein' as How You're My Boojum," is credited to him). In any case, it is Comfort's readiness to be somebody's "boojum" that defines her; the word, presumably a male construction amalgamating "boobs" and "yum-yum," on the one hand expresses her overt sexuality, on the other her consumability. Tuesday Weld's reactions (really indescribable in words—a marvelous manifestation of the McCareyan use of body language and facial expression) to the song as sung to her by the soldier from the South Opie (Tom Gilson) beautifully capture the combination of energy and subjugation.

It is fitting, then, that in the pageant Comfort is cast as Pocahontas, the betrayer of her race, her saving of Captain John Smith historically emblematic of the triumph of white imperialism.

FROM THE NUCLEAR FAMILY TO
NUCLEAR MISSILES

Although it provides one of the major narrative threads, the explicitly political issue of the film need not detain us long: McCarey's satirical treatment speaks for itself, his anarchic disrespect for the military mentality and the political authority that sustains it (and which it in turn sustains) going back at least to *Duck Soup*. Again one might note the transgeneric nature of basic thematic material: The type of accident that launches the (harmless) missile in *Rally* could, in a "serious" film, launch an atomic warhead. McCarey refuses to endorse any political position dramatized within the film, the confrontation of the military and the women of Putnam's Landing being treated as another comic setpiece in which both sides are absurd. On the one side is the gross stupidity of the military mind as represented by Captain Hoxie (Jack Carson, directed to play the role as a kind of malignant Oliver Hardy); on the other, the women are not protesting against nuclear energy (they don't know at this point that the army is building a missile base) but against the disruptive influence of soldiers on the (repressive) orderliness of the town. They are specifically motivated by concern for the safety of their daughters—who welcome the soldiers as liberators.

THE PAGEANT

It should be clear by this point that the film offers, through its complex juxtapositions, a fairly comprehensive and thoroughly negative portrayal of modern American capitalist society: the patriarchal nuclear family, alienated labor, the repression of sexuality (the root of anarchy), the repressiveness of the modern small town cum suburbia, the monstrous absurdity of military authority and technology-as-power (backed by the "democratic" political machinery). All this is linked from the outset (the opening commentary) to the founding of America, and it is that founding that becomes the subject of the Thanksgiving Day pageant, organized by Grace in the interests of peaceful coexistence. By casting Angela as Princess Flaming Teepee (taking up the time-honored association of subversive women with fire), the film makes explicit the connection between the Indians and sexuality—specifically, sexual threat, the potential disruption of monogamy/family—that haunts *Drums Along the Mohawk* as disturbing subtext. But the outcome of the pageant—planned by Grace, its narrator, to culminate in the smoking of the peace pipe, the establishment of order, hence by implication of modern America—is its collapse into ignominious chaos, a collapse that embodies the film's comedic wish-fulfillment that America had never existed. What was planned as a celebration of harmony becomes a celebration of anarchy, centered on the Indians, hence the culmination and reversal of a whole tradition of history/mythology: The progress of the film is from the unmarrying of the couple to the unmaking of America. Captain John Smith (Opie) is burned at the stake, the Indians massacre the Pilgrim Fathers, Governor John Carver (Captain Hoxie) falls off Plymouth Rock, the *Mayflower* sinks.

THE "HAPPY END"

The pageant is the film's true climax; the ensuing comic scene at the missile base (with Captain Hoxie launched into space instead of the experimental monkey), while funny enough in itself, is somewhat anticlimactic. One of its functions is to prepare the way toward the "happy ending" by facilitating the husband/wife reconciliation (anticipated by Grace's dive into the sea to rescue Harry at the pageant's end). The restoration of the norms is ideologically obligatory: It is unthinkable that a classical American comedy should end with the abolition of home/family/marriage, though the film's logic demands precisely that. Yet, given the McCareyan thematic, it is notable that the "happy ending" is only made possible by the expedient of surreptitiously eliminating the family in order to confirm the couple. In the control room at the missile base, Harry and Grace join forces (inadvertently) to send the obnoxious Hoxie into space, and Harry repeats the act of "unmarrying." First, he reveals that he thought Grace (who can't swim) was attempting suicide when she plunged into the water. In response to his mild rebuke that she wasn't thinking of their motherless children, she replies that she was "thinking of their father." This clears the way for Harry's tender "Grace Oglethorpe, home we go." But in a strikingly perfunctory coda we see the couple, not at home, but enjoying a second honeymoon in the New York hotel where they spent their first (shades of *Make Way for Tomorrow!*)—the second honeymoon that Grace's familial and social commitments had earlier prevented. The "happy ending" is of course an illusion and a cheat;

nothing in the couple's fictional situation has changed—home, family, and alienated labor are still there (if conveniently forgotten). The best one can say is that Angela's continuing presence is at least acknowledged: She telephones from her bathtub; Harry hangs up—for the time being?

Nine Great Movies

by Roger Ebert

FROM ''THE GREAT MOVIE,'' ON-LINE FEATURE COLUMN

TROUBLE IN PARADISE

When I was small I liked to go to the movies because you could find out what adults did when there weren't any children in the room. As I grew up that pleasure gradually faded; the more I knew, the less the characters seemed like adults. Ernst Lubitsch's *Trouble in Paradise* reawakened my old feeling. It is about people who are almost impossibly adult, in that fanciful movie way—so suave, cynical, sophisticated, smooth, and sure that a lifetime is hardly long enough to achieve such polish. They glide.

It is a comedy for three characters, plus comic relief in supporting roles. Herbert Marshall plays a gentleman jewel thief, Miriam Hopkins plays the con woman who adores him, and Kay Francis is the rich widow who thinks she can buy him but is content to rent him for a while. They live in a movie world of exquisite costumes, flawless grooming, butlers, grand hotels in Venice, penthouses in Paris, cocktails, evening dress, wall safes, sweeping staircases, nightclubs, the opera, and jewelry, a lot of jewelry. What is curious is how real they manage to seem, in the midst of the foppery.

The romantic triangle was the favorite plot device of Lubitsch. The critic Greg S. Faller notes that the German-born director liked stories in which "an essentially solid relationship is temporarily threatened by a sexual rival." Here it's clear from the beginning that the gentleman thief Gaston Monescu (Marshall) and the lady pickpocket Lily Vautler (Hopkins) are destined for one another—not only because they like each other, but because their professions make it impossible to trust civilians. When Gaston meets Mariette Colet (Francis), it is to return the purse he has stolen from her and claim the reward. She is attracted to him, and he gracefully bows to her lust, but there is an underlying sobriety: He knows it cannot last, and in a way so does she.

The sexual undertones are surprisingly frank in this pre-code 1932 film, and we understand that none of the three characters is in any danger of mistaking sex for love. Both Lily and Mariette know what they want, and Gaston knows that he has it. His own feelings for them are masked beneath an impenetrable veneer of sophisticated banter.

Herbert Marshall takes ordinary scenes and fills them with tension because of the way he seems to withhold himself from the obvious emotional scripting. He was forty-two when he made the film, handsome in a subdued rather than an absurd way, every dark hair slicked close to his scalp, with a slight stoop to his shoulders that makes him seem to be leaning slightly toward his women, or bowing. His walk is deliberate and noticeably smooth; he lost a leg in World War I, had a wooden one fitted, and practiced so well at concealing his limp that he seems to float through a room.

He gives a droll, mocking richness to the dialogue by Samson Raphaelson, Lubitsch's favorite collaborator. He seems to know he's in a drawing room comedy, and the actresses speak in tune with him. There are exchanges so teasing that they're like verbal foreplay. Consider the early scene in which Gaston, having stolen some jewels, returns to his hotel suite to host a private dinner for Lily. He poses as a baron. She poses as a countess.

"You know," says Lily, "when I first saw you, I thought you were an American."

"Thank you," Gaston gravely replies.

"Someone from another world, so entirely different. Oh! One gets so tired of one's own class—princes and counts and dukes and kings! Everybody talking shop. Always trying to sell jewelry. Then I heard your name and found out you were just one of us."

"Disappointed?"

"No, proud. Very proud."

And they kiss. But soon it is revealed that they have both been busily stealing each other's possessions. She has his wallet, he has her pin, and it's like a game of strip poker in which, as each theft is revealed, their excitement grows, until finally Lily realizes she has been unmasked by another criminal, and cries out, "Darling! Tell me, tell me all about yourself. Who are you?"

He is one of the boldest thieves in the world. He meets Mariette (Francis) by stealing her diamond-encrusted purse and then returning it. He insinuates himself into her trust, advising her on lipstick and on her choice of lovers (of course he has read the love letter in the handbag). The dialogue is daring in its insinuations:

"If I were your father, which fortunately I am not," he says, "and you made any attempt to handle your own business affairs, I would give you a good spanking—in a business way, of course."

"What would you do if you were my secretary?"

"The same thing."

"You're hired."

Turn up the heat under this dialogue, and you'd have screwball comedy. It's tantalizing the way Lubitsch and his actors keep it down to a sensuous simmer. In the low, caressing tones of Marshall and Francis, they're toying with the words—they're in on the joke. And Mariette is neither a spoiled rich woman nor a naive victim. She is a woman of appetites and the imagination to take advantage of an opportunity. She probably doesn't believe, even then, that this man is who he says. He has a way of smiling while he lies, to let his victims have a peek at the joke. But Mariette is an enormously attractive woman, not least because of her calm self-assurance, and he likes her even as he deceives her.

Their first meeting is a splendid example of "the Lubitsch Touch," a press agent's phrase that stuck, maybe because audiences sensed that the director did have a special touch, a way of transforming material through style. What happens, and you are surprised to sense it happening, is that in a drawing room comedy of froth and inconsequence, you find that you believe in the characters and care about them.

Ernst Lubitsch (1892–1947), short, plain, cigar-chewing, beloved, was born in Berlin, was on the stage by the time he was nineteen, worked as a silent film comedian, and in 1915 began to direct. His silent films often starred Pola Negri, who played Madame DuBarry in *Passion* (1919), which made their reputations in America. Mary Pickford brought him to Hollywood in 1923, where he quickly became successful; his best silent films include a version of Oscar Wilde's *Lady Windermere's Fan* (1925) that the critic Andrew Sarris argues actually improves on the original ("it seems incredible") by dropping Wilde's epigrams, "which were largely irrelevant to the plot."

Lubitsch ruled at Paramount in the late 1920s and 1930s (he was head of the studio for a year), embracing the advent of sound with a series of musicals that often starred Jeannette Macdonald. *Trouble in Paradise* is generally considered his best film, but there are advocates for his version of Noël Coward's *Design for Living* (1933), with Cary Grant, Fredric March, and Miriam Hopkins; *Ninotchka* (1939), with Garbo, a definitive adult; *The Shop Around the Corner* (1940), with James Stewart and Margaret Sullavan as bickering co-workers who don't realize they're romantic pen pals; and *To Be or Not to Be* (1942), with Jack Benny and Carole Lombard in a comedy aimed squarely at Hitler.

Because "the Lubitsch Touch" was coined by a publicist, no one, least of all Lubitsch, ever really defined it. It is often said to refer to his fluid camera. Watching *Trouble in Paradise,* what I sensed even more was the way the comic material is given dignity by the actors; the characters have a weight of experience behind them that suggests they know life cannot be played indefinitely for laughs. Andrew Sarris, trying to define the Touch, said it was "a counterpoint of poignant sadness during a film's gayest moments." Consider the way Gaston and Mariette say good-bye for the last time, after it is clear to both of them that he loved her, and stole from her. How gallantly they try to make a joke of it.

RED RIVER

When Peter Bogdanovich needed a movie to play as the final feature in the doomed small-town theater in *The Last Picture Show*, he chose Howard Hawks's *Red River* (1948). He selected the scene where John Wayne tells Montgomery Clift, "Take 'em to Missouri, Matt!" And then there is Hawks's famous montage of weathered cowboy faces in closeup and exaltation, as they cry "Hee-yaw!" and wave their hats in the air.

The moment is as quintessentially Western as any ever filmed, capturing the exhilaration of being on a horse under the big sky with a job to do and a paycheck at the other end. And *Red River* is one of the greatest of all Westerns when it stays with its central story about an older man and a younger one, and the first cattle drive down the Chisholm Trail. It is only in its few scenes involving women that it goes wrong.

The film's hero and villain is Tom Dunson (Wayne), who heads West with a wagon train in 1851 and then peels off for Texas to start a cattle ranch. He takes along only his wagon driver, Groot Nadine (Walter Brennan). Dunson's sweetheart, Fen (Coleen Gray), wants to join them, but he rejects her almost absentmindedly, promising to send for her later. Later, from miles away, Tom and Groot see smoke rising: Indians have destroyed the wagon train. Groot, a grizzled codger, fulminates about how Indians "always want to be burning up good wagons," and Tom observes that it would take them too long to go back and try to help. Their manner is surprisingly distant, considering that Dunson has just lost the woman he loved.

Soon after, the men encounter a boy who survived the Indian attack. This is Matt Garth, who is adopted by Dunson and brought up as the eventual heir to his ranch. Played as an adult by Montgomery Clift (his first screen role), Matt goes away to school, but returns in 1866 just as Dunson is preparing an epic drive to take nine thousand head of cattle north to Missouri.

I mentioned that Dunson is both hero and villain. It's a sign of the movie's complexity that John Wayne, often typecast, is given a tortured, conflicted character to play. He starts with "a boy with a cow and a man with a bull," and builds up a great herd. But then he faces ruin; he must drive the cattle north or go bankrupt.

He's a stubborn man; all through the movie people tell him he's wrong, and usually they're right. They're especially right in wanting to take the cattle to Abilene, which is closer and reportedly has a railroad line, instead of on the longer trek to Missouri. As the cattle drive grows grueling, Dunson grows irascible, and finally whiskey and lack of sleep drive him a little mad; there are attempted mutinies before Matt finally rebels and takes the cattle to Abilene.

The critic Tim Dirks has pointed out the parallels between their conflict and the standoff between Captain Bligh and Fletcher Christian in *Mutiny on the Bounty*. And indeed, the Borden Chase screenplay makes much of the older man's pride and the younger one's need to prove himself.

Also established, but never really developed, is a rivalry between young Matt and a tough cowboy named Cherry Valance (John Ireland), who signs up for the cattle drive and becomes Matt's rival. There's gonna be trouble between those two, old Groot predicts, but the film never delivers, leaving them stranded in the middle of a peculiar ambivalence that drew the attention of *The Celluloid Closet*, a documentary about hidden homosexuality in the movies. ("You know," Cherry says, handling Matt's gun, "there are only two things more beautiful than a good gun: a Swiss watch or a woman from anywhere. You ever had a Swiss watch?")

The shifting emotional attachments are tracked by a silver bracelet, which Dunson gives to Fen before leaving her. It later turns up on the wrist of an Indian he kills, and Dunson then gives it to Matt, who later gives it to Tess Millay (Joanne Dru), a woman he rescues and falls in love with. The three scenes with Tess are the movie's low points, in part because of her prattle (listen to how she chats distractingly with Matt during an Indian attack), in part because she is all too obviously the deus ex machina the plot needs to avoid an unhappy ending. The final scene is the weakest in the film, and Borden Chase reportedly hated it, with good reason: Two men act out a fierce psychological rivalry for two hours, only to cave in instantly to a female's glib tongue-lashing.

What we remember with *Red River* is not, however, the silly ending, but the setup and the majestic central portions. The tragic rivalry is so well established that somehow it keeps its weight and dignity in our memories, even though the ending undercuts it.

Just as memorable are the scenes of the cattle drive itself, as a handful of men control a herd so large it takes all night to ford a river. Russell Harlan's cinematography finds classical compositions in the drive, arrangements of men, sky, and trees, and then in the famous stampede scene he shows a river of cattle flowing down a hill. It is an outdoor movie (we never go inside the ranch house Dunson must have built), and when young Matt steps inside the cattle buyer's office in Abilene, he ducks, observing how long it's been since he was under a roof.

Hawks is wonderful at setting moods. Notice the ominous atmosphere he brews on the night of the stampede—the silence, the restlessness of the cattle, the lowered voices. Notice Matt's nervousness during a night of thick fog, when every shadow may be Tom, come to kill him. And the tension earlier, when Dunson holds a kangaroo court.

And watch the subtle way Hawks modulates Tom Dunson's gradual collapse. John Wayne is tall and steady at the beginning of the picture, but by the end his hair is gray and lank, and his eyes are haunted; the transition is so gradual we might not even notice he wears a white hat at the outset but a black one at the end. Wayne is sometimes considered more of a natural force than an actor, but here his understated acting is right on the money; the critic Joseph McBride says John Ford, who had directed Wayne many times, saw *Red River* and told Hawks, "I never knew the big son of a bitch could act."

Between Wayne and Clift there is a clear tension, not only between an older man and a younger one, but between an actor who started in 1929 and another who represented the leading edge of the Method. It's almost as if Wayne, who could go over a flamboyant actor, was trying to go under a quiet one: He meets the challenge, and matches it.

The theme of *Red River* is from classical tragedy: the need of the son to slay the father, literally or symbolically, in order to clear the way for his own ascendancy. And the father's desire to gain immortality through a child (the one moment with a woman that does work is when Dunson asks Tess to bear a son for him). The majesty of the cattle drive, and all of its expert details about "taking the point" and keeping the cowhands fed and happy, is atmosphere surrounding these themes.

Underlying everything else is an attitude that must have been invisible to the filmmakers at the time: the unstated assumption that it is the white man's right to take what he wants. Dunson shoots a Mexican who comes to tell him "Don Diego" owns the land. Told the land had been granted to Diego by the king of Spain, Dunson says, "You mean he took it away from whoever was here before—Indians, maybe. Well, I'm takin' it away from him." In throwaway dialogue, we learn of seven more men Dunson has killed for his ranch, and there's a grimly humorous motif as he shoots people and then "reads over 'em" from the Bible.

Dunson is a law of his own, until Matt stops a hanging and ends his reign. If all Westerns are about the inevitable encroachment of civilization, this is one where it seems like a pretty good idea.

DETOUR

Detour is a movie so filled with imperfections that it would not earn the director a passing grade in film school. This movie from Hollywood's poverty row, shot in six days, filled with technical errors and ham-handed narrative, starring a man who can only pout and a woman who can only sneer, should have faded from sight soon after it was released in 1945. And yet it lives on, haunting and creepy, an embodiment of the guilty soul of film noir. No one who has seen it has easily forgotten it.

Detour tells the story of Al Roberts, played by Tom Neal as a petulant loser with haunted eyes and a weak mouth, who plays piano in a nightclub and is in love, or says he is, with a singer named Sue. Their song, significantly, is "I Can't Believe You Fell in Love with Me." He wants to get married, she leaves for the West Coast, he continues to play piano, but then: "When this drunk gave me a ten spot, I couldn't get very excited. What was it? A piece of paper crawling with germs."

So he hitchhikes to California, getting a lift in Arizona from a man named Haskell, who tells him about a woman hitchhiker who left deep scratches on his hand: "There oughta be a law against dames with claws." Haskell dies of a heart attack. Al buries the body, and takes Haskell's car, clothes, money and identification; he claims to have no choice, because the police will in any event assume he murdered the man.

He picks up a hitchhiker named Vera (Ann Savage), who "looked like she'd just been thrown off the crummiest freight train in the world." She seems to doze, then sits bolt upright and makes a sudden verbal attack: "Where'd you leave his body? Where did you leave the owner of this car? Your name's not Haskell!" Al realizes he has picked up the dame with the claws.

Haskell had told them both the same unlikely story, about running away from home at fifteen after putting a friend's eye out in a duel ("My dad had a couple of Franco-Prussian sabers").

In Los Angeles, Vera reads that Haskell's rich father is dying, and dreams up a con for Al to impersonate the long-lost son and inherit the estate. Waiting for the old man to die, they sit in a rented room, drinking, playing cards, and fighting, until Al finds himself with another corpse on his hands, once again in a situation that makes him look guilty of murder.

Roberts is played by Tom Neal as a sad sack who seems relieved to surrender to Vera ("My favorite sport is being kept prisoner"). Ann Savage plays Vera as a venomous castrator. Every line is acid and angry; in an era before four-letter words, she lashes Al with "sucker" and "sap." Of course Al could simply escape from her. Sure, she has the key to the room, but any woman who kills a bottle of booze in a night can be dodged fairly easily. Al stays because he wants to stay. He wallows in mistreatment.

The movie was shot on the cheap with B-minus actors, but it was directed by a man of qualities: Edgar G. Ulmer (1900–72), a refugee from Hitler, who was an assistant to the great Murnau on *The Last Laugh* and *Sunrise,* and provided one of the links between German Expressionism, with its exaggerated lighting, camera angles and dramaturgy, and the American film noir, which added jazz and guilt.

The difference between a crime film and a noir film is that the bad guys in crime movies know they're bad and want to be, while a noir hero thinks he's a good guy who has been ambushed by life. Al Roberts complains to us: "Whichever way you turn, fate sticks out a foot to trip you." Most noir heroes are defeated through their weaknesses. Few have been weaker than Roberts. He narrates the movie by speaking directly to the audience, mostly in a self-pitying whine. He's pleading his case, complaining that life hasn't given him a fair break.

Most critics of *Detour* have taken Al's story at face value: He was unlucky in love, he lost the good girl and was savaged by the bad girl, he was an innocent bystander who looked guilty even to himself. But the critic Andrew Britton argues a more intriguing theory in Ian Cameron's *Book of Film Noir.* He emphasizes that the narration is addressed directly to us: We're not hearing what happened, but what Al Roberts wants us to believe happened. It's a "spurious but flattering account," he writes, pointing out that Sue the singer hardly fits Al's description of her, that Al is less in love than in need of her paycheck, and that his cover-up of Haskell's death is a rationalization for an easy theft. For Britton, Al's version illustrates Freud's theory that traumatic experiences can be reworked into fantasies that are easier to live with.

Maybe that's why *Detour* insinuates itself so well—why audiences respond so strongly. The jumps and inconsistencies of the narrative are nightmare psychology; Al's not telling a story, but scurrying through the raw materials, assembling an alibi. Consider the sequence where Al buries Haskell's body and takes his identity. Immediately after, Al checks into a motel, goes to sleep, and dreams of the very same events: It's a flashback side-by-side with the events it flashes back to, as if his dream mind is doing a quick rewrite.

Tom Neal makes Al flaccid, passive, and self-pitying. That's perfect for the material. (In real life, Neal was as unlucky as Al; he was convicted of manslaughter in the death of his third wife.) Ann Savage's work is extraordinary: There is not a single fleeting shred of tenderness or humanity in her performance as Vera, as she snaps out her pulp dialogue ("What'd you do—kiss him with a wrench?"). These are two pure types: the submissive man and the female hellion.

The movie's low budget is obvious. During one early scene, Ulmer uses thick fog to substitute for New York streets. He shoots as many scenes as possible in the front seats of cars, with shabby rear-projection (the only meal Al and Vera have together is in a drive-in). For a flashback, he simply zooms in on Neal's face, cuts the lights in the background, and shines a light in his eyes.

Sometimes you can see him stretching to make ends meet. When Al calls long-distance to Sue, for example, Ulmer pads his running time by editing in stock footage of telephone wires and switchboard operators, but can't spring for any footage of Sue actually speaking into the phone (Al does all the talking, and then Ulmer cuts to her lamely holding the receiver to her ear).

And it's strange that the first vehicles to give lifts to the hitchhiking Al seem to have right-hand drives. He gets in on what would be the American driver's side, and the cars drive off on the "wrong" side of the road. Was the movie shot in England? Not at all. My guess is that the negative was flipped. Ulmer possibly shot the scenes with the cars going from left to right, then reflected that for a journey from the east to the west coasts, right to left would be more conventional film grammar. Placing style above common sense is completely consistent with Ulmer's approach throughout the film.

Do these limitations and stylistic transgressions hurt the film? No. They are the film. *Detour* is an example of material finding the appropriate form. Two bottom-feeders from the swamps of pulp swim through the murk of low-budget noir and are caught gasping in Ulmer's net. They deserve one another. At the end, Al is still complaining: "Fate, for some mysterious force, can put the finger on you or me, for no good reason at all." Oh, it has a reason.

WRITTEN ON THE WIND

Opinion on the melodramas of Douglas Sirk has flip-flopped since his key films were released in the 1950s. At the time, critics ridiculed them and the public lapped them up. Today most viewers dismiss them as pop trash, but in serious film circles Sirk is considered a great filmmaker—a German who fled Hitler to become the sly subverter of American postwar materialism.

One cold night this winter, I went up to the Everyman Cinema in Hampstead, north of London, to see a revival of a restored print of Sirk's *Written on the Wind* (1956). This is a perverse and wickedly funny melodrama in which you can find the seeds of *Dallas*, *Dynasty*, and all the other prime-time soaps. Sirk is the one who established their tone, in which shocking behavior is treated with passionate solemnity, while parody burbles beneath.

All the reviews of this movie seem to involve lists: It's about wealth, alcoholism, nymphomania, impotence, suicide, and veiled elements of incest and homosexuality. And the theme song, by Sammy Cahn, is sung by the Four Aces. The pieces are in place for a film you can mock and patronize. But my fellow audience members sat in appreciative silence (all right, they snickered a little when Rock Hudson is told it's time to get married and replies, "I have trouble enough just finding oil").

To appreciate a film like *Written on the Wind* probably takes more sophistication than to understand one of Ingmar Bergman's masterpieces, because Bergman's themes are visible and underlined, while with Sirk the style conceals the message. His interiors are wildly over the top, and his exteriors are phony—he wants you to notice the artifice, to see that he's not using realism but an exaggerated Hollywood studio style. The Manhattan skyline in an early scene is obviously a painted backdrop. The rear-projected traffic uses cars that are ten years too old. The swimming hole at the river, where the characters make youthful promises they later regret, is obviously a tank on a sound stage with fake scenery behind it.

The actors are as artificial as the settings. They look like *Photoplay* covers, and speak in the clichés of pulp romance. Sirk did not cast his films by accident, and one of the pleasures of *Written on the Wind* is the way he exaggerates the natural qualities of his actors and then uses them ironically.

The film stars Rock Hudson as Mitch Wayne (think about that name), who grew up poor on the Texas ranch owned by oil millionaire Jasper Hadley (Robert Keith). He's been raised with Jasper's son Kyle (Robert Stack) and daughter Marylee (Dorothy Malone). Now Mitch holds an important post in the Hadley Oil empire, which requires him to wear a baseball cap and keep a yellow pencil parked over his ear, while studying geological maps. Kyle has turned into a drunken playboy, and Marylee into a drunken nympho.

As the film opens, Mitch and Kyle are in New York, where they both fall in love with the trim, intelligent Lucy Moore (Lauren Bacall). When she tells Kyle she wants to work in advertising, he picks up the phone to buy her an agency. She demurs. All three have lunch at 21 and then Kyle sends Mitch to buy cigarettes while he whisks Lucy off in a cab to the airport, where Mitch (who knows his tricks) is there ahead of them on the Hadley plane. Kyle pilots it himself, flying them to Miami Beach while confessing to Lucy, "I drink too much" and "Nobody has ever listened to me the way you do." Of Mitch Wayne, he says: "He's eccentric. He's poor." The terms are synonymous.

In Miami Beach, they check into a Hadley hotel, where the manager announces, "Miss Moore's suite," while the music swells in materialistic ecstasy, and Kyle shows Lucy closets full of designer gowns, drawers full of purses, and trays of jewelry, and asks her to prepare for dinner. Half an hour later (after dressing with Mitch in the suite they . . . share), Kyle enters Lucy's suite, calling out, "Are you decent?" Discovering she has left for the airport, he muses, "I guess she was."

Miami Beach was a painted backdrop. Texas, apart from a few shots of sports cars racing past oil derricks, is all built on the back lot. The plot heats up. Marylee has had a crush on Mitch since childhood, and wants to marry him. So great is her need, indeed, that when she sashays around in low-cut dresses, her knees almost buckle under the weight of her lust. (Malone won an Oscar for the performance.)

Kyle goes on the wagon, until a doctor unwisely informs him he is impotent. Well, not completely impotent—there is a "problem," but a baby is "possible." Kyle doesn't wait for the footnotes before racing to the country club to resume his boozing, and when Lucy tells him she's pregnant, he assumes the father is Mitch—a suspicion encouraged by Marylee, who wants Lucy off the ranch so she can regain possession of her childhood friends.

If I smile as I synopsize the plot, surely Sirk was smiling when he directed it; he's subverting the very lifestyle he celebrates. His use of artificial and contrived effects, colors, and plot devices is "a screaming Brechtian essay on the shared impotence of American family and business life," says film critic Dave Kehr, and encompasses deliberate distancing "that draws attention to the artificiality of the film medium, in turn commenting on the hollowness of middle-class American life" (*Cinebooks*). Well, yes, but it's possible to enjoy Sirk's subtleties as simple entertainment, too. Films like this are both above and below middle-brow taste. If you only see the surface, it's trashy soap opera. If you can see the style, the absurdity, the exaggeration, and the satirical humor, it's subversive of all the 1950s dramas that handled such material solemnly. William Inge and Tennessee Williams were taken with great seriousness during the decade, but Sirk kids their Freudian hysteria (that Williams's work survives is a tribute to his poetry, not his common sense).

One test of satire is: At what point do we realize the author is kidding? There's a clue here in an early remark by Mitch to Lucy: "Are you looking for laughs? Or are you soul-searching?" And in the way the old swimming hole represents lost innocence and promise for Marylee. In one of the film's more lurid sequences, Sirk uses a closeup of her face in orgiastic nostalgia, as we hear little Mitch's childish voice piping out a promise to marry Marylee when they grow up. "How far we've come from the river!" Mitch later tells her.

There's a broad wink and nudge at the end. Old Jasper Hadley is often seen behind his desk, which holds a large bronze model of an oil derrick. (A portrait on his wall shows him at the same desk with the same bronze—a barbershop mirror effect.) At the end of the film, after Marylee's rivals have won, she is left alone in her father's office, where she caresses the erect derrick—first sadly, then tenderly.

To appreciate the trashiness of *Written on the Wind* is not to condescend to it. To a greater degree than we realize, our lives and decisions are formed by pop clichés and conventions. Films that exaggerate our fantasies help us to see them—to be amused by them, and by ourselves. They clear the air.

Douglas Sirk (1900–87) had two careers. His first thirty-seven years were spent in Germany, where he worked as a stage director, specializing in classics. His first American film was *Hitler's Madmen* (1943), and his critical reputation is based on a series of enormously popular melodramas he made for Universal, including *All I Desire* (1953), *Magnificent Obsession* (1954), *All That Heaven Allows* (1955), and *Imitation of Life* (1959). He also made Westerns, musicals, and war stories, working with Hudson more often than any other star—perhaps appreciating the way Hudson's concealed homosexuality worked subtly to subvert the stock characters he often played.

Rainer Werner Fassbinder, another German obsessed with American forms of melodrama, said Sirk was the greatest influence on his work. Certainly Sirk was the father of prime-time TV soaps. "I have seen *Written on the Wind* a thousand times," the Spanish director Pedro Almodovar said, "and I cannot wait to see it again." Sirk's style spread so pervasively that nobody could do melodrama with a straight face after him. In countless ways visible and invisible, Sirk's sly subversion skewed American popular culture, and helped launch a new age of irony.

NOTORIOUS

Alfred Hitchcock's *Notorious* is the most elegant expression of the master's visual style, just as *Vertigo* is the fullest expression of his obsessions. It contains some of the most effective camera shots in his—or anyone's—work, and they all lead to the great final passages in which two men find out how very wrong they both were.

This is the film, with *Casablanca,* that assures Ingrid Bergman's immortality. She plays a woman whose notorious reputation encourages U.S. agents to recruit her to spy on Nazis in postwar Rio. And that reputation nearly gets her killed, when the man she loves mistrusts her. His misunderstanding is at the center of a plot in which all of the pieces come together with perfect precision, so that two people walk down a staircase to their freedom, and a third person climbs steps to his doom.

Hitchcock made the film in 1946, when the war was over but the Cold War was just beginning. A few months later, he would have made the villains Communists, but as he and Ben Hecht worked on the script, Nazis were still uppermost in their minds. (An opening subtitle says: "Miami, Florida, 3:20 P.M., April 20, 1946"—admirably specific, but as unnecessary as the similarly detailed information at the beginning of *Psycho.*)

The story stars Bergman as a patriotic American named Alicia Huberman, whose father is a convicted Nazi spy. Alicia is known for drinking and apparent promiscuity, and is recruited by an agent named Devlin (Cary Grant) to fly to Rio and insinuate herself into the household of a spy ring led by Sebastian (Claude Rains). Sebastian once loved her, and perhaps he still does; Devlin is essentially asking her to share the spy's bed to discover his secrets. And this she is willing to do, because by the time he asks her, she is in love—with Devlin.

All of these sexual arrangements are of course handled with the sort of subtle dialogue and innuendo that Hollywood used to get around the production code. There is never a moment when improper behavior is actually stated or shown, but the film leaves no doubt. By the time all of the pieces are in place, we actually feel more sympathy for Sebastian than for Devlin. He may be a spy but he loves Alicia sincerely, while Devlin may be an American agent but has used Alicia's love to force her into the arms of another man.

Hitchcock was known for his attention to visual details. He drew storyboards of every scene before shooting it, and slyly plays against Grant's star power in the scene introducing Devlin to the movie. At a party the night her father has been convicted, Alicia drinks to forget. The camera positions itself behind the seated Devlin, so we see only the back of his head. He anchors the shot as the camera moves left and right, following the morally ambiguous Alicia as she flirts, drinks, and tries to forget.

There are more famous shots the next morning. Alicia awakens with a hangover, and there is a gigantic foreground closeup of a glass of Alka-Seltzer (it will be paired much later in the movie with a huge foreground coffee cup that we know contains arsenic). From her point of view, she sees Devlin in the doorway, backlit and upside down. As she sits up, he rotates 180 degrees. He suggests a spy deal. She refuses, talking of her plans to take a cruise. He plays a secret recording that proves she is, after all, patriotic—despite her loose image. As the recording begins, she is in shadow. As it continues, she is in bars of light. As it ends, she is in full light. Hitchcock has choreographed the visuals so that they precisely reflect what is happening.

The film is rich with other elegant shots, the most famous beginning with the camera on a landing high above the entrance hall of Sebastian's mansion in Rio. It ends, after one unbroken movement, with a closeup of a key in Alicia's nervously twisting hand. The key will open the wine cellar, where Devlin (posing as a guest) will join Alicia in trying to find Sebastian's secret. One of the bottles contains not wine but a radioactive substance used in bombs. Of course, it could contain anything—maps, codes, diamonds—because it is a MacGuffin (Hitchcock's name for that plot element that everyone is concerned about, although it hardly matters what it is).

The Hecht screenplay is ingenious in playing the two men against one another. Sebastian, played by Rains, is smaller, more elegant, more vulnerable, and dominated by his forbidding mother (Leopoldine

Konstantin). Devlin, played by Grant, is tall, physically imposing, crude at times, suspicious where Sebastian is trusting. Both men love her but the wrong man trusts her, and the plot leads to a moment of inspired ingenuity in which Devlin is able to escort Alicia out of the Nazi mansion in full view of all of the spies, and the circumstances are such that nobody can stop him. (There is a point earlier in the film where Devlin walks up the same staircase, and if you count his steps you will find that on the way down he and Alicia descend more steps than there actually are—Hitchcock's way of prolonging the suspense.)

Throughout Hitchcock's career, he devised stories in which elegant women, usually blond, were manipulated into situations of great danger. Hitchcock was the master manipulator, with the male actors as his surrogates. *Vertigo* treats this theme so openly it almost gives the game away. But look how it works in *Notorious,* where Devlin (like the Jimmy Stewart character in *Vertigo*) grooms and trains an innocent women to be exactly who he desires her to be, and then makes her do his bidding.

The great erotic moment in *Vertigo* is the one where the man kisses the woman of his fantasy, while the room whirls around him. There is a parallel scene in *Notorious,* and it was famous at the time as "the longest kiss in the history of the movies." It was not, however, a single kiss, as Tim Dirks points out in his essay on the film (www.filmsite.org/ noto). The production code forbade a kiss lasting longer than three seconds, and so Bergman and Grant alternate kissing with dialogue and eyeplay, while never leaving each other's arms. The sequence begins on a balcony overlooking Rio, encompasses a telephone call and a discussion of the dinner menu, and ends with a parting at the apartment door, taking three minutes in all. The three-second rule led to a better scene; an actual 180-second kiss might look like an exercise in slobbering.

The choice of Ingrid Bergman for the role was ideal; she subtly combined the noble and the carnal. Consider *Casablanca* (all of the viewers of *Notorious* would have), in which she lives with a resistance hero but in her heart loves a scruffy bar owner, and yet emerges as an idealistic heroine. In *Notorious,* we never seriously doubt that she is the heroine, but we can understand why the Grant character does. She appears to be a dipsomaniac, and besides, she sleeps with Sebastian. But she does it because she loves Devlin. Devlin has difficulty in loving a woman who would do that; one is reminded of Groucho Marx, who refused to join any club that would have him as a member.

So many movies have ended in obligatory chases and shoot-outs that the ability to write a well-crafted third act has almost died out. Among its many achievements, *Notorious* ends well. Like clockwork, the inevitable events of the last ten minutes take place, and they all lend to the final perfect shot, in which another Nazi says to Sebastian, "Alex will you come in, please? I wish to talk to you." And Alex goes in, knowing he will never come out alive.

THE BIG SLEEP

Two of the names mentioned most often in Howard Hawks's *The Big Sleep* (1946) are Owen Taylor and Sean Regan. One is the chauffeur for the wealthy Sternwood family. The other is an Irishman hired by old Gen. Sternwood "to do his drinking for him." Neither is ever seen alive; Regan has disappeared mysteriously before the movie begins, and Taylor's body is hauled from the Pacific after his Packard runs off a pier. Were they murdered? And does it even matter, since there are five other murders in the film? One of the best-known of all Hollywood anecdotes involves the movie's confusing plot, based on the equally confusing novel by Raymond Chandler. Lauren Bacall recalls in her autobiography, "One day Bogie came on the set and said to Howard, 'Who pushed Taylor off the pier?' Everything stopped." As A.M. Sperber and Eric Lax write in *Bogart,* Hawks sent Chandler a telegram asking whether the Sternwood's chauffeur, Owen Taylor, was murdered or a suicide. 'Dammit I didn't know either,' Chandler recalled. And Chandler later wrote to his publisher, "The girl who played the nymphy sister (Martha Vikers) was so good she shattered Miss Bacall completely. So they cut the picture in such a way that all her best scenes were left out except one. The result made nonsense and Howard Hawks threatened to sue. After long argument, as I hear it, he went back and did a lot of re-shooting."

It is typical of this most puzzling of films that no one agrees even on why it is so puzzling. Yet that has never affected *The Big Sleep*'s enduring popularity, because the movie is about the process of a criminal investigation, not its results.

The process follows private eye Philip Marlowe (Humphrey Bogart) as he finds his way through the jungle of gamblers, pornographers, killers, and blackmailers who have attached themselves to the rich old general (Charles Waldron) and his two randy daughters (Bacall and Vickers). Some bad guys get killed and others get arrested, and we don't much care—because the real result is that Bogart and Lauren Bacall end up in each other's arms. *The Big Sleep* is a lust story with a plot about a lot of other things. That can be seen more clearly now that an earlier version of the film has surfaced. *The Big Sleep* was finished by Warner Brothers in 1945, but held out of release while the studio rushed to play off its backlog of World War II movies. Meanwhile, ongoing events greatly affected its future. Hawks's *To Have and Have Not* (1944), Bacall's screen debut, was an enormous hit, and the onscreen chemistry between her and Bogart was sizzling. ("You know how to whistle, don't you, Steve? You just put your lips together and blow.") Bacall then starred opposite Charles Boyer in *Confidential Agent* (1945) and got withering reviews. And she and Bogart were married (she was twenty, he was forty-four).

Bacall's powerful agent, Charles Feldman, who disliked the version he saw, wrote studio head Jack Warner in desperation, asking that scenes be eliminated, added, and reshot. Otherwise, he warned, Bacall was likely to get more bad reviews, damaging the career of a promising star who was married to the studio's biggest money-maker.

Warner agreed, and Hawks returned to the sound stages with his actors for reshoots. Bacall's book minimizes this process: "Howard . . . did need one more scene between Bogie and me." Actually, he needed a lot more than that. The 1945 release, now restored by archivists at UCLA, is accompanied by a detailed documentary showing what was left out and what was brand new when the movie was finally released in 1946.

What Feldman missed, he said, was the "insolence" that Bacall showed in *To Have and Have Not*. In the original version of *The Big Sleep*, the relationship between Bogart and Bacall is problematical: Marlowe isn't sure whether he trusts this cool, elegant charmer. The 1946 version commits to their romance and adds among other scenes one of the most daring examples of double entendre in any movie up until that time. The new scene puts Bacall and Bogart in a nightclub, where they are only ostensibly talking about horse racing.

Bacall: ". . . speaking of horses, I like to play them myself. But I like to see them work out a little first. See if they're front-runners or come from behind. . . . I'd say you don't like to be rated. You like to get out in front, open up a lead, take a little breather in the back stretch, and then come home free. . . ."

Bogart: "You've got a touch of class, but I don't know how far you can go."

Bacall: "A lot depends on who's in the saddle."

What you sense here is the enjoyable sight of two people who are in love and enjoy toying with one another. The new scenes add a change to the film that was missing in the 1945 version; this is a case where "studio interference" was exactly the right thing. The only reason to see the earlier version is to go behind the scenes, to learn how the tone and impact of a movie can be altered with just a few scenes. (The accompanying documentary even shows how dialog was redubbed to get a slightly different spin.)

As for the 1946 version that we have been watching all of these years, it is one of the great film noirs, a black-and-white symphony that exactly reproduces Chandler's ability, on the page, to find a tone of voice that keeps its distance, and yet is wry and humorous and cares. Working from Chandler's original words and adding spins of their own, the writers (William Faulkner, Jules Furthman, and Leigh Brackett) wrote one of the most quotable of screenplays: It's unusual to find yourself laughing in a movie not because something is funny but because it's so wickedly clever. (Marlowe on the "nymphy" kid sister: "She tried to sit in my lap while I was standing up.") Unlike modern crime movies which are loaded with action, *The Big Sleep* is heavy with dialogue—the characters talk and talk, just like in the Chandler novels; it's as if there's a competition to see who has the most verbal style.

Martha Vickers was indeed electric as the kid sister, and Dorothy Malone all but steals her scene as a book clerk who finds Marlowe intriguing. But the 1945 version makes it clear Bacall was by no means as bad as Feldman feared she was. She is adequate in most scenes, and splendid in others—but the scenes themselves didn't give her the opportunities that the reshoot did. In scenes like the "racing" conversation she has the dry reserve, the private amusement, the way of sizing up a man and enjoying the competition, that became her trademark. It's astonishing to realize she was twenty, untrained as an actor, and by her own report scared to death.

Bogart himself made personal style into an art form. What else did he have? He wasn't particularly handsome, he wore a rug, he wasn't tall ("I try to be," he tells Vickers), and he always seemed to act within a certain range. Yet no other movie actor is more likely to be remembered a century from now. And the fascinating subtext in *The Big Sleep* is that in Bacall he found his match.

You can see it in his eyes: Sure, he's in love, but there's something else, too. He was going through a messy breakup with his wife, Mayo, when they shot the picture. He was drinking so heavily he didn't turn up some days, and Hawks had to shoot around him. He saw this coltish twenty-one-year-old not only as his love but perhaps as his salvation. That's the undercurrent. It may not have been fun to live through, but it creates a kind of joyous, desperate tension on the screen. And since the whole idea of film noir was to live through unspeakable experiences and keep your cool, this was the right screenplay for this time in his *life*.

Howard Hawks (1896–1977) is one of the great American directors of pure movies (*His Girl Friday, Bringing Up Baby, Red River, Rio Bravo*), and a hero of auteur critics because he found his own laconic values in many different kinds of genre material. He once defined a good movie as "three great scenes and no bad scenes." Comparing the two versions of *The Big Sleep* reveals that the reshoots inserted one of the great scenes, and removed some of the bad ones, neatly proving his point.

THE LADY EVE

If I were asked to name the single scene in all of romantic comedy that was sexiest and funniest at the same time, I would advise beginning at six seconds past the twenty-minute mark in Preston Sturges's *The Lady Eve,* and watching as Barbara Stanwyck toys with Henry Fonda's hair in an unbroken shot that lasts three minutes and fifty-one seconds.

Stanwyck plays an adventuress who has lured a rich but unworldly young bachelor to her cabin on an ocean liner, and is skillfully tantalizing him. She reclines on a chaise. He has landed on the floor next to her. "Hold me tight!" she says, holding him tight—allegedly because she has been frightened by a snake. Now begins the unbroken shot. Her right arm cradles his head, and as she talks she toys with his earlobe and runs her fingers through his hair. She teases, kids, and flirts with him, and he remains almost paralyzed with shyness and self-consciousness. And at some point during this process, she falls for him.

That isn't part of her plan. Stanwyck plays Jean Harrington, a con woman who travels first class with her father and their valet, fleecing rich travelers in card games and whatever else comes along. She sets her sights on Charles Pike (Fonda), heir to a brewery fortune, as he comes aboard after a snake-hunting expedition in South America. She drops an apple on his pith helmet as he climbs the rope ladder to the ship, and is reprimanded by her father. "Don't be vulgar, Jean. Let us be crooked, but never common."

What is delightful about Stanwyck's performance is how she has it both ways. She is a crook, and yet can be trusted. A seductress, and yet a pushover for romance. A gold digger, and yet she wants nothing from him. And he is a naive innocent who knows only that her perfume smells mighty good to someone who has been "up the Amazon" for a year. She falls for him so quickly and so thoroughly that she's even frank about her methods; just before he kisses her in the moonlight in the ship's bow, she tells him, "They say a moonlit deck's a woman's business office."

Howard Hawks once said that the flaw in his *Bringing Up Baby*, one of the great screwball comedies, is that everyone in it is a screwball; there's no baseline of sanity to measure the characters against. *The Lady Eve* (1941), which in its way is just as preposterous as the Hawks picture, doesn't make that mistake. Fonda is the rock. He remains vulnerable and sincere throughout the picture because, like all young men who are truly and badly in love, his consciousness is focused on one thing: the void in his heart that only she can fill.

That frees Stanwyck for one of her greatest performances, a flight of romance and comedy so graceful and effortless that she is somehow able to play different notes at the same time. The movie establishes Jean Harrington in an inspired early scene, as she joins her father, a phony colonel, in the ship's lounge. Using the mirror in her compact, she spies on Charlie Pike as he sits alone and reads a book (its title, *Are Snakes Necessary?*, is a sly addition to the movie's phallic imagery). Sturges cuts to the view reflected in the mirror, and Jean provides a tart voice-over narration for her father, describing the attempts of every woman in the room to catch the handsome bachelor's eye. Then, as Charlie leaves the room, she simply sticks out a foot and trips him; as he picks himself up she blames him for breaking off the heel of her shoe.

He escorts her to her stateroom and she tells him to pick out a new pair of shoes and put them on her feet. "You'll have to kneel down," she says, and swings her nyloned leg almost in his face. His vision blurs with passion, and Sturges comes within an inch of violating the production code, the way her toe swings dangerously close. Poor Charlie falls for her, soon finds himself playing poker with Jean and her father, wins $600 as part of their setup, and then undergoes the exquisite torment of her ear-and-hair caress.

The plot unfolds as screwball invention, except that after boy meets girl and boy loses girl, boy wins what he only thinks is another girl. Jean, hurt by the way he has not trusted her, gets herself invited to a dinner at his father's palatial mansion by posing as "Lady Eve Sidwich." Charlie is struck by how much Eve resembles Jean. "It's the same dame!" says his faithful valet Muggsy (William Demarest). But Charlie can't believe it, and follows her moon-eyed through a series of pratfalls.

Sturges says in his memoirs that the studios were always trying to get him to limit his pratfalls, and at the sneak previews he crossed his fingers as Demarest fell into the bushes and Fonda tripped over a couch and a curtain before getting a roast beef in his lap. But they all worked. "That couch has been there fifteen years and nobody ever fell over it before!" exclaims Charlie's father. Lady Eve: "Oh, well—now the ice is broken!"

Barbara Stanwyck (1907–90) was known primarily as a gifted dramatic actress (*Golden Boy*, *Stella Dallas*, *Double Indemnity*). Preston Sturges (1898–1959), who in the early 1940s made one inspired comedy after another (*Sullivan's Travels*, *Palm Beach Story*) and scarcely seemed able to step wrong, had promised her a comic role, and gave her one for the ages.

Although the movie would be inconceivable without Fonda, *The Lady Eve* is all Stanwyck's; the love, the hurt, and the anger of her character provide the motivation for nearly every scene, and what is surprising is how much genuine feeling she finds in the comedy. Watch her eyes as she regards Fonda, in all of their quiet scenes together, and you will see a woman who is amused by a man's boyish shyness and yet aroused by his physical presence. At first she loves the game of seduction, and you can sense her enjoyment of her own powers. Then she is somehow caught up in her own seduction. There has rarely been a woman in a movie who more convincingly desired a man.

Her father is played by Charles Coburn (1877–1961), a valuable character actor from the 1930s through the 1950s, who in appearance was sort of a toned-down Charles Laughton. Here Coburn and Sturges make a crucial right decision: "Colonel" Harrington is not blustering and broad, but a smart and perceptive man, not loud, who loves his daughter.

Their relationship is established in a quiet scene the morning after Jean first meets Charlie. She is in her stateroom, still in bed. Her father enters in dressing gown, sits on her bed, and plays with a deck of cards while questioning her. At this point we have a good notion, but no hard evidence, that he is a fraud. "What are you doing?" she asks. "Dealing fives," he says. She wants to see. He shows her four aces, puts them on top of the deck, and then deals four hands without dealing a single ace—dealing the fifth card every time. (It's hard to be sure, but here and elsewhere it looks as if Coburn himself is handling the cards.)

The scene establishes him as a shark, makes it clear they're confederates, and underlines, by the way she calls him "Harry," that they're two adults and not locked into a narrow daddy-daughter relationship. The scene also sets up the hilarious scene that night, where the Colonel tries to cheat Charlie at cards, and Jean outcheats him to rescue the man she loves.

A movie like *The Lady Eve* is so hard to make that you can't make it at all unless you find a way to make it seem effortless. Preston Sturges does a kind of breathless balancing act here, involving romance, deception, and physical comedy. Consider the scenes where Jean masquerades as the Lady Eve. She throws Charlie off the scent by her very lack of a disguise. Brazenly entering his house looking exactly like herself, she adds a British accent and dares him to call her bluff. She knows he cannot, and the masquerade sets up the two final lines of the film, which I will not mention here—except to say that for my money, either one is equal to the classic line "Nobody's perfect!" at the end of *Some Like It Hot*.

M

The horror of the faces: That is the overwhelming image that remains from a recent viewing of the restored version of *M*, Fritz Lang's famous

1931 film about a child murderer in Germany. In my memory it was a film that centered on the killer, the creepy little Franz Becker, played by Peter Lorre. But Becker has relatively limited screen time, and only one consequential speech—although it's a haunting one. Most of the film is devoted to the search for Becker, by both the police and the underworld, and many of these scenes are played in closeup. In searching for words to describe the faces of the actors, I fall hopelessly upon "piglike."

What was Lang up to? He was a famous director, his silent films like *Metropolis* worldwide successes. He lived in a Berlin where the left-wing plays of Bertolt Brecht coexisted with the decadent milieu re-created in movies like *Cabaret*. By 1931, the Nazi Party was on the march in Germany, although not yet in full control. His own wife would later become a party member. He made a film that has been credited with forming two genres: the serial killer movie and the police procedural. And he filled it with grotesques. Was there something beneath the surface, some visceral feeling about his society that this story allowed him to express?

When you watch *M,* you see a hatred for the Germany of the early 1930s that is visible and palpable. Apart from a few perfunctory shots of everyday bourgeoisie life (such as the pathetic scene of the mother waiting for her little girl to return from school), the entire movie consists of men seen in shadows, in smoke-filled dens, in disgusting dives, in conspiratorial conferences. And the faces of these men are cruel caricatures: fleshy, twisted, beetle-browed, dark-jowled, out of proportion. One is reminded of the stark faces of the accusing judges in Dreyer's *Joan of Arc,* but they are more forbidding than ugly.

What I sense is that Lang hated the people around him, hated Nazism, and hated Germany for permitting it. His next film, *The Testament of Dr. Mabuse* (1933), had villains who were unmistakably Nazis. It was banned by the censors, but Joseph Goebbels, so the story goes, offered Lang control of the nation's film industry if he would come on board with the Nazis. He fled, he claimed, on a midnight train—although Patrick McGilligan's new book, *Fritz Lang: The Nature of the Beast,* is dubious about many of Lang's grandiose claims.

Certainly *M* is a portrait of a diseased society, one that seems even more decadent than the other portraits of Berlin in the 1930s; its characters have no virtues and lack even attractive vices. In other stories of the time we see nightclubs, champagne, sex, and perversion. When *M* visits a bar, it is to show closeups of greasy sausages, spilled beer, rotten cheese, and stale cigar buffs.

The film's story was inspired by the career of a serial killer in Dusseldorf. In *M*, Franz Becker preys on children—offering them candy and friendship, and then killing them. The murders are all offscreen, and Lang suggests the first one with a classic montage including the little victim's empty dinner plate, her mother calling frantically down an empty spiral staircase, and her balloon—bought for her by the killer—caught in electric wires.

There is no suspense about the murderer's identity. Early in the film we see Becker looking at himself in a mirror. Peter Lorre at the time was twenty-six, plump, baby-faced, clean-shaven, and as he looks at his reflected image he pulls down the corners of his mouth and tries to make hideous faces, to see in himself the monster others see in him. His presence in the movie is often implied rather than seen; he compulsively whistles the same tune, from *Peer Gynt,* over and over, until the notes stand in for the murders.

The city is in turmoil: The killer must be caught. The police put all their men on the case, making life unbearable for the criminal element ("There are more cops on the streets than girls," a pimp complains). To reduce the heat, the city's criminals team up to find the killer, and as Lang intercuts between two summit conferences—the cops and the criminals—we are struck by how similar the two groups are, visually. Both sit around tables in gloomy rooms, smoking so voluminously that at times their very faces are invisible. In their fat fingers their cigars look fecal. (As the criminals agree that murdering children violates their code, I was reminded of the summit on drugs in *The Godfather.*)

M was Lang's first sound picture, and he was wise to use dialogue so sparingly. Many early talkies felt they had to talk all the time, but Lang allows his camera to prowl through the streets and dives, providing a rat's-eye view. One of the film's most spectacular shots is utterly silent, as the captured killer is dragged into a basement to be confronted by the city's assembled criminals, and the camera shows their faces: hard, cold, closed, implacable.

It is at this inquisition that Lorre delivers his famous speech in defense, or explanation. Sweating with terror, his face a fright mask, he cries out: "I can't help myself! I haven't any control over this evil thing that's inside of me! The fire, the voices, the torment!" He tries to describe how the compulsion follows him through the streets, and ends: "Who knows what it's like to be me?"

This is always said to be Lorre's first screen performance, although McGilligan establishes that it was his third. It was certainly the performance that fixed his image forever, during a long Hollywood career in which he became one of Warner Bros.' most famous character actors (*Casablanca*, *The Maltese Falcon*, *The Mask of Dimitrios*). He was also a comedian and a song-and-dance man, and although you can see him opposite Fred Astaire in *Silk Stockings* (1957), it was as a psychopath that he supported himself. He died in 1964.

Fritz Lang (1890–1976) became, in America, a famous director of film noir. His credits include *You Only Live Once* (1937, based on the Bonnie and Clyde story), Graham Greene's *Ministry of Fear* (1944), *The Big Heat* (1953, with Lee Marvin hurling hot coffee in Gloria Graham's face), and *While the City Sleeps* (1956, another story about a manhunt). He was often accused of sadism toward his actors; he had Lorre thrown down the stairs into the criminal lair a dozen times, and Peter Bogdanovich describes a scene in Lang's *Western Union* where Randolph Scott tries to burn the ropes off his bound wrists. John Ford, watching the movie, said, "Those are Randy's wrists, that is real rope, that is a real fire."

For years *M* was available only in scratchy, dim prints. Even my earlier laserdisc is only marginally watchable. This new version, restored by the Munich Film Archive, is not only better to look at but easier to follow, since more of the German dialogue has been subtitled. (Lorre also recorded a soundtrack in English, which should be made available as an option on the eventual laserdisc and DVD versions.)

Watching the new print of *M*, I found the film more powerful than I remembered, because I was not watching it through a haze of disintegration.

And what a haunting film it is. The film doesn't ask for sympathy for the killer Franz Becker, but it asks for understanding: As he says in his own defense, he cannot escape or control the evil compulsions that overtake him. Elsewhere in the film, an innocent old man, suspected of being the killer, is attacked by a mob that forms on the spot. Each of the mob members was presumably capable of telling right from wrong and controlling his actions (as Becker was not), and yet as a mob they moved with the same compulsion to kill. There is a message there somewhere. Not "somewhere," really, but right up front, where it's a wonder it escaped the attention of the Nazi censors.

MY DARLING CLEMENTINE

"What kind of town is this?" Wyatt Earp asks on his first night in Tombstone. "A man can't get a shave without gettin' his head blowed off." He gets up out of the newfangled barber's chair at the Bon Ton Tonsorial Parlor and climbs through the second-story window of a saloon, his face still half lathered, to konk a gun-toting drunk on the head and drag him out by the heels.

Earp (Henry Fonda) already knows what kind of town it is. In the opening scenes of John Ford's greatest Western, *My Darling Clementine* (1946), he and his brothers are driving cattle cast to Kansas. Wyatt, Virgil, and Morgan leave their kid brother James in charge of the herd and go into town for a shave and a beer. As they ride down the main street of Tombstone, under a vast and lowering evening sky, gunshots and raucous laughter are heard in the saloons, and we don't have to ask why the town has the biggest graveyard west of the Rockies.

Ford's story reenacts the central morality play of the Western. Wyatt Earp becomes the town's new marshal, there's a showdown between law and anarchy, the law wins and the last shot features the new schoolmarm—who represents the arrival of civilization. Most

Westerns put the emphasis on the showdown. *My Darling Clementine* builds up to the legendary gunfight at the OK Corral, but it is more about everyday things—haircuts, romance, friendship, poker, and illness.

At the center is Henry Fonda's performance as Wyatt Earp. He's usually shown as a man of action, but Fonda makes him the new-style Westerner, who stands up when a woman comes into the room and knows how to carve a chicken and dance a reel. Like a teenager, he sits in a chair on the veranda of his office, tilts back to balance on the back legs, and pushes off against a post with one boot and then the other. He's thinking of Clementine, and Fonda shows his happiness with body language.

Earp has accepted the marshal's badge because when he and his brothers returned to their herd they found the cattle rustled and James dead. There is every reason to believe the crime was committed by Old Man Clanton (Walter Brennan) and his "boys" (grown, bearded, and mean). An early scene ends with Clanton baring his teeth like an animal showing its fangs. Earp buries James in a touching scene. ("You didn't get much of a chance, did you, James?") Then, instead of riding into town and shooting the Clantons, he tells the mayor he'll become the new marshal. He wants revenge, but legally.

The most important relationship is between Earp and Doc Holliday (Victor Mature), the gambler who runs Tombstone but is dying of tuberculosis. They are natural enemies, but a quiet, unspoken regard grows up between the two men, maybe because Earp senses the sadness at Holliday's core. Holliday's rented room has his medical diploma on the wall and his doctor's bag beneath it, but he doesn't practice anymore. Something went wrong back East, and now he gambles for a living, and drinks himself into oblivion. His lover is a prostitute, Chihuahua (Linda Darnell), and he talks about leaving for Mexico with her. But as he coughs up blood, he knows what his prognosis is.

The marshal's first showdown with Holliday is a classic Ford scene. The saloon grows quiet when Doc walks in, and the bar clears when he walks up to it. He tells Earp, "Draw!" Earp says he can't—doesn't have a gun. Doc calls for a gun, and a man down the bar slides him one. Earp looks at the gun, and says, "Brother Morg's gun. The other one, the good-lookin' fellow—that's my brother, Virg." Doc registers this information and returns his own gun to its holster. He realizes Earp's brothers have the drop on him. "Howdy," says Doc. "Have a drink." Twice Doc tells someone to get out of town, and twice Earp reminds him that's the marshal's job. Although the Clantons are the first order of business, Doc and Earp seem headed for a showdown. Yet they have a scene together that is one of the strangest and most beautiful in all of John Ford's work. A British actor (Alan Mowbray) has come to town to put on a play, and when he doesn't show up at the theater, Earp and Holliday find him in the saloon, on top of a table, being tormented by the Clantons. The actor begins Hamlet's famous soliloquy, but is too drunk and frightened to continue. Doc Holliday, from memory, completes the speech, and could be speaking of himself: ". . . but that the dread of something after death, the undiscovered country from whose bourn no traveler returns, puzzles the will. . . ."

The gentlest moments in the movie involve Earp's feelings for Clementine (Cathy Downs), who arrives on the stage from the East, looking for "Dr. John Holliday." She is the girl Doc left behind. Earp, sitting outside the hotel, rises quickly to his feet as she gets out of the stage, and his movements show that he's in awe of this graceful vision. Clementine has been seeking Doc all over the West, we learn, and wants to bring him home. Doc tells her to get out of town. And Chihuahua monitors the situation jealously.

Clementine is packed to go the next morning when the marshal, awkward and shy, asks her to join him at the church service and dance. They walk in stately procession down the covered boardwalk, while Ford's favorite hymn plays: "Shall We Gather at the River?" When the fiddler strikes up, Wyatt and Clementine dance—he clumsy but enthusiastic, and with great joy. This dance is the turning point of the movie, and marks the end of the Old West. There are still shots to be fired, but civilization has arrived.

The legendary gunfight at the OK Corral has been the subject of many films, including *Frontier Marshal* (1939), *Gunfight at the O.K. Corral* (1957), *Tombstone* (1993, with Val Kilmer's brilliant performance as Doc), and *Wyatt Earp* (1994). Usually the gunfight is the centerpiece of the film. Here it plays more like the dispatch of unfinished business; Ford doesn't linger over the violence.

There is the quiet tenseness in the marshal's office as Earp prepares to face the Clantons, who've shouted their challenge that they'd be waiting for him at the corral. Earp's brothers are with him, because this is "family business." Earp turns down other volunteers, but when Doc turns up, he lets him take part, because Doc has family business, too (one of the Clanton boys has killed Chihuahua). Under the merciless clear sky of a desert dawn, in silence except for far-off horse whinnies and dog barks, the men walk down the street and take care of business.

John Ford (1895–1973) was, many believe, the greatest of all American directors. Certainly he did more than any other to document the passages of American history. For him, a Western was not quite such a "period film" as it would be for later directors. He shot on location in the desert and prairie, his cast and crew living as if they were on a cattle drive, eating out of the chuckwagon, sleeping in tents. He filmed *My Darling Clementine* in his beloved Monument Valley, on the Arizona-Utah border.

He made dozens of silent Westerns, met the real Wyatt Earp on the set of a movie, and heard the story of the OK Corral directly from him (even so, history tells a story much different from this film). Ford worked repeatedly with the same actors (his "stock company") and it is interesting that he chose Fonda rather than John Wayne, his other favorite, for Wyatt Earp. Maybe he saw Wayne as the embodiment of the Old West, and the gentler Fonda as one of the new men who would tame the wilderness.

My Darling Clementine must be one of the sweetest and most good-hearted of all Westerns. The giveaway is the title, which is not about Wyatt or Doc or the gunfight, but about Clementine, certainly the most important thing to happen to Marshal Earp during the story. There is a moment, soon after she arrives, when Earp gets a haircut and a quick spray of perfume at the Bon Ton Tonsorial Parlor. Clem stands close to him and says she loves "the scent of the desert flowers." "That's me," says Earp. "Barber."

A WOMAN UNDER THE INFLUENCE

John Cassavetes is one of the few modern directors whose shots, scenes, dialogue, and characters all instantly identify their creator; watch even a few seconds of a Cassavetes films, and you know whose it is, as certainly as with Hitchcock or Fellini. They are films with a great dread of silence; the characters talk, fight, joke, sing, confess, accuse. They need love desperately, and are bad at giving it and worse at receiving it, but God how they try.

Cassavetes (1929–89) is the most important of the American independent filmmakers. His *Shadows* (1959), shot in 16-mm on a low budget and involving plausible people in unforced situations, arrived at the same time as the French New Wave and offered a similar freedom in America: not the formality of studio productions, but the spontaneity of life happening right now. Ironically, it was by starring in such mainstream films as *Rosemary's Baby* and *The Fury* that Cassavetes raised the money to make his own films.

Because his work felt so fresh, it was assumed that Cassavetes was an improvisational filmmaker. Not true. He was the writer of his films, but because he based their stories on his own emotional experience, and because his actors were family or friends, his world felt spontaneous. There was never the arc of a plot, but the terror of free-fall. He knew that in life you do not often improvise, but play a character who has been carefully rehearsed for a lifetime.

A Woman Under the Influence (1974) is perhaps the greatest of Cassavetes's films (although a case can be made for *Love Streams* in 1984). It stars his wife and most frequent collaborator, Gena Rowlands, and his friend Peter Falk, in roles perhaps suggested by his own marriage (how closely may be guessed by the fact that the two characters' mothers are played by Lady Rowlands and Katherine Cassavetes).

Falk plays a construction foreman named Nick Longhetti, and Rowlands is his wife, Mabel. They have three children, and live in a house with so little privacy that they sleep on a sofa bed in the dining room. (The bathroom door has a large sign: PRIVATE. People are always knocking on it.) Mabel drinks too much and behaves strangely, and during the film she will have a breakdown, spend time in a mental institution, and star at her own welcome-home party. Only by the end of the film is it quietly made clear that Nick is about as crazy as his wife is, and that in a desperate way their two madnesses make a nice fit.

Rowlands won an Oscar nomination for her performance, which suggests Erma Bombeck playing Lady Macbeth. Her madness burns amid the confusions of domestic life. Nothing goes easily. Her first words are "No yelling!" Sending the three kids to spend the night with her mother, she hops around the front yard on one foot, having lost her shoe. When her husband unexpectedly arrives home early in the morning with ten fellow construction workers, her response is direct: "Want some spaghetti?" But she tries too hard, and is eventually embracing one embarrassed worker, asking him to dance, until Nick breaks the mood with "Mabel, you've had your fun. That's enough." The workers quickly clear their places and leave, while Mabel crumples into the ashes of another failed attempt to please.

Mabel has no room of her own. Her entire house belongs at all times to the other members of her family, to her relatives and in-laws, to the neighbors, to unexpected visitors like Dr. Zepp (Eddie Shaw), who turns up to eyeball her and decide if she's a suitable case for treatment. There is a quiet moment early in the film when Mabel is left alone for a while, and stands in the middle of the front hallway, smoking, thinking, listening to opera, drinking, and making gestures toward the corners of the rooms, as if making sure they are still there.

Later we see her guzzling whiskey in a bar, and spending the night with a guy she can't get rid of. (The guy leaves just before Nick arrives with his crew; Cassavetes avoids the obvious payoff of having them meet, while establishing the possibility that such meetings with stray men may have occurred in the past.) Nick and Mabel, alone for a moment, are fond and loving, but soon the kids burst in and join them on the bed, along with Mabel's mother, and Nick leads everyone in the manic whistling of "Jingle Bells."

Waves of noise and chaos sweep in and out of this house. "In her view," writes critic Ray Carney, "for things to stop moving even for a pulsebeat is for them to begin to die." That's true of most of Cassavetes's characters. Living in constant dread of silence or insight, unsure of her abilities as wife or mother, rattled by booze and pills, Mabel tries to enforce a scenario of happiness. Just meeting the school bus is a daily crisis, and in the house the kids are always being prompted to perform, to play, to sing, to bounce, to seem happy. "Tell me what you want me to be," she tells Nick. "I can be anything."

While Mabel is offstage, we see Nick's own madness, masked by macho self-assurance. Consider the scene where he arrives at his children's school in a city truck, yanks the kids out of classes, and takes them to the beach, where they are instructed to run up and down and have a good time. On the way home, he even lets them sip from his six-pack. Nothing Mabel has done is as crazy as this.

And consider the welcome that Nick stages for Mabel on her return from the institution. It is strained in countless ways, but underneath everything is the sense of an actress returning to reclaim the role she made her own, in a long-running play. She may be well, she may still be ill, but the people in her life are relieved that at least she is back, taking up the psychic space they are accustomed to her occupying. A dysfunctional family is not a nonfunctional family; it functions after its fashion, and in its screwy routine there may even be a kind of reassurance. There is no safe resolution at the end of a Cassavetes film. You feel the tumult of life goes on uninterrupted, that each film is a curtain raised on a play already in progress. The characters seek to give love, receive it, express it, comprehend it. They are prevented by various addictions, booze, drugs, sex, self-doubt. Self-help gurus talk about "playing old tapes." Cassavetes writes characters whose old tapes are like prison cells; their dialogue is like a call for help from between the bars.

Carney suggests that *A Woman Under the Influence* is the middle film of a "marriage trilogy" by Cassavetes. The first in the emotional sequence is *Minnie and Moskowitz* (1971), with Rowlands and Seymour Cassel in the goofy intoxication of first love, and the third is *Faces* (1968), with Rowlands and John Marley in the last stages of a disintegrating marriage. *A Woman Under the Influence* comes in the full flood of marriage and parenthood, with an uncertain balance between hope and fear.

Cassavetes cut many other films from the bolt of his quest and exhilaration. I thought *Husbands* (1970) was unconvincing, with Cassavetes, Falk, and Ben Gazzara mourning a friend by holding an extended debauch. *The Killing of a Chinese Bookie* (1976, with Gazzara as the operator of a strip club) is the sleeper, a portrait of a shifty, charming operator. *Opening Night* (1977) stars Rowlands in one of her best performances, as an alcoholic actress coming to pieces on the first night of a new play. *Gloria* (1980) is more conventional, with Rowlands as a mob-connected woman who hides a kid whose parents have been rubbed out. Then comes the greatness of *Love Streams* (1984), but by then Cassavetes's health was failing and after a few more jobs he descended into a painful terminal illness.

One of the things we can ask of an artist is that he leave some record of how it was for him, how he saw things, how he coped. Movies are such a collaborative medium that we rarely get the sense of one person, but Cassavetes at least got it down to two: himself and Rowlands. The key to his work is to realize that it is always Rowlands, not the male lead, who is playing the Cassavetes role.

A World of Fewer Words

by E. L. Doctorow

FROM *THE NEW YORK TIMES*

The effect of a hundred years of filmmaking on the practice of literature has been considerable.

As more than one critic has noted, today's novelists tend not to write exposition as fully as novelists of the nineteenth century. Where the first chapter of Stendahl's *Red and the Black* (1830) is given over to the leisurely description of a provincial French town, its topographic features, the basis of its economy, the person of its Mayor, the Mayor's mansion, the mansion's terraced gardens, and so on, Faulkner's *Sanctuary* (1931) begins this way: "From beyond the screen of bushes which surrounded the spring, Popeye watched the man drinking."

The twentieth-century novel minimizes discourse that dwells on settings, characters' C.V.'s, and the like. The writer finds it preferable to incorporate all necessary information in the action, to carry it along in the current of the narrative, as is done in movies.

Of course there are nineteenth-century works, Mark Twain's *Tom Sawyer,* for example ("'Tom?' No answer."), that jump right into things, and perhaps American writers have always been disposed to move along at a snappier pace than their European counterparts. But the minimal use of exposition does suppose a kind of filmic compact between writer and reader, that everything will become clear eventually.

Beyond that, the rise of film art is coincident with the tendency of novelists to conceive of compositions less symphonic and more solo voiced, intimate personalist work expressive of the operating consciousness. A case could be made that the novel's steady retreat from realism is as much a result of film's expansive record of the way the world looks as it is of the increasing sophistications of literature itself.

Another crossover effect has to do with film's major device, the instantaneous reposition in space and time: the cut. Writers today derive all sorts of effects from scanting the interstitial explanations or transitions that get their story from one character to another, or their characters from one place to another, or from yesterday to next year. More daring uses of discontinuity have occurred from violations of the grammatical protocols of person or tense.

But after a hundred years or so it may be that movies can do nothing more for, or to, literature than they have already done. By now film has begun to affirm its essentially nonliterate nature and to make of its conventions an art form detached and self-contained, like painting.

Movies began in silence. The early filmmakers learned to convey meaning apart from the use of language. For the most part the title cards of the silent films only nailed down the intelligence given to the audience nonverbally. (Young couple on porch swing at night. He removes a ring from his vest pocket. He gazes into her eyes. Title card: "Milly, will you be my wife?")

In the modern audible feature film, especially as made by Hollywood, spoken dialogue tends more and more to function as the old title cards of the silents. The genre of the film is indicated with the portentous opening credits. The beginning shots site the film and identify its time period. A given scene is lighted and the camera is positioned to create mood or inform the audience as to how it is to regard what it is seeing, how serious or unserious the story may be, how objectively we may regard the characters, how intimately we are being asked to share their adventures.

The film stock is color coordinated with its subject. The actors are dressed, and their hair is cut or coiffed, to indicate age, economic class, social status, education, and even degree of virtue. They're directed to demonstrate their characters' states of mind with bodily attitudes, gestures, facial expressions, and the movements of their eyes. Given all this, the weight of the scene is carried nonverbally. What is seen and felt is a signifying context for any words actually spoken. In some of today's film dramas ninety-five percent of a scene's meaning is conveyed before a word is uttered; ninety-eight percent if you add music.

Of course recent filmmakers—Eric Rohmer, for example, or Louis Malle—have made highly verbal films. And as a generalization, the assemblage of visual effects that make of dialogue a capstone is less true of comedy. The art of the television sitcom, for example, is highly verbal. Its standing sets, and its inclination to celebrate character, provide the impetus for wordplay, gags, and verbal economies that can verge on the aphoristic. On the other hand the sitcom's mostly interior scenes and its limited scope for camera setups suggest it is closer to a filmed stage play than it is to movies.

In the 1930s and 1940s when stage plays and books were a major source of film scripts, the talkies were talkier (as adaptations of Shakespeare are still). Films of that period were, by comparison with today's products, logorrheic. Even action films, the Bogart film noir, the Errol Flynn swashbuckler, abounded with dialogue. Now, after a century of development, the medium of film generates its own culture. Its audience is as schooled in its rhythms and motifs and habits of being as Wagnerians are in der Nibelungen. Films work off previous films. They are genre referential and can be more of what they are by nature.

Literary language extends experience in discourse. It flowers to thought with nouns, verbs, objects. It thinks. That is why the term "film language" may be an oxymoron. Film de-literates thought; it relies primarily on an association of visual impressions or understandings. Moviegoing is an act of inference. You receive what you see as a broad band of sensual effects that evoke your intuitive nonverbal intelligence. You understand what you see without having to think it through with words.

What shall we make of this? Today, at the end of the century, film is ubiquitous. There are more movies than ever. They are in theaters, on television; they are cabled, videotaped, CD'd and DVD'd. They are sent around the world by satellite transmission; they are dubbed and translated and available from all their periods for consumers to choose as books are chosen from the library. Their enormous popularity reaches all classes and all levels of education. And their primary producers are major entertainment conglomerates that put lots of money into them and expect even more money in return.

It is not that great and important films will no longer be made. But one can imagine a merger of film esthetics and profit-making incentives that, apart from the efforts of this or that serious and principled filmmaker, effects a culture of large, beautifully dressed, tactically pigmented, stimulating, and only incidentally verbal movies that excite predetermined market tastes and offer societal myths that slightly vary with each recycling: films composed artfully from the palette of such basic elements as car drive-ups, interiors, exteriors, faces, chases, and explosions.

Just as significant for the culture of the future may be the declining production costs of computerized, digitally made movies. It is not hard to understand the lure to the creative young when making a film will be as feasible as writing a story.

That pictograms, whether corporately or privately produced, may eventually unseat linguistic composition as the major communicative act of our culture is a prospect I find only slightly less dire than global warming.

Some of the most thoughtful if not ingenious criticism written today is written by critics of film who, often as not, address themselves to work that is hardly worth their attention. The most meretricious or foolish movie will elicit a cogent analysis. Why? It may be a film's auspices that obligate the critics. But it may be that, however unconsciously, they mean to reaffirm or defend print culture by subjecting the nonliterate filmgoing experience, good or bad, to the extensions of syntactical thought.

The Movie of the Century

It Looks Both Backward to Everything Hollywood Had Learned About Westerns and Forward to Things Films Hadn't Dared Do

by Geoffrey O'Brien

FROM *AMERICAN HERITAGE*

It is a phrase so high-concept it ought to be the title of a movie, or at least the slogan for a marketing campaign, the ultimate coming attraction. Never mind *Intolerance* or *Citizen Kane,* the real Movie of the Century would be a will-o'-the-wisp, always just about to be revealed, a hundred years in the making, cast of millions, coming soon to a theater near you. What drove movies in the past was anticipation of what the future held. In the years when Hollywood was actually producing a fairly steady flow of good-to-great movies, there was scarcely time or inclination for a backward glance.

Or else—for this impossible honor—one might take any representative slice of the old Hollywood's product, from the Twenties or the Thirties or the Forties according to preference. Profusion was, after all, the point. At the height of the American public's romance with moviegoing, a night at the Orpheum was as fundamental and recurrent an activity as having dinner or going to bed; a reliable flow of cinematic pleasures was more important than any particular presentation. Tonight a double bill of a pirate adventure and a murder mystery; starting Wednesday, the screen version of a best-selling love story and a college musical. All the movies were somehow interrelated, so that even the humblest Mr. Moto thriller or Gene Autry Western had its part in the mix that likewise encompassed *Gone With the Wind*. Movies were not meant to live alone any more than people were.

Pushed, however, to propose a single movie for such unnatural solitary eminence, I'd have to pick the one I've ended up watching oftenest, John Ford's *The Searchers*. Released in 1956, it's a product of just that moment when—with the breakup of its distribution monopolies and the erosion of its audience by television—the studio machine finally began to come apart. It looks both ways in time, embodying all the traditional virtues of storytelling and technical command, yet expanding established limits to suggest a world of possibility beyond what Hollywood had permitted itself. It's an extraordinarily generous and exploratory work, made by a director who had just turned sixty-one. *The Searchers* might be taken as the outermost extension of everything that John Ford—and who else but John Ford could have made the American Movie of the Century?—had learned in the forty years of filmmaking that preceded it, from the time he made what probably was his acting debut by playing a character named Dopey in his brother Francis Ford's two-reeler *The Mysterious Rose*, filmed just as World War I was breaking out.

A career like Ford's was conceivable only in the old Hollywood. Born in 1894, he had already directed more than fifty films when he achieved his first major success at age thirty with the epic Western *The Iron Horse*. He went on to turn out seventy-two more, not counting a range of shorts and documentaries undertaken for the U.S. government. Laden with honors for such prestige pictures as *The Informer*, *The Grapes of Wrath*, and *How Green Was My Valley*, Ford expended more of his creative energy on quirkier personal projects, Westerns like *My Darling Clementine*, *Fort Apache*, and *Wagon Master*. Outwardly straightforward entertainments, noted for their splendid landscapes and the vigorous presence of Ford's stock company of character actors, these were films that undermined conventional movie structure in favor of a looser, more generically mixed form in which slapstick could adjoin tragedy and plot development might be suspended at any moment for a dance or a brawl or a serene stroll.

The Searchers was in many ways an atypical project for Ford. Derived from an excellent novel by Alan LeMay, it had all the earmarks of the newer "adult" Westerns that were Hollywood's answer to the onslaught of TV gunslingers: a psychologically conflicted hero, adulterous (if repressed) passion, rape, massacre, interracial sex. The dramatic action was far more violent and overt than in Ford's previous Westerns, and he rose to the challenge by forging a style unique to this film. All the amplitude and laid-back atmospherics of his earlier masterpieces are put under a pressure that takes Ford beyond himself; the garrulous impulse that often led to extended bouts of knockabout comedy and ceremonial pageantry is reined in, although hardly absent. It's as if two contradictory approaches to filmmaking operated simultaneously. The characteristic Fordian desire to open things up, to slow down the story to allow the margins and backgrounds to be fully felt— his capacity for letting minor characters become momentarily central—works together here with a contradictory impulse toward ruthless concision and relentless forward impetus. For all its seven-year time span and sprawling geographic range, *The Searchers* works like a suspense movie.

When the film came out, in 1956, I was a little too young to be exposed to its elements of rape and massacre, but by reputation it extended a whiff of the forbidden. This was a movie, the word went, with a profound violation at its core and implacable rage stemming from that violation. It took me a few years to catch up with it; this was before the era when directors like Martin Scorsese and Wim Wenders helped elevate *The Searchers* to the canonical status it currently enjoys. Only in Times Square—at the eponymous Times Square theater, devoted exclusively to old Westerns—did it surface periodically.

What was most immediately striking about *The Searchers* was what it didn't have in common with other Westerns, those on which Fifties kids became experts by dint of being exposed to them Saturday after Saturday. It wasn't about the deed to the mine, or the coming of the railroad, or the first great cattle drive, or a hotheaded young gunslinger out to make a name for himself; the standard-issue one-street cowboy-picture town didn't come into it at all. No recourse was had to the comforting rituals of the genre, those depredations and confrontations that recur with a lulling predictability made all the more cozy by the assortment of wonderfully familiar character actors who recirculate endlessly as sheriffs, bankers, outlaws, barmaids, schoolmarms, and ranch hands.

In the course of the Fifties the Western became increasingly pre-occupied with Indians, a trend that gave the genre fresh energy and fresh complications. Some Indian Westerns were notably liberal in their stance, determined to expose past injustices; some were rooted in implacable hostility. Here again *The Searchers* managed to avoid stock situations; there were to be none of the tiresome conflicts be-tween sympathetic "friendlies" and fanatical "hostiles," no scenes of besieged cavalrymen sweating it out in the stockade while waiting for a dawn attack.

Nor was there any of the usual dialogue about learning to live in peace together, or the earnest speeches decrying broken treaties. Cu-riously, considering that its story revolved entirely around Indians, the film didn't seem to have anything particular to say about them. It pursued a course of omission and elision, as if to admit that there were places it was not capable of entering. There were no attempts at re-alistic vignettes of Comanche life; everything was overtly filtered through white perception and white imagination, the viewpoint of isolated settlers "out on a limb somewhere, maybe this year, maybe next," enraged at their own vulnerability. The issue was not civilization versus savagery but how to protect life and property under makeshift circumstances and how to react after it's too late for protection.

The long opening scene manages, without a superfluous touch, to introduce seven characters (four of whom do not have long to live), to sketch in the history of the Edwards family, including their adoption of young Martin Pawley (Jeffrey Hunter), himself part Cherokee, after his parents were killed in an Indian raid, and to begin elaborating the characterization of John Wayne as the embittered Confederate veteran Ethan Edwards, a performance all the more vivid for its intractable contradictions. The plot, as far as we can grasp it at the outset, has to do with Ethan's return to his brother's Texas homestead after years of mysterious postwar drifting, during which he acquired, by whatever means, a sackful of fresh-minted Yankee dollars. Some scattered remarks and furtive glances suffice to establish that Ethan's arrival is a source of unease. There is mistrust between the brothers; Ethan and his sister-in-law love each other, may even have been lovers. (This possibility is never put into words, resting entirely on a couple of reaction shots, but it subtly informs Wayne's whole portrayal.) The scene accomplishes a necessary job of misleading the audience into thinking that the movie is going to be about the individuals it has just met. On repeated viewings, nothing is more powerful than Ford's grouping of the unwittingly doomed Edwards family in a single splendid composition, as if to frame them for all time before they vanish.

The next morning, before any suggestion of daily routine is allowed, we are off with Ethan, Martin, and a posse of neighbors on a chase after stolen cattle. This breathless interruption is the first in a long chain; we are to have an interrupted funeral, an interrupted meal, an interrupted wedding, countless interrupted conversations. It becomes apparent that the cattle theft was a ruse to give a band of Comanches the opportunity to massacre those left behind; we spend the moments before the massacre with its victims. The close-up of the Comanche war chief Scar blowing his buffalo horn signals the film's most important event, which we are not allowed to witness. That the massacre must remain unseen is essential to Ford's sense of decorum. It goes without saying that this offscreen event is far more powerful than any overt depiction could be. Any contemporary remake would be likely to revel in the details, with the help of half a century of prosthetic technology; how could the temptation be resisted?

In a shot famously copied by George Lucas in *Star Wars*—Jeffrey Hunter staring in horror at the smoky ruins—we intrude on the aftermath. All are dead except for the two young girls; we move abruptly to the funeral, which is cut short angrily by Ethan: "Put an amen to it. There's no more time for praying. Amen!" In this atmosphere of indecent haste, Ford is able to rapidly introduce another indispensable group of characters, the neighboring Jorgensens, whose farm becomes the film's image of home, now that the primal home has been burned. Ethan and Martin, initially with a party of others, then on their own, set out to find the girls. The elder is found raped and killed; the younger, Debbie, becomes the sole object of their quest. Seasons pass; years pass. A secondary plot line emerges: Ethan doesn't want to rescue Debbie; he wants to kill her because by now she will have been married off to a Comanche and "ain't white anymore." In a sense it is the most linear of films, although its flashbacks, time lapses, and frequent changes of scene make it feel uncannily protracted and complex. They search; they find; Ethan has a sudden change of heart and doesn't kill Debbie when he gets the chance; Debbie comes home; Ethan goes away by himself.

Much has been made of Ethan's abrupt turnaround, encapsulated in a single image of Wayne lifting the rescued Debbie (Natalie Wood) into his arms, but moving though it is, it is also the most Hollywoodish moment in the film. In LeMay's novel, Ethan has no such change of heart and is conveniently killed before he can carry out his murderous intentions. In order for Wayne to play the part, things had to come out differently, but Ford and his screenwriter, Frank S. Nugent, wisely resisted the impulse to offer any explanation for Ethan's sudden conversion. At the same time, one can't make too much of it; it's a sudden reversal of everything else we know about the character, perhaps even a momentary weakening of purpose he might come to regret. This is, after all, the same person who shoots out the eyes of a dead Comanche because "by what that Comanch believes, ain't got no eyes he can't enter the spirit land, has to wander forever between the winds." Ethan stands with James Stewart's Scotty Ferguson in *Vertigo* as one of the great inscrutable obsessives of American film. Just as we don't know where Ethan has been before the movie began, so we have no real sense of what kind of person he will become. The only certainty is that he will be alone.

Ethan's change of heart, although it neatly resolves the situation, is no more the point of the movie than any of the other things that happen in *The Searchers*. It is a movie in which things change irrevocably between the beginning and the end, in which a world is created only to be wrecked. After the first few scenes the worst has already happened, and the only remaining dramatic action can be an attempt to retrieve a remnant. Finding Debbie will not restore the family that has been destroyed or erase the memory of devastation.

The Searchers' primary power derives from the vast stretches of space and time that it strings together on a single thread. I don't mean the mere bigness that money can buy, the splendid scenery, sweeping music, and sheer duration of, say, William Wyler's otherwise empty *The Big Country*. *The Searchers*, magnificently shot by Winton C. Hoch, is an object of incomparable beauty, a fact never more evident than when New York's Papp Public Theater a few years ago unveiled an immaculate print and projected it under optimum conditions on a properly vast screen. If I returned to *The Searchers* repeatedly, it was beyond anything else in order to see certain images again: Ethan and Martin crossing an icy plain at night, or riding downhill through deep snow, or silhouetted against a red sky as they travel along a ridge; the 7th Cavalry, fresh from slaughtering a Comanche encampment, crossing a newly thawed stream, the camera moving down a narrow crevasse, the whole Vista Vision image given over to a singular moment of rocky abstraction. Not one shot felt like an interpolation or interlude; the visual life of the film was a continuous balancing of immensity and intimacy. Movement through space, whether of a hand in close-up or of an army in long shot, was always in the center of the drama.

The operatic dimension of the movie exists not so much in the dialogue, or in Ford's masterly deployment of on-screen singing (the hymn "Shall We Gather at the River" is heard twice, at a funeral and a wedding), as it does in that succession of vast light-paintings. The film's center and culmination is the famous shot in which, while Ethan and Martin converse in the foreground, the newly found Debbie emerges as a tiny speck at the ridge of a sand dune, running downhill toward the two men, Ethan oblivious, Martin suddenly aware of her presence and standing frozen in astonishment just as she reaches the edge of the creek by which they are standing. The coordination of movement and framing within this composition is a species of music that can be attended to an infinite number of times.

The visual splendors do tend to focus attention unfairly away from Frank Nugent's script, the most cunning of screenplays, with its telegraphed subplots, reiterated phrases (Wayne's famous "That'll be the day"), and recurring actions. The structure suggests a world of cyclical rhythms and irrevocable losses; the return to the point of departure is never a true recurrence, since it always registers a fundamental change. The superbly laconic dialogue—discreetly flecked with archaisms and folksy locutions—is a major component of the film's feeling of density. There is so much to be covered that there is scarcely time for verbal elaboration, so that relatively brief speeches have the effect of lengthy soliloquies. Ethan's character is built up out of a few one-liners: "I still got my saber. Didn't turn it into no plowshare neither." "You speak pretty good English for a Comanch, somebody teach you?" Nobody has time for speechmaking. The emotional burden of Martin's final confrontation with Ethan is reduced to four words: "I hope you die."

The Searchers gives the impression of expending the material for a whole film in a single scene. Ethan and Martin's trajectory is a passage through various spheres—the world of the Comanches, of the 7th Cavalry, of old Hispanic aristocracy and new European immigrants—lingering just long enough in each to let us know that there is much more that cannot be shown. The restless forward movement permits unresolved mysteries: We are never to be told where Ethan got those fresh-minted Yankee dollars or what was the secret mission of Martin's accidentally acquired Indian wife. Most of everything gets lost, and the little that is left at the end—the small band of survivors facing who knows what difficulties of communication and readjustment—is swallowed up in blackness by a closing door.

Most of the important events around which the film revolves occur elsewhere: the years of Wayne's wanderings before the movie begins, the massacre of the Indians on whose aftermath Wayne and Hunter intrude, Debbie's years of captivity. Of the heroes' seven years of searching, we see only a few representative moments, vaulting in Shakespearean fashion over intervals of many years at several points. The holes and absences and elisions are put to superb use throughout. Because so much is left blank, the characters retain their mystery. In a fundamental way the movie does not deign to explain itself.

Mystery here is not a matter of erasing distinctions. Ford was at bottom a profoundly antiromantic filmmaker, and his appeals to old loyalties always involve a precise calculation of the costs and tradeoffs of such allegiances. Some have found the flirtatious byplay between Jeffrey Hunter and Vera Miles (as the long-suffering Laurie Jorgensen) a concession to the Hollywood demand for "love interest," but essentially it reinforces the film's disconsolate view of things. Laurie's anger at Martin is designed to force an acknowledgment that an understanding exists between them; love, or the possibility of love, has something to do with it, but mostly the theme is contractual agreement, just as the crucial flare-up between Ethan and Martin revolves around division of property. If the settlers are inordinately concerned with nailing things down, it is because they live in a territory not wholly theirs, among those already dispossessed (the old Spanish ruling class) or in the process of being dispossessed (the Comanches), and under the monitoring eye of an army serving the interests of a distant national government.

But in the interstices of all that cold-eyed pragmatism and latent rage, sheer human oddity has a way of tilting the balance. Ford's neatest trick in *The Searchers* is his enlisting of an apparently insignificant character—the alternately canny and halfwitted drifter Mose Harper—to serve as messenger, chorus, and comic relief. Mose seems like extra flavoring, with his goofy outbursts (hollering, "I've been baptized, Reverend, I've been baptized," in the middle of a skirmish with the Comanches) and his yearning for "a roof over old Mose's head and a rocking chair by the fire"; only in retrospect does he emerge as the engine of the story, the true discoverer, not once but twice, of the lost girl. In Hank Worden's magical interpretation, Mose becomes the secret hero of the film, the man who can cross all boundaries and who intuits or randomly picks up the information that counts. The others search without finding; he finds without searching.

CONTRIBUTORS' NOTES

Elizabeth Abele is a Ph.D. candidate in English at Temple University. Her work has been featured at meetings of the Popular Culture Association and the Mid-Atlantic Popular Culture Association.

Richard Alleva is the film critic for *Commonweal.*

Douglas Brinkley is a staff writer for *The New Yorker.*

John Brodie is a senior writer at *GQ.*

Chris Chang is the film critic for *New York Sidewalk.*

David Denby, staff writer for *The New Yorker* and former film critic for *New York* magazine, is the author of *Great Books: My Adventures with Homer, Rousseau, Woolf, and Other Indestructible Writers of the Western World,* a National Book Critics Circle Award finalist. He is also the editor of *Awake in the Dark: An Anthology of American Film Criticism, 1915–1977,* among other books.

E. L. Doctorow's novels include *Ragtime, Billy Bathgate, World's*

Fair, The Book of Daniel, The Waterworks, and *Loon Lake,* among others. He is also the author of the play *Drinks Before Dinner,* a collection of stories, *Lives of the Poets,* and two books of essays, among other publications. His awards include the National Book Award, the National Book Critics Award, and the National Humanities Medal.

Roger Ebert, film critic for the *Chicago Sun-Times,* is the recipient of the Pulitzer Prize for distinguished criticism—the first and only time the award was given to a film critic. His books include *A Kiss Is Still a Kiss* (biographies of film stars), *The Perfect London Walk,* and, most recently, *Roger Ebert's Book of Film.* Although no longer cohosting *At the Movies* with Gene Siskel (who died in 1998), he continues to appear on the national television program.

Molly Haskell's books include *From Reverence to Rape: The Treatment of Women in the Movies* and *Holding My Own in No Man's Land.* Her film writings appear regularly in national magazines and newspapers.

Robert Horton's film commentary appears regularly in *The Herald* of Evertt, Washington.

Phillip Lopate is the author of three essay collections, *Portrait of My Body, Against Joie de Vivre,* and *Bachelorhood;* two novels, *The Rug Merchant* and *Confessions of Summer;* and an educational memoir and text book, *Being with Children.* He is also the editor of *The Art of the Personal Essay.*

James Mangold has directed several movies, including most recently *Copland.*

Mia L. Mask's writings have appeared in *The Village Voice, Cineaste, The Insider,* and other publications nationwide. She teaches film studies and communications at CUNY/Staten Island.

Joseph McBride's books include *Steven Spielberg: A Biography* and *Frank Capra: The Catastrophe of Success*, and a forthcoming biography of John Ford.

Geoffrey O'Brien's books include *The Phantom Empire* and *The Times Square Story*. He is editor in chief of the *Library of America*.

Terrence Rafferty is a critic at large for *GQ*.

Rex Reed's film criticism appears regularly in leading publications nationwide, including *Vogue, Playboy, Esquire, Harpers, GQ, New York Daily News*, and *The New York Observer*. His books include *Big Screen, Little Screen; Travolta to Keaton;* as well as the novel *Personal Effects*.

Jonathan Rosenbaum's books include *Moving Places: A Life at The Movies, Midnight Movies* (with J. Hoberman), *Film, The Front Line*, and *Placing Movies: The Practice of Film Criticism*. He is the film critic for the *Chicago Reader* and has published film commentary in periodicals nationwide.

Andrew Sarris's books include *You Ain't Heard Nothin' Yet: The American Talking Film, History and Memory, 1927–1949*. A former film critic for *The Village Voice*, he now writes film commentary for *The New York Observer* and teaches film studies at Columbia University.

Martin Scorsese is the award-winning director of such films as *Mean Streets, Taxi Driver, Raging Bull, King of Comedy, Goodfellas, The Color of Money, The Last Temptation of Christ*, and, most recently, *Kundun*.

Steven Spielberg is the Academy Award–winning director of such films as *Schindler's List, Jurrassic Park, Jaws, E.T.*, and, most recently,

Saving Private Ryan. He is one of the three founders and partners of DreamWorks SKG, an entertainment megastudio.

Cliff Thompson is an editor and freelance writer.

Gore Vidal's novels include *Williwaw, The City and the Pillar,* and *Myra Breckenridge;* the historical novels *Julian; Washington, D.C., Burr, Lincoln,* and *Hollywood;* and the essay collections *Reflections on a Sinking Ship, The Sexual American Revolution,* and *Armageddon.*

Bruce Wagner is the author of the novel *Force Majeure* and the comic strip *Wild Palms.* A frequent contributor to leading periodicals, he is the author of the screenplays *A Nightmare on Elm Street* (with Wes Craven) and *Scenes from the Class Struggle in Beverly Hills.*

Robin Wood's books include *Hitchcock's Films, Personal Views: Explorations in Film, The American Nightmare: Essays on the Horror Film,* and, most recently, *Sexual Politics and Narrative Film.*

William Zinsser's books include *On Writing Well, Spring Training, American Places, Speaking of Journalism,* among many others. A regular contributor to leading publications nationwide, he is also the editor of *Worlds of Childhood: The Art and Craft of Writing for Children* and *They Went: The Art and Craft of Travel Writing,* among other collections.

NOTABLE AMERICAN MOVIE WRITINGS
OF 1998

Kent Jones   "Easy Targets: Ragging Skells," from
                              Film Comment

Lucy Kaylin   "The Bo Show," from *GQ*

Donald Lyons   "Fathers and Sons and American Cin-
                              ema," from *Film Comment*

Scott MacDonald   "The City as the Country: The New
                              York City Symphony from Rudy Bur-
                              chardt to Spike Lee," from *Film Com-
                              ment*

Kathi Maio   "The Soul (or Lack Thereof) of the New
                              Monster," from *The Magazine of Science
                              & Fantasy*

John R. May   "Close Encounters: Hollywood and Reli-
                              gion After a Century," from *Image*

James C. McKelly   "*Do the Right Thing* and the Culture of
                              Ambiguity," from *African American Re-
                              view*

Rebecca Mead   "Cheeze Whiz: Sam Rami," from *The
                              New Yorker*

Paula Parisi   "Obsessed: Jim Cameron," from *Wired*

Alexandra Stanley   "The Funniest Italian You've Never
                              Heard Of: Roberto Benigni, Italy's
                              Robin Williams," from *The New York
                              Times Magazine*

Jack Stevenson   "A Secret History of American Gay Sex
                              Cinema," from *Beloit Journal*

Anne Thompson   "Chick Flicks Nix Chicks," from *Premiere*

David Thompson   "Killing Time," from *Esquire*

David E. Williams   "Leader of the Pack: Director of Photography, Conrad Hall," from *American Cinematographer*

Michael Wilmington   "The Wild Heart," from *Film Comment*

Armond White   "Against the Hollywood Grain," from *Esquire*

Rick Worland   "OWI Meets the Monsters: Hollywood Horror Films and War Propaganda," from *Cinema Journal*

Michael Yhara   "Blacklist Whitewash," from *The New Republic*

DIRECTORY OF FILM MAGAZINES

The following is a select directory of magazines published in the United States dedicated primarily to film writing. Whenever possible, phone and fax numbers and e-mail addresses have been provided.

After Midnight, Tod Buttery, 5023 Hilltop Acres Road, Perry Hall, MD 21128

Alternative Cinema, P.O. Box 371, Glenwood, NJ 07418

American Cinematographer, P.O. Box 2230, Hollywood, CA 90078

Asian Cult Cinema, P.O. Box 16-1919, Miami, FL 33116

Bad Azz Mo Fo, Angziety Productions, P.O. Box 40649, Portland, OR 97240-0649

Cashiers du Cinemart, P.O. BOX 401, Riverview, MI 48192-2401

Cineaste, P.O. Box 2242, New York, NY 10009-8917

Cinefantastique, P.O. Box 270, Oak Park, IL 60303

Classic Images, 301 East 3rd Street, Muscatine, IA 52761

Communication Arts, P.O. Box 10300, Palo Alto, CA 94303; phone: (650) 326-6040, fax: (650) 326-1648

Communication Review, The, Professor Robert B. Horowitz, Department of Communication, University of California, 9500 Gilman Drive, San Diego, CA 92093-0503

ComNotes Editor, Department of Communication, University of California, 9500 Gilman Drive, San Diego, CA 92093-0503

Critical Inquiry, 202 Wieboldt Hall, 1050 East 59th Street, Chicago IL, 60637; phone: (773) 702-8477, fax: (773) 702-3397

Cue, P.O. Box 2027, Burlingame, CA 94011-2027

Cult Movies, 6201 Sunset Boulevard, Suite 152, Hollywood, CA 90028

Cultronix, English Department, CMU, 259 Baker Hall, Pittsburgh, PA 15213-3890; fax: (412) 268-7989, e-mail: cultsubmissions@oserver.org

Current's, 1612 K Street N.W., Suite 704, Washington, DC 20006; phone: (202) 463-7055, ext. 38, fax: (202) 463-7056, e-mail: current@ix.nctcom.com.

Deep Red, Chas Balun, 8456 Edinger Ave., Suite 111, Huntington Beach, CA 92647

Dreadful, Pleasures, 650 Prospect Avenue, Fairview, NJ 07022

Ecco, Charles Kilgore, P.O. Box 65742, Washington, DC 20035; e-mail: killgore@mindspring

Enculturation, David Rieder, 1701 Hidden Bluff Trail #3032, Arlington, TX 76006; e-mail: ENCULTURATION@uta.edu.

Entertainment Ave!, 931 West 75th Street, Suite 137-303, Naperville, IL 60565–1294

Entertainment Employment Journal, Department 1000W, 5632 Van Nuys Boulevard, Suite 320, Van Nuys, CA 91401-4600

Etc, P.O. Box 5367, Kingwood, TX 77325

Exploitation Journal, 40 South Brush Drive, Valley Stream, NY 11581

Fair/Extra!, P.O. Box 170, Congers, NY 10920

Fangoria, Starlog Group, Inc., 475 Park Avenue South, New York, NY 10016

Femme Fatales, P.O. Box 270, Oak Park, IL 60303

Film & History, Peter C. Rollins, Editor, Route 3, Box 80, Cleveland, OH 74020

Film Comment, 70 Lincoln Center Plaza, 4th Floor, New York, NY 10023

Film Culture Magazine, 32 Second Avenue, New York, NY 10003; phone: (212) 979-5663, fax: (212) 979-1683

Film Quarterly, Ann Martin, Editor, University of California Press, 2120 Berkeley Way, Berkeley, CA 94720

Film Score, 5545 Wilshire Boulevard, Suite 1500, Los Angeles, CA 90036-4201

Filmeax/Outré, P.O. Box 1900, Evanston, IL 60202; phone: (847) 866-7155, e-mail: editor@fincartforum.org

Giant Robot, P.O. Box 642053, Los Angeles, CA 90064

HKEM, 601 Van Ness Avenue, E3728, San Francisco, CA 94102

Iam Magazine, P.O. Box 523, Melbourne, FL 32902-0523; phone: (407) 773-3615, fax: (407) 773-9951, e-mail: iam@iammagazine.com

Iconomania, Department of Art History, 100 Dodd Hall, UCLA, Los Angeles, CA 90095-1417; phone: (310) 206-6905, e-mail: esegal@ucla.edu

Images, 111 East 66th Terrace, Kansas City, MO 64113: e-mail: info@imagesjournal.com

IndieZine, Queso Productions, P.O. Box 1007, Telluride, CO 81435

Inquisitor, P.O. Box 132, New York, NY

It's Only a Movie, Michael Flores, P.O. Box 14683, Chicago, IL 60614-0683

Journal of Aesthetics and Art Criticism, The, JAAC Office, Department of Philosophy, University of Louisville, Louisville, KY 40292; phone: (502) 852-4768

Kaiju Review, Dan Reed, 301 East 64th Street New York, NY 10021

Los Angeles Weekly, P.O. Box 4315, Los Angeles, CA 90078-9810

Make-Up Artist Magazine, P.O. Box 4316, Sunland, CA 91041-4316; phone: (818) 504-6770

Millennium Film Journal/Millennium Film Workshop, 66 East 4th Street, New York, NY 10003; phone: (212) 673-0090

Monster Scene, GOGO Entertainment Group, Inc., 1036 South Ahrens Avenue, Lombard, IL 60148

Movieline, 1141 South Beverky Drive, Los Angeles, CA 90035

Movie Maker Magazine, 2265 Westwood Boulevard, 479, Los Angeles, CA 90064; phone: (888) MAKE-MOVies, fax: (626) 584-5752

New York Screenwriter Monthly, The, 655 Fulton Street, Suite 276, Brooklyn, NY 11217

Other Voices, Attn.: Vance Bell, P.O. Box 31907, Philadelphia, PA 19104-1907

Outre, P.O. Box 1900, Evanston, IL 60204

Pacific Coast Studio Directory, The, P.O. Box VCA, Pine Mountain, CA 93222-0022; phone: (805) 242-2722, fax: (805) 242-2724

Pagoda, 2 Holworthy Terrace, Cambridge, MA 02138

Postmodern Culture, Johns Hopkins University Press, Baltimore, MD 21218

Premiere, 1633 Broadway, New York, NY 10019; phone: (212) 767-5400, fax: (212) 767-5444

Production Weekly, P.O. Box 10101, Burbank, CA 91510-0101

Res, 109 Minna Street, CA, Suite 390, San Francisco, CA 94105; phone: (415) 437-2686, fax: (415) 437-2687, e-mail: editor@resmag.com

Rewinder, The, John Hudson, Box 148111, Nashville, TN 37214

Ritz Filmbill, c/o Entropy Design, 46 North Front Street, Philadelphia, PA 19106

San Francisco Chronicle, 901 Mission Street, San Francisco, CA 94103

Saturday Evening Post Society, The, 1100 Waterway Boulevard, Indianapolis, IN 46202, Phone: (317) 636-8881

Science Fiction Weekly, 5 Lyons Mall, Suite 665, Basking Ridge, NJ 07920

Script, Shelly Geatty, 5683 Sweet Air Road, Baldwin, MD 21013

Screem, Daryl Mayeski, 490 S. Franklin Street, Wilkes-Barre, PA 18702-3765

Screenwriter's Insider Report, 16752 Bollinger Drive, Pacific Palisades, CA, 90272

Shock Cinema, c/o Steven Puchalski, P.O. Box 518, Stuyvesant Station, New York, NY 10009

Shocking Images, Mark Jason Murray, P.O. Box 7853, Citrus Heights, CA 95621

Sinema Brut, Keith T. Ryer Breese, R-1041771 South Quebec Way, Denver, CO 80231

Spex, 70 West Colombus Avenue, Palisades Park, NJ 07650

Starlog, 475 Park Avenue South, New York, NY 10016

Story and Myth, Great Bridge Internet, Inc., P.O. Box 16131, Chesapeake, VA 23328

Tiger Beat, Sterling/Macfadden, N.Y., 35 Wilbur Street, Lynbrook, NY 11563

Velvet Light Trap, The, University of Wisconsin–Madison, Department of Communication Arts, 821 University Avenue, Madison, WI 53706-1497

Vex, P.O. Box 319, Roselle, NJ 07203

Viden Eyeball, 122 Montclair Avenue, Boston, MA 02131-134

Video Watchdog, P.O. Box 5283, Cincinnati, OH 45205-0283; phone: (800) 275-8395, fax: (513) 471-8989, e-mail: videowd@aol.com

Videomaker Magazine, P.O. Box 4591, Chico, CA 95927; phone: (530) 891-8410, fax: (530) 891-8443

Videoscope, P.O. Box 216, Ocean Grove, NJ 07756

Wired Digital, 660 Third Street, 4th Floor, San Francisco, CA 94107; phone: (415) 276 8400, fax: (415) 276 8499

World of Fandom, P.O. Box 9421, Tampa, FL 33604

Written By, Writers Guild of America West, 7000 West Third Street, Los Angeles, CA 90048

Xeromorphic, Terrance Jennings Wharton, P.O. Box 481, Lancaster, OH 43130

Peter Bogdanovich began his filmmaking career as one of America's most distinguished, versatile, and remarkable directors with *Targets* (1968), followed by the Academy Award–winning *The Last Picture Show* (1971), which received eight Academy Award nominations, including one for Larry McMurtry and Bogdanovich for best screenplay; *What's Up Doc?* (1972); *Paper Moon* (1973), which garnered a Best Supporting Actress Academy Award for eight-year-old Tatum O'Neal; *Daisy Miller* (1974); *At Long Last Love* (1975); *Nickelodeon* (1976); *Saint Jack* (1979); *They All Laughed* (1981); *Mask* (1985); *Texasville* (1990); *Noises Off* (1992); *The Thing Called Love* (1993); *Two Women* (1997); and the forthcoming *Wait for Me*. Throughout his film career, he has published some of the most illuminating books about film, including *The Cinema of Orson Welles* (1961), *The Cinema of Howard Hawks* (1962), *The Cinema of Alfred Hitchcock* (1963), *John Ford* (1967), *Fritz Lang in America* (1969), *Allan Dwan: The Last Pioneer* (1970), *Pieces of Time* (1985), *The Killing of the Unicorn: Dorothy Stratten* (1984), *This Is Orson Welles* (1992), *A Moment with Miss Gish* (1995), *Who the Devil Made It: Conversations with Legendary Film Directors* (1997), and the forthcoming books *Movie of the Week* and *Who the Hell's in It*.

ABOUT THE SERIES EDITOR

Jason Shinder's books include the poetry collections *Every Room We Ever Slept In* (1994) and the forthcoming *Among Women* (2000). He is the editor of *Lights, Camera, Poetry: American Movie Poems* (1996), *First Books: A Resource for Writers* (1998), and the forthcoming *Tales from the Couch: Writers on the Talking Cure* (2000), among other books. His first volume of interviews with poets on poets of the past, *What Lovest Well Remains*, is also forthcoming in 2000. Founder and national director of YMCA of the USA Arts and Humanities and the YMCA National Writer's Voice, a network of literary arts centers at YMCAs nationwide, Shinder teaches in the graduate writing programs at Bennington College and the New School for Social Research.

(continued from page iv)